Praise for
Cut Your Grocery Bill in Half

"Many people think that it's impossible to reduce your grocery bill by 50 percent. But you can. Steve and Annette Economides provide step-by-step instructions in *Cut Your Grocery Bill in Half*. Tools that are practical and easy to follow. No special shopping or cooking skills required. Anyone can see a surprising reduction in their grocery budget if they follow the Economides' methods. And, best of all, the savings begin right away. You don't need to finish the whole book to benefit. You'll find money-saving ideas that you can put to use in the first chapter and every chapter thereafter. Normally I advise people to check books out of the library and save the cost of the book. But this is one do-it-yourself guide to lower grocery bills that you'll want to have on your bookshelf or kitchen countertop."

GARY FOREMAN, PUBLISHER OF THEDOLLARSTRETCHER.COM

"This book is loaded with fresh ideas to slash your grocery bills."

RICHARD EISENBERG, SENIOR EDITOR, CBS MONEYWATCH.COM

"If you are eager to save on groceries, but don't always have the time to clip coupons, this book is for you! It's perfect if you're interested in more ways to cut costs, reduce waste, and get organized. This is an awesome book for the novice or the skilled cook."

TAWRA KELLAM AND JILL COOPER, EDITORS OF LIVINGONADIME.COM
AND AUTHORS OF *DINING ON A DIME COOKBOOK*

"An amazing insight into the life of a family that is daily living out this book. Following these grocery concepts will not only make a difference in your family's budget, but it will also help you unite with a common goal in mind; spending your money with a purpose by following a plan. The end result is having more money every month to invest in your family's future."

JEFF JONES, DRUMMER, BIG DADDY WEAVE, AND FOUNDER OF CUSTOMSTIX.COM

"*Cut Your Grocery Bill in Half* is a must-read if you're serious about saving money at the supermarket. Steve and Annette detail step-by-step how to save hundreds or even thousands of dollars a year on your food shopping. The book is not a compilation of abstract theories on grocery shopping, but strategies and tactics that work in the real lives of busy families. You'll not only save money but save time and stress too."

GREGORY KARP, AUTHOR OF *LIVING RICH BY SPENDING SMART*

"From the basics of couponing to many other advanced strategies, the Economides prove why they are the King and Queen of cheap! Beginners, intermediates, and even experts will find insightful strategies that will help them SAVE MONEY. More than a great read, this book is a resource I will keep coming back to over and over."

ASHLEY NUZZO, FOUNDER OF FRUGALCOUPONLIVING.COM

"Shopping for and feeding three boys (four if you count my husband) can be a full-time job and eat up my whole paycheck. But, thanks to *Cut Your Grocery Bills in Half*, I've discovered practical, simple strategies to save precious time and money and keep my ALWAYS hungry boys' tummys filled."

JEAN BLACKMER, AUTHOR OF *BOY-STEROUS LIVING*
AND PUBLISHING MANAGER FOR MOPS INTERNATIONAL

"I've known Steve and Annette for several years and they definitely live what they believe. If you're serious about spending less money at the grocery store, this book offers some practical ways to achieve your goal. When it comes to stretching your dollar, I know of no one with more experience than Steve and Annette."

JJ HELLER, SINGER/SONGWRITER

Cut Your Grocery Bill in Half with America's Cheapest Family®

*Includes So Many Innovative Strategies
You Won't Have to Cut Coupons*

Steve and Annette Economides

(aka America's Cheapest Family®)

THOMAS NELSON
Since 1798

NASHVILLE   DALLAS   MEXICO CITY   RIO DE JANEIRO

Cut Your Grocery Bill in Half with America's Cheapest Family*

© 2010 by Steve and Annette Economides

Published in Nashville, Tennessee, by Thomas Nelson. Thomas Nelson is a registered trademark of Thomas Nelson, Inc.

Thomas Nelson, Inc., titles may be purchased in bulk for educational, business, fund-raising, or sales promotional use. For information, please e-mail SpecialMarkets@ThomasNelson.com.

Library of Congress Cataloguing-in-Publication Data

Economides, Steve.
  Cut your grocery bill in half with America's cheapest family : includes so many innovative strategies you won't have to cut coupons / Steve and Annette Economides.
      p. cm.
  Includes bibliographical references and index.
  ISBN 978-1-4002-0283-6 (alk. paper)
  1. Grocery shopping—United States. 2. Consumer education—United States. 3. Low budget cooking—United States. 4. Finance, Personal—United States. I. Economides, Annette. II. Title.
  TX356.E36 2010
  640.73—dc22

                              2010025077

Printed in the United States of America

10 11 12 13 VG 6 5 4 3

JUN 2 8 2011

We dedicate this book
to three very influential people in our lives:

To Annette's best friend, Dianne Guastella, you were always better
at junior high social studies, high school chemistry,
and coupon savings at the grocery store.

To Steve's college gymnastics coach, Don Robinson, you taught me
to persist until I succeeded and to "want to" rather than "have to."

And to the memory of recording artist Keith Green,
who lived his passion and ignited ours.

Contents

Acknowledgments

No book is ever the work of just one or two people. We are so grateful for the hundreds of friends who have supported and encouraged us along our frugal journey and through the writing of this book.

To our AmericasCheapestFamily.com family—thank you for buying our books and recommending them to your friends. You inspire us with your frugal tips and success stories.

To booksellers across the world who have carried and recommended our book—thanks for the vote of confidence.

Steve Laube—thank you for being an awesome literary agent and believing that every family in the world would want to save money on groceries.

Thomas Nelson staff—thank you for trusting our message of frugality and working diligently to produce an awesome book.

Win Holden—how can we thank you for your patience and kindness. Your excellent advice has been a lifesaver to us and foundational to our success.

To our media friends in TV, newspapers, magazines, radio, and online—thank you for embracing our message and helping us spread the word that frugality frees and debt destroys.

Lyn—our office simply wouldn't run without your part-time help. Thanks for doing whatever is needed at the moment. You're a gem!

To our advisory board and prayer team—thank you for your encouragement, support, and wise counsel.

To our kids—as you all leave the nest and venture into independence we are nothing but proud parents. Thank you for proving to the world that frugal values can be "caught" and enjoyed.

1

Cut Your Grocery Bill in Half (or More)

Cut my grocery bill in half? You've got to be kidding!

When you hear the phrase, "Cut your grocery bill in half," what do you envision? Do you see a harried homemaker, spending hours each day running from one grocer to another, piling her cart with a mountain of sale items? Or is it the coupon queen—clipping coupons for hours on end—and then standing in line for thirty minutes while the checker scans her 2-inch pile of coupons? Or could it possibly be that you see a family eating rice and beans every day?

Please put those images out of your mind and imagine a pantry stocked with all of your favorite foods and a checkbook with a positive balance. Imagine that you come home to be greeted by the wonderful aroma of dinner ready to be served. Imagine a family eating delicious meals and laughing together at the dinner table.

No, this isn't a daydream—this is our reality, and it can be yours too!

We know many families are struggling with unending to-do lists, failing finances, and flagging energy levels. The thought of learning *all* of the strategies contained in this book, just to save some money at the grocery store, could be overwhelming.

We'll make you a promise. If you select one chapter in this book to start and apply just one or two of the ideas we present, you'll start saving money right away—this week. You'll easily save enough to cover the price of this book and probably much more! We've heard from many people around the world who have literally cut their grocery bill in half by applying our grocery strategies. You can too.

WHAT WOULD YOU DO IF?

If we gave you $3,000 to read this book, would you do it? What would you do with the extra money? And if we could guarantee you that you could save that much money each year (tax free), would you be interested?

And, if we could give you a few more hours each week to spend any way you wanted, what would you do? Would you relax and watch a movie, spend time with your kids or some friends, or maybe take a college class to improve your skills?

And if we could reduce your stress level by giving you a few practical efficiency tools, would you be interested?

Look, we aren't selling a multilevel marketing membership, and this isn't some sort of Ponzi scheme. We're selling you on *you* and your ability to learn and think and act differently. Don't worry though, we aren't going to tell you to do anything that we haven't already done ourselves. And when you hear how we started out, and you realize that we aren't professional shoppers, gourmet chefs, financial gurus, or infomercial stars, we're sure that you'll believe that you can do what we do and probably do it better.

WHO IS AMERICA'S CHEAPEST FAMILY?

We're Steve and Annette Economides (econo mee dis). Yes, that's really our last name. It's Greek and means "son of a steward." We're an ordinary family with kids, but we're living out the American Dream in a very un-American way—without debt. We live in a large house on three-quarters of an acre surrounded by citrus trees. But when we married in 1982, we lived on near-poverty wages—Steve was earning $6.50 an hour ($838 per month take-home) working as a printing company paste-up artist. Annette's domestic ability was limited to boiling water and scrambling eggs. In spite of her limitations, she was determined to excel, so she took every penny we had and stretched it until it begged for mercy.

Three years later, after living on one income, having one baby (John) and with another on the way (Becky), our frugal efforts started to bear fruit. We had saved enough money to put 15 percent down on a repossessed, four-bedroom, two-bath home. With careful planning and some sacrifice, we paid off that home in nine years on an average income of only $35,000.

By the time we moved into our current home, our family had grown to include five kids (John, Becky, Roy, Joe, and Abbey), two dogs, three turtles, and a couple of hamsters. By learning to plan and shop and cook smarter, we were able to feed our family of seven for $350 each month (including paper goods and personal care items). And we weren't living on ramen noodles.

We don't buy a lot of prepackaged foods, but we do buy some. We don't buy a lot of soda or chips, however every once in a while we indulge in those also—but only when they're on sale. We eat steak, lamb, and lots of Italian and Greek dishes. We spend less by implementing lots of different little strategies that, when combined, add up to huge savings.

In 2004 our money-saving habits caught the eye of a producer at *Good Morning America*. Charlie Gibson conducted the interview and introduced us to the viewing public as *America's Cheapest Family* (you can watch that first interview on our website). The name stuck and since that time we've shared our frugal habits on TV, radio, and the Web as well as in magazines and newspapers, worldwide. We are on a crusade to convince the world that frugality produces freedom (and fun) while a debt-riddled lifestyle only produces distress (and destruction).

In our first book, *America's Cheapest Family Gets You Right on the Money*, we covered money-saving strategies from practically every budget category in a household budget. Of the fifteen chapters, only one was devoted to the topic of saving on groceries. Despite the varied content of the book, invariably every time we talked to the media, the interviewer wanted to know how we manage to spend so little on groceries with such a large family. In a three- to five-minute interview we can barely scratch the surface of the subject, merely offering a couple of specific examples and a few overarching principles to encourage consumers to save money. Even in our two-hour seminar, Stretching Your Grocery Dollars Without Becoming a Coupon Queen, we have to rush to get through a myriad of money- and time-saving strategies, and we still can't cover everything. This book is a wonderful opportunity to share it *all* with you. We invite you into our kitchen, to tour our pantry and freezers, and to follow us through the grocery store as we give you a one-on-one tutorial of how we have fine-tuned the art of saving money. This isn't going to be a book that you will read before bedtime to help you sleep. This is a clarion call to action. It's time to stop being a casualty of your grocer's marketing strategies and to become a savvy, super-saving shopper, or as Annette has been called, a diva of the discount.

WHY IS A BOOK ON GROCERY SAVINGS IMPORTANT?

According to a 2009 US Department of Labor report, the average American family of three spends about $6,133 per year on groceries. That's $511 each month and breaks down to $170 per person!

If you're like the average family and we could help you reduce your food bill just 20 percent, at the end of the year you'd have over $1,200 in the bank. Wow, that's not just pocket change—that's some real savings. And if you learn to use a few more strategies, you'll easily save 50 percent or more. (There's your $3,000 for reading this book!)

We can hear you saying, "Right! Sure, I can understand your math, but how much time is it going to take me to save all this money? I've seen the news stories about those coupon-clipping women who buy $200-worth of groceries for $1.72— I'm not buying it. It's not worth my time and effort." We agree. Clipping coupons is only one of many ways to save, but it is time-consuming and not something we can do every month. And going to the store is something we just don't like to do (we try to shop only once each month). Look, we've all got to eat, and to eat we have to shop. Our goal is to give you so many options for savings that you can pick the ones that fit your lifestyle and bank the savings! Not just one-time savings, but savings that will continue every week, year in and year out, for the rest of your life.

Even though we all have to eat, we don't all like to eat the same foods. Some like meat and potatoes, others like vegan. Some like hot and spicy, others like bland. There's low-fat or high protein, generic or gourmet—the list could go on forever. Just as there are numerous types of eating habits, there are almost as many choices for buying what you want to eat, from convenience marts, supermarkets, and super-stores, to warehouse clubs, ethnic stores, hypermarkets, online shops, and superettes. The one constant is that grocers are in business to make a profit.

With most families spending 10 to 15 percent of their take-home pay on grocer-ies, a lot of money is at stake here. Saving money on groceries is one of the quickest ways to start making a positive difference in your family's financial future. The money you save can be used to pay off debt, survive unemployment, manage a divorce, get through college without loans, raise your family, or fund retirement accounts.

This book will teach you about some of the tactics grocers use, but more impor-tantly, it will give you proven, winning strategies that you can implement to not only beat the grocer at his own game, but also help *your household* turn a bigger profit.

HOW SHOULD YOU USE THIS BOOK?

Because we are all unique in our diets, our shopping habits, and our lifestyles, there isn't just one way for us all to achieve grocery savings. Some people hate the idea of clipping coupons, while others revel in the challenge and love watching their gro-cery bill plummet at the checkout. Some people love spending hours each day cooking to create a delectable gourmet meal, while others look at cooking as a chore to be endured, but certainly not enjoyed.

Since we all approach food differently, we have divided this book into chapters that will address the many different methods we employ to achieve savings with feeding our families. You may want to review the table of contents and pick an area of interest to you.

We've attempted to order the chapters in a logical sequence from planning your shopping to eating what you've purchased—and everything in between. Each chapter builds on a previous one, but they can also stand alone. If, for instance, you're super-motivated to use coupons or learn about bulk cooking, you can read those chapters first, start perfecting those methods, and then come back to the other chapters later.

No matter where you start, you'll find ways to save money. One thing to remember is that while our saving methods are great for us, they may not be perfect for you. Please don't simply toss the idea if it doesn't work for you the first time. The best savings ideas we've found have been tried repeatedly, modified, reviewed, and modified again until we're satisfied with them. You'll need to do the same thing—take what we've done and make it your own. Modify, scrutinize, test, and then celebrate when it works.

GROCERY PRICES CAN VARY

We've discovered that there are major differences in prices for groceries depending on where you live, how much competition there is, and current economic and weather conditions. Please use any prices we share as a guideline—not as a goal for you to achieve in your area. The minute this book hits the shelf, many of these prices will be obsolete, but the principles we share will still be effective in helping you cut your grocery bill in half.

WHO ARE THE TIMID MOUSE, WISE OWL, AND AMAZING ANT?

Everyone who reads this book is coming from a different life experience. Some of you are new to the idea of saving money; others are old pros at it. Because of these differences, at the end of each chapter we offer three different levels of action items you can start applying right away. The names of these levels may seem strange, but they have significance, so keep reading . . .

The Timid Mouse

Mice don't like to be seen by humans. They scurry around the edge of rooms at night, looking for morsels of food to take back to their nests.

If you're just starting on your frugal journey, you may not want to be seen by other people as you search for bargains either. We understand that concern, so we've tailored our suggestions at the end of each chapter to help you start saving money without feeling embarrassed.

The Wise Owl

A family of great horned owls often visits our neighborhood. At night we hear their low "hoo-hoo" sounding from the tops of our tall pine trees. They sit and watch with their keen eyes until they spy their prey. With their quarry sighted, they swoop down making barely a sound, scoop up their victim, and are gone.

More experienced shoppers are similar to the owl family. They know how to watch and wait for great deals, then scoop them up and take them home to enjoy. They don't tarry in the grocery store; they get in, get what they want, and get out. We'll share tips for you too!

The Amazing Ant

Ants don't care who sees them. They lay a scent trail to a great find, and many of the colony's workers follow to bring home the food. They work tirelessly until the job is done. They are efficient, diligent, and always work together with others.

If you've been living the frugal life for a while, you are similar to the amazing ant. You don't care who sees you shopping; in fact, you love to tell your friends and anyone who asks how they can save money too. Being a smart shopper, you realize that you can always hone your skills—so we have tips for you too!

HOW DO WE WRITE?

This book, like our lives, is a team effort. We (Annette and Steve) have written every word in this book together. Working together presents a unique problem—how do we address you, our reader? For the most part, we write in first person plural (e.g., "We sort coupons and go shopping"). When we talk about things we do individually, we switch to third person—"Annette clips coupons," rather than, "I (Annette) clip coupons."

Because most books on frugal living are written by one spouse or the other, you might be left wondering how the author's partner really feels about this sometimes-quirky lifestyle. While we don't always agree on how to do things, we do agree that together we will accomplish much more than we could separately. We are in this life together, we shop together, we work together, and we've found a way to write together.

WHAT IS IT GONNA TAKE?

Many people are looking for one simple thing they can do to magically change their spending habits and instantly save them thousands of dollars. Throughout this book, we are going to be brutally honest with you, and we're going to start right now.

There is no magic bullet or fairy godmother with a magic wand to instantly change your life or your habits. *We wish there were, but it just isn't so.*

But we are going to share lots and lots of skills, habits, and tools that can work like magic on your situation . . . *if* (why is there always an "if" associated with magic?) . . . if you're willing to do three things:

Practice

The most effective habits require repetition to perfect. You aren't going to decide today to apply some of our shopping tips and instantly be transformed into a grocery guru. You're going to make some mistakes, but you're also going to discover some phenomenal deals. Focus on practicing and perfecting the habits that work for you, and if you do fail once in a while, don't condemn yourself. You'll improve over time.

Be Persistent

Sometimes we're both dog tired and the thought of inventorying the freezer or planning a month's worth of meals is the last thing either of us wants to do. We know that you've got incredible demands on your time, but if any of us are going to score a big win at the grocery store, we've got to stay in the game. We've got to do what we know is best, even if we don't *feel* like it. We promise you, if you persist in practicing what we share with you, you *will* save money and lots of it!

Be Patient

None of us would expect a baby who is just learning to walk to do it perfectly the first, second, or even third time. With our kids, we would cheer when they took their first wobbly steps, and cheer even louder when they plopped down on their diaper-clad posteriors. We knew that each fall brought them one step closer to being confident and capable walkers.

Be patient with yourself too. Old habits surrender to new routines slowly—but surrender they will. Day by day, month by month, your new habits will become the new normal. And soon you'll be standing in the checkout lane, arms raised as the checker smiles and reads your final total—*ahh, sweet victory!*

Yes, it's going to take some practice, persistence, and patience, but the payoff of banking thousands of dollars each year is a huge motivation to persist until you succeed.

A FEW WORDS OF CONCERN

What we've written comes from our life experience and those of visitors to our website. You need to make your own decisions as to whether what we have done is a fit for you.

Be Careful

We know that frugal-minded people are trailblazers, going places where others may not venture. Please do your own research and be safe in your frugal pursuits. In other words, don't eat green meat, "yellow snow," or anything else that just doesn't look, smell, or taste right.

Have Fun

As you perfect your saving methods, you'll experience the same euphoria that we have when we stumble across a killer deal. Give your war whoop, spike a football, or do a victory dance, and then tell a few friends about your great success. We've got to spread the word that saving money is a worthwhile and fun hobby.

LET'S GET STARTED!

There is no time like the present. No matter how overwhelming life is, you have at your disposal the greatest power in the universe—the power to choose. So make the choice now to look over the table of contents, pick a chapter that interests you, and focus on that one area of savings. By making one choice and applying one thing, you'll move from feeling like a victim to being a victor. *Any* one thing you do today to improve yourself will return benefits for many years to come.

Okay, enough of the pep talk, it's game time! So get your sneakers on, find your pencil and paper, pull out the grocery ads, oil up your shopping cart, and let's start cutting your grocery bill in half.

We interrupt this book to bring you an unannounced Pop Quiz. We really do apologize for doing this to you, but before you start any journey it's always good to assess exactly where you stand. If you don't, it would be like using MapQuest.com for a cross-country driving trip without putting in your home address—you really wouldn't have a clear picture of where to start.

TEST YOUR GROCERY GENIUS (GG)

We all come from different places when it comes to shopping for groceries. Few of us have had any formal shopper training, and most of us feel less than adequately prepared for the task. If we're going to improve, we've got to have a rough idea of our ability to bring home the deals (and the bacon too!). Just how savvy are you when it comes to shopping smarter? Take this short quiz to determine your GG. Then retake it six months from now to chart your progress.

Put a check mark next to any statement that describes how you shop.

- ☐ I go to the grocery store several times each week.
- ☐ I regularly go to the store around dinnertime, or some other time when I'm hungry.
- ☐ I never use a list—I can remember everything I need to pick up, in my head.
- ☐ I don't use an official list, I just use a piece of scrap paper or an old envelope and jot down a few items to pick up as I'm heading out the door.
- ☐ I don't have time to plan a menu. And anyway, once I get to the store I just pick up what I feel like eating.
- ☐ I don't bother looking at the grocery store ads in the newspaper, I just buy what we normally eat.
- ☐ I always take my kids with me to the store. Sure, they grab a few things and throw a tantrum or two, but I'm only going in to pick up a few items—how harmful can that be?
- ☐ I only food shop whenever I'm out and about running errands or driving from one kid's activity to another.
- ☐ I always have a grumbling spouse or elderly parent with me when I go shopping, even though they hate running this errand.
- ☐ I usually don't have time to put all of the groceries away, wash the produce, or divide the larger quantities into meal-sized portions when I get home.
- ☐ I don't bother checking what I have in my pantry. It's just easier to buy new stuff than to take the time to inventory what I already have.

☐ At the checkout, I'd rather relax, look at the magazines, or do anything but watch the cashier and the prices as my order is processed.

☐ I know I should be concerned about saving money, but what's the big deal about using a coupon to save 50 cents on a box of cereal?

☐ My life is already too structured, and planning all this grocery stuff is simply too much! Anyway a spontaneous dinner is so fun and romantic.

☐ It would take me days to organize my kitchen, refrigerator, and freezer. If I really need something I can't find, I can just run to the store to pick it up.

Okay, we know this was a pop quiz, and you didn't have time to study. How did you do? You get one point for every check mark.

10 or more points—There is room for saving a huge amount on your grocery expenses. Start your action plan by following the Timid Mouse tips at the end of each chapter.

6 to 9 points—You can find some significant savings by making a few changes. Check out the Timid Mouse and Wise Owl tips at the end of each chapter.

3 to 5 points—Pat yourself on the back; you're well on your way to becoming a super saver. Improve your skills by focusing on the Wise Owl and Amazing Ant tips at the end of each chapter.

0 to 2 points—Congratulations, you are an Amazing Ant! This book will encourage you and fine-tune your skills even further.

You'll find answers to each of the fifteen statements throughout this book (if you want to read our specific responses to these statements, go to this page on our website—AmericasCheapestFamily.com/GroceryQuiz). And as you practice and perfect the skills we outline, your grocery genius will increase, your pantry will be packed with great deals, and your bank account will be busting with cash. *It just doesn't get much better than this!*

Throughout the book, you'll see some comments from frugal friends who have visited our website or e-mailed us after reading our newsletter or first book. We've included these comments to encourage you that there are lots of other people like you who are finding success in saving money at the grocery store. If they can do it, so can you! Here is an excellent example of a smart lady who decided to improve her Grocery Genius.

Love the Website

I really love your website. It's just what I've been needing all these years. It's really helped me in more ways than one. I'm a single mom and for years it's always been easier for me to go to a fast food place or restaurant for breakfast, lunch, and dinner. And of course, I never had money for other things we needed. But thank God you opened up my eyes! I have since started looking through the ads on Wednesdays and I've gone to the grocery store (something I haven't done for years). My fridge, freezer, and pantry are overstuffed and boy is my family happy. Mom is cooking again!!! Not only that, I've saved money and been able to take care of our other needs that I didn't have money for before. Thanks for your help!

JEAN—DALLAS, TX

2

The Power of the Plan

Every successful business employs planning. They've got one-year plans, two-year plans, and five-year plans. They hire consultants to help them evaluate and fine-tune their plans. They hold meetings and retreats to focus on planning. They even plan the planning meetings. Why? Why do businesses spend all of this time, money, and effort on planning? Simply this—they know that the more they plan, the more they will accomplish. The more they plan, the more they will stay focused on their goals. The more they stay focused on their goals, the more often they'll reach those goals. Shooting from the hip may win TV gunfights, but in business it spells disaster.

But will planning in the home yield the same benefits as in business? Most of us would say something like, "We just don't have time to plan—we've got too much to do." But if we're ever going to get control of this thing called life, we've got to get off the wildly spinning carnival ride. We've got to stop the noise and stop running long enough to sit for a few minutes and look at where we are and decide where we want to go. The funny thing is that if we just take a few minutes for planning each day, we'll actually accomplish more and be less stressed.

In 2000, A. C. Nielsen produced a study showing that consumers were slightly reducing their trips to the grocery store. The trend went from 94 trips per year (1.8 trips per week) in 1997 to 90 trips per year (1.73 per week) in 2000. In 2008 a Food Marketing Institute and Nielsen survey revealed that the decline in grocery store visits has stopped. Now they have found that Americans are going to the store more than previously: 98 trips per year or 1.9 trips per week. Our family does a major shopping trip 12 times each year—once each month, with a supplemental trip to the store or a produce market midmonth to restock fruits and veggies. The only way to *shop less* is to *plan more*.

So step into our kitchen to get a behind-the-scenes look at the planning Annette does. Remember you don't have to start by doing *everything* we do. Just implementing one or two new planning habits or strategies is going to free up loads of time each week and plenty of cold, hard cash.

This chapter will focus on how you can plan your menu for one week, two weeks, or a whole month and eliminate most of your last-minute meal panics. We'll also show you how we plan our monthly grocery trip so we can capitalize on sale items to achieve the most delicious and least expensive meals possible. And, if you have kids, we'll address two topics where you've got to have a solid plan: dealing with picky eaters and school lunches.

MENU MANIA: BASIC MENU PLANNING

Even though Annette was committed to learning to manage our home and made it her full-time job, in 1983 when Steve suggested that she develop a weekly menu plan, she bristled. Her response was, "I don't need to do it! I don't want to do it! My mother didn't do it and none of my friends do it!" Eventually she decided to give it a try. To be honest, her first attempt took hours, but over time, she learned to streamline the process, and now she can crank out a monthly menu in about half an hour. Annette now says that menu planning is one of the greatest time-saving and mind-freeing tools she employs in the kitchen.

Before you start waving red flags and shouting objections about how unworkable this idea is or how domestically challenged you are, you've got to know that when we were first married, Annette was no domestic diva. As a teenager she wanted nothing to do with cooking or housework—she much preferred the mall and parties. In our first year of marriage, Annette's mom, Carol, could almost set her clock by Annette's inevitable phone call around ten in the morning. "Mom, I want to cook Aunt Harriet's pork chops and rice. How do I do it?" Each day was an adventure in learning, but it wasn't very efficient, and there was no long-range planning involved. As she learned to cook, she also started to realize that she could become more efficient in the kitchen. Planning was a natural progression in her domestic education.

Menu planning can be started simply and developed into an art form that rivals any five-star restaurant. For our family, Annette's menus fall somewhere in the middle, as she has found a way to combine our favorite tasty meals with our oftentimes hectic schedule. However, our kids will tell you that Annette's cooking is often much better than the food they've eaten at restaurants. As a result of her planning and cooking ability, we eat dinner at home together almost every night.

According to the Food Marketing Institute's 2006 survey, the average American family is eating dinner away from home 1.4 times each week. We know several families who are either so busy, hate cooking so much, or feel so incompetent in the kitchen that eating out or picking up a carryout dinner is a daily occurrence. If you fall into one of these categories, stay with us. We'll share some simple menu solutions so you can start feeding your family at home without having to spend your life in the kitchen.

Initially, Annette planned only the dinner meals, but over time she included a rotation of breakfast and lunch meals also. Having a menu planned takes the stress out of end-of-day meal preparation: she's no longer a victim of the money-sucking, "It's 5 p.m., what should I make for dinner? Nothing sounds good—let's order a pizza," dilemma.

We are going to approach planning meals much differently than most people do. For the masses, meal planning and preparation are emotional decisions, "What do I feel like eating or making tonight?" Based on those feelings, the chef does the shopping or meal preparation at that time. We're going to help you set emotion aside—you'll still have the freedom to cook and eat what you want, but you won't have to run to the store every day to shop, spending precious minutes of your life, just so you can eat. Be prepared, though, because this method is almost completely opposite of what most people do.

We want to help you be successful, so we're going to provide you with plenty of examples and tools to get you started. Eventually, planning a menu for your family will be as easy as getting dressed in the morning.

We've broken down our menu planning process into five easy steps:

Step One: Taking stock of what you already have
Step Two: Researching and listing sale items
Step Three: Listing daily events
Step Four: Selecting the meals
Step Five: Making the shopping list

STEP ONE: TAKING STOCK OF WHAT YOU ALREADY HAVE

Before we embark on our once-a-month grocery trek, Annette takes stock of what we have in our pantry and refrigerator, and Steve inventories the freezer. Annette records items in a number of categories, noting what we'll need to buy in order to make it through the month. If you go shopping once each week or twice a month, you may not have to do a full inventory each time. But this step is still critical for making sure your pantry and freezer are fully stocked so you won't have to make a special trip to just pick up one missing item for a meal you are preparing. Taking stock also helps us minimize duplicate purchases and reminds us to use the things we already have in the house.

Using a blank sheet of scrap paper, we make note of the following items and quantities we have in stock (of course, your list will differ):

- **Breakfast Foods**: Eggs, milk, juice, oatmeal, farina, cold cereal, bagels, and ingredients for waffles, pancakes, and French toast. Annette also makes sure our pantry is well stocked with baking soda, flour, baking powder, vanilla, cinnamon, and commonly used spices.
- **Lunch Foods**: Peanut butter and jelly, tuna, bread, lunch meat, eggs for

egg salad, tortillas and shredded cheese for cheese crisps, hot dogs, cottage cheese, yogurt, salad fixings, and plenty of fruit.

- **Dinner Foods**: Steve takes almost everything out of our chest freezer, and gets a count of the number of items in each of the following categories: pork/ham, sausage, chicken/turkey, beef, lamb, and lunch meat. He also notes how much margarine, milk, bread, and butter we have, along with frozen vegetables. Finally we check our supply of beans, pasta, and other items for meatless meals or side dishes.

A Stocked Pantry

Early in our writing career we had a TV news reporter and cameraman standing in our pantry room. As the reporter looked over the three sets of floor-to-ceiling, heavy-duty, grey metal shelves, he looked at Annette and asked, "So how much did it cost you to fill these shelves with food?" She kind of shook her head and realized that he really didn't understand our methods. She told him, "We spend $350 each month for food. Over time, as we pick up bargains, the shelves get filled with the things you see here. It's not a onetime expense." He nodded, but we could tell from the glazed look in his eyes that he still didn't understand.

If you follow the principles in this chapter, your pantry will be bursting with an abundance of great food purchased at rock-bottom prices. We'll share more about what we stock in our pantry in Chapter 6, "Stocking Up and Organizing."

Once you know what you have in your pantry and freezer, you have two choices to make:

1. Go on to the next step of reviewing the food ads so you can decide which stores have the best prices and decide where you will shop for the items you'll eat in the next week or weeks. Or . . .
2. Plan your menu from what you already have in stock and just go to the store to pick up a few of the things that you are out of and items that are steeply discounted. There have been a few times when we've been so well stocked and the sales so poor, that our monthly shopping trips have either been delayed or we've just picked up some produce and dairy products and gone home.

STEP TWO: RESEARCHING AND LISTING SALE ITEMS

Once Annette knows what we have in stock, she carefully reviews the grocery store ads with a black marker in hand, circling items that we need and items that are at or below our "Buy Price." In our city, food ads from most of the grocery stores arrive either in the mail or in the Wednesday newspaper. If for some reason a particular store's flyer doesn't arrive, we review its ad on the Internet. But it's always easier for Annette to evaluate the sales flyers while sitting at the kitchen table with *all* of the printed ads in front of her.

Once she has reviewed and circled all of the ads, Annette takes out a sheet of loose-leaf paper and writes a list of the best deals. But she doesn't just write one long list of items she wants, she lists the sale items by store. Just because an item is put on the list doesn't mean that it will be purchased—they are just written down, to note the price as a possible purchase and for easy price comparison.

She lists one store at a time on a sheet of loose-leaf paper, recording the best sale items each is advertising under the store's name. Then she lists the next store and the sale items. The stores we shop at in our area are: Albertsons, Bashas', Fresh & Easy, Fry's (Kroger), Safeway, Sprouts, and Smart & Final (we don't list Walmart because they don't publish a specific grocery ad). Many reporters and people at our seminars ask us which store has the best prices. Annette always says, "There is no one store that always has the best prices. You have to shop around to save."

STORE 1:		
ITEM	PRICE	COUPON

STORE 2:		
ITEM	PRICE	COUPON

She keeps listing stores until she has covered all of the best sale items.

Here is an actual example of Annette's loss-leader list:

|ALBERTSONS|

GM Cereal 9-13oz 1.77
Betty Crocker Cake Mix 59¢
Light br Sugar 2# 1.00
Cornstarch 16oz 1.00
Evap milk 12oz 79¢
Nature Valley Granola Bars 2.00
Broccoli Crowns/Cauliflower 99¢lb
Cilantro 33¢ bunch

|BASHAS|

Tomatoes 99¢
Baguette Bread 50¢
Whole milk 1.49 L2 (40.00 purchase)
Bananas 39¢ lb
pineapples 2.00
40% off Shamrock (Egg Nog?) whipping cream cottage cheese
Bars, Hotdogs, lunch meat, bacon 40% off
Food Club cereals 1.99
Pillsbury Grand Biscuits 16oz 1.66
Bashas ice cream/sherbet 1.75qt 2.00
fritos/cheetos 10oz 1.50
zucchini or yellow squash 89¢lb
McIntosh Apples .50 lb

|SAFEWAY|

* Boneless Beef Chuck Steak, Chuck Roast 1.49 lb
* Corn on Cob 10-2.00
  Best Foods Mayo 30oz 1.88
* Kraft Singles 99¢ L1
* Doritos 1.50 L2
  ✓ Hillshire Farm Smoked Sausage 16oz 2.00 L2
* Starkist Tuna 50¢ 6oz
  Kraft salad dressing 16oz 1.50
* Van Camps pork + beans 50¢
  Arm + Hammer Laundry det 100oz 3.50
  Natures Cupboard breads 24oz 1.50
  Lucerne Eggs 18ct B1G1F
* Potatoes 10# russets 2.99

|SPROUTS|

* Watermelons 99¢ each
  Bartlett Pears 2lbs-1.00
  gr peppers 3-1.00

This list serves three purposes:

1. It helps us determine the store or stores where we will shop. We usually shop two in one night, the first one for the bulk of our shopping and the second for loss leaders.
2. It allows us to more easily see prices on the items we want, without having to flip through numerous pages of store ads.
3. If we are short on time, it allows us to go to Walmart and more easily "ad-match" the best prices from all of the other stores' sales.

Some of the sale items purchased on this shopping trip will not be incorporated into the menu now, but will be saved for future months. This stockpiling concept allows us to always be eating food purchased at the lowest prices.

The Savings Add Up with Ad-Match

It was February 2007 a few weeks after our first book had launched and life had been *crazy*. We'd had two trips to New York in two months—we were tired and didn't have a lot of time for shopping. Annette made her list of the loss leaders from the various stores in our area, and we grabbed the walkie-talkies and drove to the Super Walmart near our home.

When we do a full-fledged ad-match shopping trip at Walmart, we each take two carts and head out. One cart is for regularly priced items and a second for the items that we are asking Walmart to match the price on. This practice of segregating the items really helps at the checkout. Most checkers are accustomed to shoppers having three or four ad-matched items, but never a full cart. It can be overwhelming for them, and *we* could possibly forget which items we want to get a discount on.

This particular time, right in front of us, was a guy in his thirties with one shopping cart filled with groceries. He checked out and paid with cash—$265. Our four-cart order took about fifteen minutes to ring up, but in the end after we had everything bagged in our paper bags (brought from home), and the cashier totaled the order, we paid out $278.10. The cashier was amazed at the amount of groceries we had purchased for just a few dollars more than her previous customer.

Using ad-match, over half of our order was steeply discounted. We also saved on gas and driving time. There is one disadvantage to shopping at Walmart and that is they don't double coupons. But if you're strapped for time and have few or no coupons—whew—this is the way to go.

STEP THREE: LISTING DAILY EVENTS

Having determined what sale items Annette will buy, she starts to create the month's meal plan by pulling out her calendar and a menu planning sheet.

Why the calendar? Simple. She plans the menu based on our family's schedule for each night. She doesn't want to cook a roast on a night when Abbey has to be out the door early for her 4H Club meeting or a night when the boys do weight training. On busy nights she plans a simpler meal, and on nights when we have more time and nothing is scheduled after dinner, she'll plan a more complex meal like a turkey or roast. The bottom line is to plan meals that fit with the schedule so we rush less and enjoy sitting down together for dinner more.

Here's what a typical week of activities looks like:

DAY	ACTIVITY	DINNER MEAL
Sunday	Home night—schedules and kids' payday	
Monday	Early dinner: 4H clogging for Abbey, everyone else weight training	
Tuesday	Joe work	
Wednesday	Joe baseball	
Thursday	All weight training	
Friday	Young adult/singles group	
Saturday	Home—work on projects day	

Here's an actual menu sheet from the end of June and the beginning of July 2009:

Menu Planner

Sunday	6/21 Leftovers	6/28 Leftovers
Monday	6/22 Clogging/Paps Beef Stroganoff rice gr. beans	6/29 Clogging/Paps Sesame chicken rice beets
Tuesday	6/23 Econ Fake Bay Chicken Cashew rice onion celery water chestnuts	6/30 Ham & gravy potatoes broccoli
Wednesday	6/24 Cheese, sausage, spinach pie applesauce	7/1 Sloppy Joes Buns tater tots, pickles or fruit
Thursday	6/25 Spaghetti & meatballs Salad or squash	7/2 Eggplant parmesan spaghetti
Friday	6/26 Julie home Hash – potatoe onion carrot	7/3 Chicken fajitas rice, tortillas peppers, onions
Saturday	6/27 YAS tower of Babel night Pizza veggies + dip	7/4 YAS pool party hamburgers, hot dogs, pork ribs veggies baked beans fruit corn on cob

Cake for June
Bdays

desserts

Use the following blank menu planning sheet to start planning your next two weeks of meals. You can either make a copy of this sheet or create your own version in a word processing program.

Menu Planner

DATE	WEEK 1	DATE	WEEK 2
Sun __ / __	Activity - Meal	Sun __ / __	Activity - Meal
Mon __ / __	Activity - Meal	Mon __ / __	Activity - Meal
Tues __ / __	Activity - Meal	Tues __ / __	Activity - Meal
Wed __ / __	Activity - Meal	Wed __ / __	Activity - Meal
Thurs __ / __	Activity - Meal	Thurs __ / __	Activity - Meal
Fri __ / __	Activity - Meal	Fri __ / __	Activity - Meal
Sat __ / __	Activity - Meal	Sat __ / __	Activity - Meal

STEP FOUR: SELECTING THE MEALS

A while back we did an interview with Vicky Thornton and Jen Rehberger for their podcast, *What Matters Most* (visit www.vickyandjen.com and search for a show entitled *Everyday Frugal Living*). We were talking about grocery shopping when Steve decided to turn the tables on our interviewers by asking them a question. He asked Jen to quickly name her three favorite meals. She rattled off chicken enchiladas, grilled cheese with tomato soup, and chicken cordon bleu. It took fifteen seconds for her to come up with her list. Our point in asking the question was to show listeners how easy it is to create a simple dinner menu. Give it a try at home; just pull out a blank sheet of paper and list some of your favorite meals. It won't take long, and over time you can add to that list and end up with a catalog of meals you love to prepare and eat. If you're having trouble getting started, here's a little help.

Sample Beginner Menu

This is a simple beginner menu that Annette presents at our seminars. It's not perfectly nutritious, but it will give you an easy target to hit—so you start off being successful.

Monday: Tacos—lettuce, tomato, cheese, meat, and taco shells or tortillas
Tuesday: Mac & cheese, carrots—cooked or raw
Wednesday: Hot dogs, beans, pickles
Thursday: BBQ chicken, corn on the cob, applesauce
Friday: Spaghetti & meatballs, salad
Saturday: Hamburgers, baked potatoes, green beans
Sunday: Vegetable soup with muffins

List Your Side Dishes

Over the years Annette has been transformed from being a culinary-challenged cook to a menu-planning machine. She isn't one of these women who just loves to be in the kitchen cooking from morning to night. She views it more as an exercise in efficiency: "I want to feed my family good-tasting, healthy meals. So how can I achieve this goal without spending my life doing it?" It's not that Annette hates to cook, but that she has so many other things she wants to do with the kids and Steve that she wants to minimize the time spent preparing meals. It helps to break down meal planning into various components (veggies, starches, and main dishes) so you can create nutritionally balanced meals.

Before you select your meals, it's a good idea to create a reference list of all the veggies, fruits, and starches that are available for you to choose from. You can use this list to combine with main dishes to complete your meals. It's a lot easier to have a list in front of you than to have to try to remember all of your options. Here's our list; it's not exhaustive, but it should give you a jump-start. Don't worry about including everything, you can always add more as time goes on.

VEGGIES / FRUITS	STARCHES
Applesauce	Beans
Asparagus	Biscuits / rolls
Baked apples	Butternut squash
Beets	Corn—frozen kernel
Broccoli	Cornbread
Brussels sprouts	Corn on the cob
Cabbage	Muffins
Carrots	Noodles / pasta
Cauliflower	Potato or tortilla chips (special occasions only)
Green beans	Potatoes (baked, mashed, or oven fried)
Green salad	Rice (brown or white)
Pickles	Yams
Spinach	
Squash (patty pan, yellow crookneck, zucchini)	
Add your own family favorites	

We eat very few one-dish/casserole meals. Consequently, Annette prepares side dishes each night to accompany the main dish (which was usually prepared and frozen on our once-a-month cooking day—more about this in Chapter 5, "Cooking"). These side dishes generally take about a half hour or less to put together. And because the main dish only needs reheating, once the side dish is prepared, we can eat.

The meal combinations are determined based on a number of factors:

1. **Seasonal**: Almost all of the fruits and vegetables we eat are in season—and inexpensive. So if we have a hankering for asparagus or some other seasonal fruit or veggie, but the price is outrageous, we wait for it to be in season. That is, unless we have previously purchased a fruit such as blueberries and stored them in the freezer. If you're not sure when particular fruits or veggies are in season in your area, consult with your local county extension service; they should be able to provide you with accurate information. Another great source would be to stop by a farmers market—they'll know for sure.

2. **Variety**: We try not to repeat the same veggies or starches two days in a row. We once heard of a mom who didn't like the idea of planning meals, so she fed her family the same meal every day for two weeks! We know that's an extreme example, but planning a little variety into your menu will go a long way to helping you really enjoy the process.

3. **Nutrition**: Having a menu planned with three categories—proteins, starches, and vegetables—provides a balanced diet and helps kids understand the food groups so they can develop healthy eating habits from a young age.

Here's the completed week's worth of activities with dinner meals:

DAY	ACTIVITY	DINNER MEAL	IN FREEZER	FROM SCRATCH
Sunday	Home night—schedules and kids' payday	Shepherd's pie with broccoli	X	
Monday	Early dinner: 4H clogging for Abbey, everyone else weight training	Chicken enchiladas, rice, and carrots	X	
Tuesday	Joe work	Cooked ham, mashed potatoes, green beans		X
Wednesday	Joe baseball	Baked ziti with green salad	X	
Thursday	All weight training	Chicken vegetable soup with blueberry muffins	X	
Friday	Young adult / singles group	Tacos including lettuce, tomato, cheese, and meat		X
Saturday	Home—work on projects day	Leftovers		

Another time saver in selecting the meals is to compile a list that contains all of the meals you currently know how to cook. Annette's list has grown over the years from just a handful of meals to over one hundred. The meals are categorized by types: beef, pork/ham, chicken/turkey (we use them interchangeably), ethnic Greek or Italian, and meatless meals. Many people have asked if we have recipes available for all of these meals. There are some in the Bonus Material at the back of this book, and others are posted at AmericasCheapestFamily.com in our subscriber-only section. Someday we hope to compile an entire cookbook of the recipes we use.

From this list, Annette selects and "plugs in" meals on her menu planner sheet, always being mindful of the amount of preparation time required for the meal and the events of each particular evening. She even includes the judicious use of leftovers—knowing that many of the meals are prepared in large enough quantities to serve again. Planning the daily meals is probably the most time-consuming and mentally intense part of menu planning. It's also the step that will give you the most freedom throughout the week or month because you'll have a plan, written down. With this step completed, you've just taken dinner out of panic mode and planned it to perfection.

Annette usually plans fifteen to eighteen dinner meals to be cooked on our once-a-month cooking day. We view this much like our once-a-month food shopping trek—it is efficient and helps make the household run smoother throughout the month. These meals are stored in the freezer to be used later in the month when the menu calls for them. Once she has the freezer meals planned, she fills in the remaining days with leftovers or roasted chicken, pasta with homemade spaghetti sauce, pork chops, steaks on the grill, or other meals cooked on the day they are eaten.

Here are more options for some easier dinner combinations:

MAIN DISH	STARCH	VEGETABLE
BEEF MEALS		
Beef brisket with mustard and onion	Baked potatoes	Cooked carrots
Beef stroganoff	Rice	Green beans
Meat loaf	Corn (frozen)	Broccoli
Shish kebab	Oven-fried potatoes	Cauliflower
Shepherd's pie	Dough crust	Squash—zucchini
Salisbury steaks	Baked potatoes	Broccoli
CHICKEN MEALS		
BBQ chicken	Corn	Green salad
Cashew chicken	Rice	Celery and onions
Chicken fajitas	Tortillas and rice	Peppers and onions

Oven-fried chicken	Mashed potatoes	Creamed spinach
Marinated chicken	Baked potatoes	Beets
PORK MEALS		
Breaded pork chops	Oven-fried yams	Asparagus
Sweet and sour ham	Rice	Pineapple, carrots, onions, and green peppers in recipe
Ham	Scalloped potatoes	Cooked carrots
Ham & split pea soup	Cheese muffins or biscuits	Carrot, celery, and onion in soup
MISC. MEALS		
Marinated lamb shoulder chops	Yams	Green beans
Vegetable lentil soup	Banana bread	Veggies in soup
Hot dogs	Beans	Applesauce

Can you see how having a written plan can really reduce your stress level? Once you have all of the components laid out, it becomes more like piecing together a jigsaw puzzle than creating an entire menu from scratch.

Annette also creates a rotation of meals for breakfasts and lunches. We have included several tips for packing school and office lunches in the next section of this chapter.

Breakfast. We have a set rotation of various meals for breakfast—with a few substitutions if we are running low on a particular supply or type of meal. This is an example from one week a while back:

Monday: Hot cereal with grapefruit/or bagels (in the summer)
Tuesday: Cold cereal with fresh fruit
Wednesday: Over-easy eggs with toast and grapefruit
Thursday: Pancakes (made from scratch or from the freezer) and sausage

Friday: Bagels with fruit or cold cereal with fruit

Saturday: French toast, pancakes, or waffles (made fresh or from the freezer) with ham

Sunday: Scrambled eggs with potatoes, cheese, and sausage with fruit juice to drink.

When we cook French toast, pancakes, or waffles, we usually prepare a quadruple batch. The leftovers are neatly packed into freezer storage bags and frozen. Then they are put into the rotation of meals during that month.

Lunch. This rotation varies greatly depending on what we have purchased on sale and what leftovers we have in the refrigerator. Here's a sample:

Monday: Yogurt with fruit and pretzels (on the side)

Tuesday: Mac & cheese and bananas (on the side)

Wednesday: Tuna fish sandwiches and apples

Thursday: PB&J with orange slices

Friday: Lunch-meat sandwiches and pickles

Saturday: Leftovers

Sunday: Bacon, lettuce, and tomato sandwiches (BLTs)

The Bad Ad Day

But, what do you do if your budget is limited, your pantry is bare, and the sales are uninspiring?

About a year after Annette had started menu planning, she hit a bump in the road. The food ads were really "boring," and although we did have a few cuts of meat in the freezer, there just wasn't much variety. The only meat sale that even slightly appealed to her tastes and our budget was on Italian sausage at $1.50 per pound. Previously she had only used Italian sausage in spaghetti sauce. What do you do in an instance like this? Well, Annette thought for a few minutes and then pulled out her cookbooks and searched for recipes that used Italian sausage. As a result of this inconvenient situation she discovered one of our all-time favorite meals—cheese sausage spinach pie (nope, it doesn't sound like a gourmet meal, but it sure tastes great!). Today you could easily search for recipes on the Internet. A quick search on www.Cooks.com resulted in over six hundred suggestions for meals that include Italian sausage. (The recipe for cheese sausage spinach pie is in the Bonus Material section in the back of this book.)

If you make a commitment to living within your means and using menu planning as a helpful tool, you might have to put in some extra effort and research, but the rewards can be incredibly delicious as you save money and expand your culinary expertise.

Help for the Recipe-Challenged

You may be saying, "Sure, menu planning is easy for you, but I only know how to cook five different meals!" Here's what Annette did when she discovered she was "recipe-challenged."

Initially, each day she would phone her mom to figure out how to cook the day's dinner. After a few months she had her basic recipes down and was feeling more comfortable with cooking and planning. Then she hit a plateau. She grew tired of the ten to twelve different meals in our diet. We'd been to a potluck dinner with some friends and tasted some really yummy recipes. That's when she came up with the idea of hosting a recipe swap. She invited some friends over and asked each one to bring a few of their favorite recipes to share. It was a lot of fun: they were like little kids playing "Go Fish." ("Got any really easy dessert recipes?" "I need a pork recipe.") The event was so successful that Annette felt totally recharged and enthusiastic about trying some new things. Out of this particular recipe swap came a delicious family classic, Doreen's Christmas pumpkin bread.

Find Reference Materials

Cookbooks are an invaluable resource. Make sure to have at least a couple of basic ones, such as *Better Homes and Gardens New Cook Book*—the red and white–checkered one—or the bright red *Betty Crocker Cookbook*. Annette's mom gave her the *Good Housekeeping Illustrated Cookbook* at one of our wedding showers. It was one of the best "tools" Annette could have received because every recipe is accompanied by a full-color picture and line drawings of each step. A picture is worth a thousand words—unless it's cheese blintzes; they're worth a couple thousand . . . calories. Don't forget your public library. Ours has an entire section of cookbooks—13 feet long and 8 feet high—with every kind of ethnic and lifestyle variety imaginable.

Steve loves to research recipes on the Internet. This is where he discovered our recipe for beef jerky. (This stuff is so good it almost disappears as soon as it's made.) Twara Kellum hosts a website with lots of inexpensive recipes—visit www.LivingOnADime.com/free-recipes.htm for some great ideas. Make a game of it and try to find one new recipe each month. Some of the new recipes will be winners, and others will be quickly forgotten or become the stuff of family legends.

Our Cooking Bible

We received *1000 Best Recipes* from Cook's Illustrated when we got married. We've since renamed it *The Bible*. The Cook's Illustrated food testers walk you through all the various ways they tried to cook the meal. Not only do you get a professional, foolproof recipe (which saved us tons of money from not having to throw out meals), but you actually learn how to cook in the process—not just follow a recipe. Anyone looking to increase their cooking skills and have a near 100 percent success rate right out of the gate ought to have this book.

BRYAN—NASHVILLE, TN

After many years of planning, researching, and experimenting, Annette has an outstanding catalog of meals to choose from. Since Annette's repertoire of meals is so large now, it allows enough variety for our family to enjoy, and she rarely feels the need to look for something new. The same thing applies to side dishes and desserts. With a little practice, patience, and perseverance, you can expand your repertoire too. Planning a menu is a skill that can be easily learned and will definitely become easier as it is repeated and fine-tuned.

Still not sure? Okay, so you've got the idea of planning a rotation of nutritionally appropriate meals that fit with your family's schedule. But you feel uncertain about pulling this whole thing off. It takes practice, but you can do it. Just don't try planning a whole month at first. Begin with one week of meals, then expand from there.

As your cooking improves and you get the quantities right for your family, you'll discover the value of leftovers. About once each week, Annette plans a dinner of leftovers. The only downside is that the best stuff goes first, so those late to the table have to do some serious negotiating. Leftovers also make great lunches for those who work outside of the home—just ask Becky—her coworkers are always jealous of her great-smelling lunches.

Nothing can derail the best-laid plans of a menu-planning maven faster than a picky eater in your house. We've dealt with this issue at *our* house, and maybe what we've tried can help you stay on track.

Pickin' on Picky Eaters

"Come on, Jimmy, eat your Brussels sprouts." "*Rrrrrrr-Rrrrooorr,* here comes the airplane. Make sure you open the hangar doors nice and wide." Oh, the games we play to get kids to eat what is served. There must be an easier way.

Let's talk about picky eaters—kids *and* adults. In the US, UK, and Australia many studies have shown that we throw away between 20 and 30 percent of the food we buy. That is a terrible waste of money. But even worse is when you don't help your kids learn to appreciate a wide variety of foods. We know families where the kids (and one or both of the parents) won't eat anything green, or they need to put ketchup on everything they eat, or their favorite food is hot dogs and they eat them every day. None of these choices is healthy. So how do you get your family to be adventuresome and try different foods like Brussels sprouts, or beets, or some other food they find "disgusting"? We have read that it takes about fifteen exposures to a new food to acquire a taste for it—and we've seen this to be true in our own family. You've got to have a plan and stick to it. Consistency is the key to learning to enjoy what is served. We are going to focus on helping kids expand their culinary boundaries, but everything we share can also apply to adults.

The Three-Bite Rule. If you're serving a food your kids don't seem to like, try serving it with something they really *do* enjoy. Then enact the "three-bite rule," but make sure you have a yummy dessert planned to get the greatest effect out of the rule. Here's how we implemented it. Initially we required our kids to take three small bites of the new food. If they complied with three (or more) bites, then they got to have dessert. Eventually we said that they could have dessert if they ate an entire (small) serving of the food. It's sort of like raising the bar on a pole vaulter. Just remember that kids have eagle eyes, and if the parents won't eat the food, then why should they? This is the reason Steve endures eating beets. He's never appreciated the finer points of beet eating. He can't get past the fact that, as he says, "They taste like dirt!" Nevertheless, he perseveres and eats them as an example to the kids . . . ugh! Actually, over time he has acquired a taste for them. Now he says that they taste more like "sweet dirt."

We've used the three-bite rule for years and have seen it work wonders for our kids. Grapefruit and Joseph didn't agree the first time he ate it. He gagged and carried on as if he would die. We persevered, and over time he began to appreciate it. Now when it is served, he devours it and asks for more—sometimes without brown sugar on it! Becky, who's now twenty-four, took a trip to Ecuador a few years ago and had the wonderful opportunity to try some of their native cuisine. She even ate goat . . . and liked it. Thanks to Nana's influence, Roy has learned to love all kinds of seafood.

Help with Meal Preparation. Another way to beat the picky-eater syndrome is to involve your kids in meal preparation. We'll give you plenty of tips in Chapter 9, "Feeding Your Kids for Less."

The Meal Is the Meal. In many families one or both of the parents have become short-order chefs, preparing several different options for those who don't want to eat what is served. We simply aren't willing to do this. There is only one meal offered, and while it may not be Joe's favorite tonight, we always assure the kids that their favorite meal is coming soon and that they can endure this one and survive. Having a menu plan to back up this promise is always helpful.

With a menu plan in hand and the picky-eater problem managed, you'll be able to enjoy your meals and have much less stress in the preparation and the eating.

Hey, don't just take our word for it when it comes to picky eaters. Here's what Dr. Vincent Iannelli, a pediatric expert on About.com, says regarding picky eaters and new foods:

> While you should provide three well-balanced meals each day, it is important to keep in mind that many younger children will only eat one or two full meals each day. If your child has had a good breakfast and lunch, then it is okay that he doesn't want to eat much at dinner. Although your child will probably be hesitant to try new foods, you should still offer small amounts of them once or twice a week (one tablespoon of green beans, for example). Most children will try a new food after being offered it 10-15 times.
>
> You should also not prepare more than one meal for your child. If he doesn't want to eat what was prepared for the rest of the family, then he should not be forced to, but you should also not give him something else to eat. He will not starve after missing a single meal, and providing alternatives to the prepared meal will just cause more problems later. Talk to your pediatrician if mealtime has become a battle though and your child never wants to eat what the rest of the family is eating.[1]

When Abbey was three years old, she also detested the taste of grapefruit—a staple at our house in the winter and spring. (We have an orchard of citrus trees on our property.) How did she learn to like it? She says, "Daddy would put a red cherry in the center and sprinkle some of the red cherry juice on the grapefruit. It looked fun and tasted good." Now at age sixteen, she eats her grapefruit with just a little brown sugar and a smile.

We're not expecting you to have worked out all of the issues with picky eaters at this point in time, but it is helpful to at least recognize if this is an issue in your household. Before we get to the final step in your grocery plan—making a shopping list—we've got a few tips for parents with school-aged kids who need help packing a lunch every day. These suggestions could easily work for anyone who is employed and regularly buys lunch every day (a $2,000 or more annual habit). If you fail to plan for lunches, you could easily fritter away much of the money you saved with your newly found planning skills.

Avoiding the School Lunch Crunch

The same principles of menu planning and preparation may be successfully applied to school lunches. Many people tell us that their kids don't have time to eat a hot lunch at school. Many schools limit "lunch hours" to no more than twenty minutes, due to student behavioral issues and cafeteria size. By the time kids stand in line, pay for their lunch, and find a place to sit—without gum on the seat—the lunch period is just about over. So sending your kids to school with a prepared lunch not only saves money, but allows them to have the time to eat the more nutritious food you've packed.

By doing a little brainstorming you can easily come up with a five-day (or more) rotation of meals that your kids like, which you can easily stock up for and prepare. With some planning, many parts of these meals can either be prepared on weekends or the night before. This will make getting kids out the door on school mornings much less stressful.

Here's a sample lunch rotation:

DAY	"MAIN DISH"	FRUIT	DESSERT / EXTRA
Monday	Egg salad sandwich	Apple	Homemade cookie
Tuesday	Tuna fish sandwich	Pear	Pretzels
Wednesday	Yogurt in small plastic container	Raisins	Tortilla chips
Thursday	Peanut butter & jelly	Carrots	Homemade trail mix
Friday	Lunch meat sandwich	Pineapple chunks	Cookies

Here are some tips from other families:

~

The Grab Bag Lunch

Prepackage smaller servings of chips, nuts, crackers, pretzels, or cookies (purchased in bulk bags) into zippered bags. Do the same thing with cut-up veggies—carrots and celery. When it comes time to assemble lunches just grab a bag of *this* and a bag of *that* along with a sandwich and they're ready to go.

NANCY—PHOENIX, AZ

~

Thermos Lunches

During the colder months, send your child to school with a thermos full of a hot meal—soup, stew, mac and cheese, chili, spaghetti, and even hot dogs and beans. Another idea is to fill the thermos with taco meat with the cheese mixed in. Pack a tortilla and some shredded lettuce and tomato slices and they can easily assemble their own soft taco.

SANDY—SALT LAKE CITY, UT

~

Recycle

This is a great way to include leftovers into your lunch schedule. Just preheat in the morning, place in the thermos, and it will still be warm a few hours later at lunch. Include plastic utensils and encourage your child to bring them home to be washed and reused. If they are lost, it's no big deal, but teaching them to keep track of reusable things is a good lesson and helps the environment too.

NICOLE—ARLINGTON, VA

Make It Small

Kids like small things. Baby carrots, mini celery, little pieces of broccoli. Send a small plastic container with some ranch dip in it too. If you bake cookies or brownies, make them mini-sized. Cut their sandwiches in quarters. Smaller is easier to handle and more their size.

ROBERT—LOMBARD, IL

Creativity Rules!

There's no need to purchase prepackaged extremely overpriced single-serving chips, cracker meals, and yogurts. They may seem easy, but they don't provide the best nutrition and, at three to five times the cost of the larger packages, they're no deal. Plus the amount of packaging that you'll be adding to landfills is astronomical on these little goodies. You can "prepackage" your own chips in zippered plastic bags and purchase a larger container of yogurt to spoon into smaller portable plastic containers.

JAN—ROUND ROCK, TX

Not on Bread Alone

To make lunch more interesting try some different approaches to typical sandwich bread like: pita bread, mini bagels, raisin bread, dinner rolls, croissants, soft flour tortillas or lettuce leaves used for a "wrap," and hamburger or hot dog buns. I've even used a cookie cutter on a "regular" sandwich bread to give it a fun and unique shape. The kids love the variety (and I love the fun).

ANGELA—QUEBEC, CANADA

~

Think Beyond the Sandwich

Try alternatives to sandwiches. Try packing some string cheese and rolls of sliced turkey, ham, or roast beef. Include a small container of flavored BBQ sauce or honey mustard sauce for dipping.

Robyn—Welch, MN

Kids can help! If your kids are school-age, they can help prepare their own lunches. Involve them! They may complain, but in the long run, they'll feel better about helping and learn a valuable life skill—that planning ahead can actually result in "deliciousness."

Now that you've got a solid menu mapped out and your whole family is buying into the plan, you're ready for the final step before heading out the door to the store.

STEP FIVE: MAKING THE SHOPPING LIST

With inventory taken, the ads reviewed, the daily events listed, and the menu planned, Annette prepares her final shopping list. Our list is a check-off type form that we've developed, listing the items we most often use at home. It is available as a free modifiable word processing document on our website—AmericasCheapestFamily.com. It contains items that we regularly stock in our pantry or purchase each month. It serves as a reminder so that the essentials are not overlooked. Your list will be different from ours, and that's why we've made the modifiable version available—you can customize it to your family's tastes.

SHOPPING LIST

ITEM	QTY	ITEM	QTY	ITEM	QTY	ITEM	QTY
CONDIMENTS		Baking soda	___	**FROZEN FOOD**		Chuck steak	___
Jelly/jam	___	Salt/pepper	___	Ice cream	___	Round steak	___
Peanut butter	___	Garlic powder	___	Orange juice	___	Roast beef	___
Honey	___	Spices	___	Apple juice	___	Chicken—whole	___
Shortening	___	Bouillon	___	Grape juice	___	Chicken—cut-up	___
Oil	___	**HOUSEHOLD**		Cranberry	___	Turkey	___
Vinegar	___	Dishwasher soap	___	Misc. juice	___	Turkey ham	___
Maple syrup	___	Dish soap	___	Spinach	___	Lamb—leg	___
Ketchup	___	Laundry detergent	___	Peas	___	Lamb—chops	___
Mustard	___	Bleach	___	Corn	___	Pork—chops	___
Mayonnaise	___	Bath spray	___	Green beans	___	Pork—roast	___
Pickles	___	Soap	___	Brussels sprouts	___	Italian sausage	___
Relish	___	Sponges	___	Mixed veggies	___	Ham	___
Salad dressing	___	Furniture polish	___	**PERSONAL**		**VEGGIES**	
Olives	___	Lightbulbs	___	Toothpaste	___	Avocado	___
Tomato paste	___	Vacuum bags	___	Shaving Cream	___	Broccoli	___
Tomato sauce	___	Glass cleaner	___	Razors	___	Cabbage	___
Tomatoes diced	___	Comet	___	Deodorant	___	Carrots	___
Gravy	___	**BREAKFAST**		Floss	___	Cauliflower	___
CANNED FRUIT		Cold cereal	___	Shampoo	___	Celery	___
Pineapple	___	Oatmeal	___	Conditioner	___	Corn	___
Applesauce	___	Hot cereal	___	Kotex maxi	___	Cucumbers	___
Mandarin oranges	___	Coffee/Tea	___	Thins	___	Green onions	___
Raisins	___	**PAPER GOODS**		Light days	___	Green pepper	___
CANNED GOODS		Tissues	___	Vitamins	___	Lettuce	___
Tuna	___	Toilet paper	___	Stockings	___	Mushrooms	___
Cream chicken	___	Napkins	___	**DAIRY**		Potatoes	___
Cream mushroom	___	Saran wrap	___	Milk	___	Radishes	___
Tomato soup	___	Foil	___	Margarine	___	Squash	___
Asparagus	___	Wax paper	___	Whipping cream	___	Tomato	___
Beets	___	Zip bags, large	___	Whipped cream	___	Yellow onions	___
Sauerkraut	___	Small	___	Sour cream	___	Zucchini	___
STARCHES		Freezer bags, large	___	Cottage cheese	___	**FRUIT**	
Spaghetti	___	Small	___	Yogurt	___	Apples—red	___
Fettuccini	___	Sandwich bags	___	Eggs	___	Apples—green	___
Rice, brown	___	Toothpicks	___	**CHEESE**		Apricots	___
Rice, white	___	Paper plates	___	Cheddar	___	Bananas	___
Stuffing	___	Paper cups	___	Swiss	___	Berries—blu/blk/ras	___
Dry beans	___	**BREADS**		Mozzarella	___	Cantaloupe	___
BAKING SUPPLIES		Crackers	___	Monterey Jack	___	Cherries	___
White flour	___	Chips—tortilla	___	Ricotta	___	Grapes	___
Wheat flour	___	Chips—potato	___	Parmesan	___	Honeydew	___
Sugar	___	Bread	___	**PROCESSED MEATS**		Nectarines	___
Yeast	___	Buns	___	Hot dogs	___	Oranges	___
Nuts	___	Cookies	___	Turkey franks	___	Peaches	___
Jell-O	___	**DOGS**		Bacon	___	Pears	___
Hot cocoa	___	Bones	___	Lunch meat	___	Plums	___
Pudding	___	Rawhide chews	___	**MEAT**		Strawberries	___
Coconut	___	Food	___	Ground beef	___	Watermelon	___
Cocoa powder	___						

Combining your handwritten list of loss leaders with your checked-off shopping list provides you with a complete plan for your trip. We'll pick up this plan in Chapter 3, "Shopping to Win," where we'll discuss getting in, getting what you need, and getting home from the store. We view shopping as more of a military strike than a daily chore. If you follow our advice, you'll spend less time and money at the store, which in turn will allow you to spend more time doing the things you enjoy with the people you love.

We've covered a lot of ground in this chapter. You now know the five steps to creating a plan that works, and you're also prepared to get your whole family on board with that plan. Just remember that planning takes time and practice. Don't start off trying to plan too much. Start in one area, grow from there, and you'll be successful. With your plan in hand, you're now ready to head to the store. Read the next chapter before you grab your cart and sprint through those automatic doors at the grocery store.

WHAT YOU CAN DO NOW ABOUT PLANNING

 Timid Mouse

1. Sit down for about ten minutes sometime today (heck, if you can, do it right now) and write down five of your favorite dinner meals that you can easily cook.

2. Arrange the meals by day, based on your evening schedule, to create a complete menu for this week.

3. If you haven't yet learned to cook, write down five of your favorite restaurant meals and find the recipes and directions at your public library or online. If you're still overwhelmed, find someone who knows how to cook and ask that person to help you learn.

 Wise Owl

1. Make a master list of all of the meals you can cook. Arrange them by type of meat or ethnicity.

2. Take stock of what you have in your pantry and freezer—don't just look at it, write it down.

3. Plan a one-week (seven-day) menu based on what you have in your pantry and what is on sale this week at the store. Make a list of what you are missing and go to the store only once this week. Commit to not going back to the store *no matter what*. If you run out of something like a spice or an accompanying vegetable, substitute with something else.

 Amazing Ant

1. Take your planning to the next level. If you are menu planning one week at a time, do it for two weeks. If you're already menu planning for two weeks, try to do it for a whole month! The more you plan, the more you'll save. Go for it, it really gets easier with practice.

2. Review the grocery ads and make a listing, by store, of the loss leaders. Plan your shopping trip based on the store with the best prices and see how much money you can save.

3

Shopping to Win

Grocery stores are not set up as charitable organizations designed to help harried shoppers get what they need at the lowest price and then get home. If you think that they are, you've been lulled into a sense of complacency by spending too much time listening to that carefully orchestrated, canned music in the stores. Grocery stores are strategically designed to encourage you to buy the products on which the grocer makes the greatest profit. If you are going to win at the grocery game, you've got to know how to take your plan and stick to it. Just as a marathon runner has to navigate through a maze of other runners as well as up and down hills and valleys to get to the goal of the finish line, you've got to be prepared to navigate through various distractions and detours at the grocery store to reach your goal of feeding your family for less.

PACE YOURSELF

This chapter is the largest in the entire book. It's so full of money-saving ideas, strategies, and things to watch for that you may not be able to absorb it all in one sitting. So, being a smart marathon runner, you'll have to pace yourself. But we promise you that as you apply and master each of the skills we describe, you'll cross the finish line and win a gold medal (or the equivalent in cash)!

We're going to share seventeen strategies that we employ to get the best quality food at the lowest prices possible. Over time every winning athlete learns "tricks of the trade" to give them the upper hand on their opponents. We're going to share some of the tricks we use to score incredible savings in several departments of the store. If you follow our advice, you'll not only save a ton of money, but you'll reduce your stress level and the amount of time you spend gathering food for your family.

If you're at all like us, reading a detailed list of things we can do to lose weight, make more money, or have healthier skin completely overwhelms you, and as a result you just don't know where to start, so you don't do anything. To help you get some traction, we're going to use a couple of rating symbols:

 Time: on a scale of one (not much time) to three (many hours), we'll give you an idea of what we think the amount of time you'll need to commit to see maximum savings as a result of using a particular strategy.

 Return: On a scale of one (a little money) to three (lots of money), we'll give you an idea of how much money you can save by implementing a particular strategy. We look at it as a return on our investment of time.

By looking at our rating system you can gauge if you are ready to try one of the several ideas we are going to suggest. To be honest, some will take quite a bit of time before you see a return, but the return, once you master the skill, will be high. Others will take less time and will only return a small amount of money. Remember that pennies add up to dollars and dollars add up to hundreds of dollars. Your cumulative savings will snowball even when you utilize the simpler strategies.

Are you ready? Grab your shopping cart—the race is about to begin—runners take your mark—get set—let's go!

STRATEGY 1:
COMMIT TO SPENDING LESS TIME SHOPPING

How many times have you said, "I'm running to the store to pick up something for dinner—be back in a few minutes"? If you're like most families, this is a commonly used phrase and is music to a grocer's ears. We try not to sing that song at our house. For over twenty-five years we've done one major shopping trip for groceries each month. Limiting our trips to the store is one of the many ways we have managed to keep our food budget at $350 per month (including all food items, paper goods, personal care items, and cleaning supplies) for the past decade. Limiting our shopping trips saves time and money. But before we get into how we find deals in different departments of the grocery store, we're going to describe how our monthly shopping trek came about and how we actually accomplish it.

When we were first married, Annette did what her mother did—she went to the store once a week to pick up the food we were going to eat that week. She looked at the ads, made a list, and usually only went to one store. In 1984 a neighbor in our small apartment complex offered to let us share her freezer. She had a 17-cubic-foot upright freezer that wasn't full. Allowing us to fill a shelf helped her freezer to run more efficiently and allowed us more space to store food—especially sale items. With that one change, Annette went from shopping once a week to once every other week. As a result she cut her shopping time in half! The use of our neighbor's freezer was the start of our economizing journey. There were drawbacks though. We could only access the freezer when she was home. This required Annette to think ahead. If she wanted to cook a roast, she'd have to get it from the freezer the night before because our neighbor worked and wasn't home during the day.

A year later we purchased a used, 9-cubic-foot freezer from a family friend and were able to store even more frozen food. That's when Annette decided to try shopping once a month. She was pregnant with our second child, Becky, and found that the task was pretty arduous, so she enlisted the help of a single friend. The two of them spent four hours shopping at the store and came back physically and mentally exhausted.

Steve was working as a graphic designer for a large graphics studio in Phoenix that did package design for Dial Corporation. He helped redesign Purex detergent, Old Dutch cleanser, and lots of Decker meat labels. When Annette asked him to help her grocery shop for the month, it was less of a sacrifice and became more of a research project to see how the products he had helped design stood up to the competition on the shelves of the store. That was in 1985, and we've been shopping together ever since.

The Outer Loop and the Inner Aisles

Initially Steve was a "go-fer." Annette would have the list and coupons in her cart and would have Steve "go for" various items and bring them back to the cart. Eventually, as his proficiency increased, he graduated from "go-fer" to having his own cart and then his own set of coupons.

Our way of shopping now is similar, but definitely more efficient. We each have areas of the store we are responsible for canvassing and collecting bargains from.

We divide up the list with Steve assigned to pick up items in the dairy section, wall deli (lunch meat, cheese, etc.), meat, and produce departments. Annette picks up items located on the inner aisles (where most of the coupons are used). With our list of items to pick up, we split up and get to work.

The media have really latched onto the idea that we use walkie-talkies to communicate in the store. We don't do it for the attention; we do it for the efficiency. Our eldest son, John, was working at a sporting goods store and got an employee discount on a clearance pair of Motorola walkie-talkies, and we decided to give them a try.

We used to shop on Friday nights, and Steve would be pretty wiped out after a fifty-plus-hour week as an advertising account exec. So the walkie-talkies saved him having to walk all over the store, looking down each aisle for Annette, when he came across an unadvertised sale or needed clarification on a quantity for an item on the list. Now we use them to crow about the great deals we find. When we speak at conferences, Annette says that if you want your husband to help you shop, giving him an electronic toy like a walkie-talkie is a great way to get him to "play." Today with the proliferation of cell phones, if you have enough spare minutes, you could just as easily use them.

If you don't have a willing spouse or you're single, you can still shop once a month. If your family is smaller, the task can be accomplished alone, but if you have a larger family, you might have to enlist the help of a friend or one of your children. Teaching your kids to shop efficiently is really helping them practice a great life skill. If you have several kids, take them one at a time once they are old enough to be helpful.

Using our aisle and loop system with our lists and walkie-talkies, we can usually visit two stores in one night. Why two stores? Easy. In our area we have a lot of grocery competition—over eight different choices. After Annette has fully reviewed the store ads, she usually picks two or three stores with the best sales and that's where we shop. Like we said earlier, one store is picked solely for its loss-leader sales and the second store is selected because it has some good sale prices, but overall better prices or better selections. If a third store must be visited, Steve usually goes there on Saturday morning while Annette starts her once-a-month cooking ritual.

Take the Shop-Less Challenge

If you're going to the store several times each week, commit to going only once this next week. Even if all you have is a small freezer attached to your refrigerator, you can still limit your trips to the store by planning a weekly menu. Okay, here's the tough part, but we know you can do it. If you run out of an ingredient or forget an item, substitute it with something else, borrow it from a neighbor, or make a different meal—*just don't go back to the store*. You *can* do it—it may take some time to perfect your system, but eventually it will be as easy as breathing.

Recently, Annette was making a homemade pot of spaghetti sauce and realized that she was out of celery. So she called our neighbor Rob to see if she could borrow a few stalks. He said, "No problem, come on over and get it." Then Annette asked if he would like her to send over a quart of sauce when it was made. Rob said, "Wow! I'm getting the better end of this deal." Rob did end up getting a good deal, but so did we. Annette didn't have to run to the store for a couple of stalks of celery, and we were able to continue to strengthen a relationship with a great neighbor.

If you've been able to limit your trips to the store to once each week, try taking the next step and stretch your trips to once every two weeks. Step-by-step you can refine your planning and shopping skills to the point that you are able to minimize the time you spend shopping and *maximize* the amount of money you can sock away. Repeat this over and over: The less I shop, the *more* I save!

Read what a friend of ours has accomplished by taking our advice:

Shopping Less, Saving More

I took your advice and reduced my trips to the store. I was one of those people who would shop two or three times each week—spending 75 to 100 dollars each time. I now shop one time each week spending a total of 100 dollars. This change has cut my weekly food bill at least 100 dollars—that's about 400 dollars each month ($4,800 per year)!

JENNIFER—TROY, MI

STRATEGY 2: GET YOUR TOOLS TOGETHER

We also have a checklist of things we take to the store to help us work quickly and efficiently:

- ☐ **The Shopping List.** Yup, it's been forgotten a couple of times. It's hard to execute your plan . . . without the plan.
- ☐ **Sale Flyers.** We bring these just in case the advertised items are priced differently in the store or if we see a special price and are not sure if it is less expensive at another store.

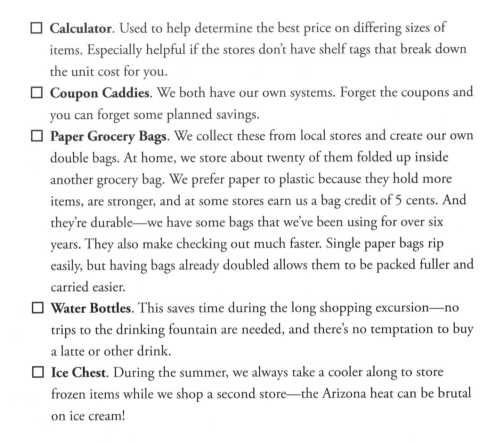

☐ **Calculator**. Used to help determine the best price on differing sizes of items. Especially helpful if the stores don't have shelf tags that break down the unit cost for you.

☐ **Coupon Caddies**. We both have our own systems. Forget the coupons and you can forget some planned savings.

☐ **Paper Grocery Bags**. We collect these from local stores and create our own double bags. At home, we store about twenty of them folded up inside another grocery bag. We prefer paper to plastic because they hold more items, are stronger, and at some stores earn us a bag credit of 5 cents. And they're durable—we have some bags that we've been using for over six years. They also make checking out much faster. Single paper bags rip easily, but having bags already doubled allows them to be packed fuller and carried easier.

☐ **Water Bottles**. This saves time during the long shopping excursion—no trips to the drinking fountain are needed, and there's no temptation to buy a latte or other drink.

☐ **Ice Chest**. During the summer, we always take a cooler along to store frozen items while we shop a second store—the Arizona heat can be brutal on ice cream!

If you're a more visual person, visit our website—AmericasCheapestFamily.com—and go to the "In the News" section, where you can click on several videos of our grocery shopping habits.

Okay, so you've got a plan. You've got your menu, shopping list, and all of your "tools." And you've got a goal—to just go to the store once and get all the groceries that you need. But you need to know that there are sinister plans afoot, which have been devised by many cunning and calculating individuals (better known as grocery merchandisers and product marketers) to induce you to buy the items *they* want you to buy. They want your money and they want *their* plan for you to become *your* plan for you. Beware of impulse buying! *In reality, we know that these marketers are just everyday people like us, trying to do their jobs, but we need to be aware of their techniques so we can do our job and live within our means.*

STRATEGY 3: AVOID IMPULSE BUYS

How many times have you gone to the store to pick up one or two forgotten items and ended up with seven to fourteen items in your cart? You get home and explain to your spouse or kids that you thought of a few more things you needed or just couldn't pass up this great bargain. Grocers have strategically designed their stores to cause you to walk past things they want you to buy on the way to the most commonly purchased items that you came in for. Did you ever wonder why the milk and eggs are always at the back of the store? Still skeptical—we aren't anymore—we learned this lesson in an unusual way.

Years ago when Steve was working in the graphics field he had a client (Bill) who marketed cheese products on military bases worldwide. Steve was responsible for producing point-of-sale materials, shelf danglers, and coupons—millions and millions of coupons. One particular point-of-sale promotion they worked on was called "Pasta Tonite." The concept was to produce a commissary display featuring products from the cheese manufacturer—particularly Parmesan cheese—along with products from other cooperating manufacturers. Things like: Italian salad dressing, croutons, spaghetti sauce, tomato paste, tomato sauce, Italian bread, pasta, and a few other products that would help a harried shopper pick up all that was needed to have "Pasta Tonite." Steve also produced a large colorful banner announcing "Pasta Tonite" and a coupon sheet that was distributed at the display. There were no special prices posted with the display. The coupon sheet was the only thing that mentioned price and it was intentionally designed to be confusing—it featured nine different coupons from several manufacturers, and to use any one coupon you had to buy at least three of the products on display.

Sales of the items on the display increased 38 percent, while coupon redemptions were less than 1 percent. The manufacturers loved this. They saw a huge increase in sales and it cost them very little. Remember that manufacturers not only reimburse the grocer for the face value of the coupon, and seven or eight cents—to process the coupon, plus they pay a coupon clearinghouse to process the coupons. This promotion was so successful that it was run for five consecutive years.

Why was the promotion so successful? The large product display—mountains of pasta, sauce, Parmesan cheese, and other items—was attractive and took up a good amount of space. You couldn't miss it when you walked through the store. But more important, it made it easy for the shopper to pick up (on impulse) all of the ingredients needed to make a complete meal. The items looked appealing—mmmm, the thought of a tasty, easy, cozy spaghetti dinner—and it played perfectly to an unsuspecting shopper's impulsiveness.

If you walked by the display without a plan or without a menu, you could easily be seduced into buying the whole deal. Remember there were no sale prices, no big savings, just a convenient way to pick up an entire meal without having to visit several aisles of the store.

It is a standard practice of grocers to put displays of sale items at the entry of their stores. The sooner you start putting things in your cart, the more likely you are to continue to put things into your cart. We know we've only presented our experience, but keep reading—we've got some extensive statistics to back up what we have learned.

Steve read in a grocery marketing magazine about a research study called "Where the Rubber Meets the Road: A Model of In-Store Consumer Decision Making."[2] The study was produced by J. Jeffrey Inman and Russell S. Winer (if you want to read their entire findings, go to our website and search for "Inman"). These two men researched the effects of in-store marketing, promotions, signage, and displays on the purchases that consumers made. The data for this well-funded study was provided by the Point-of-Purchase Advertising Institute (POPAI), which spent in excess of $400,000 gathering the information. They surveyed over four thousand shoppers in fourteen different cities. In total this represented over fifty thousand items purchased. Shoppers were surveyed on fifteen different variables, including: use of a list, number of people shopping, the number of aisles shopped, number of trips to the store each week, whether they were basing their purchases on a store ad or not, the number of items picked up from end-of-aisle displays versus in-aisle, and several more variables. The thirty-eight-page report written by Inman and Winer goes into great detail about the factors that influenced the purchasing habits of these consumers. But to summarize, here's what we gleaned from the report:

- Shoppers who run to the store for a "quick trip," planning only to buy a few specific items, will end up putting 54 percent more items in their carts than they expected.
- Larger households picked up 20 percent more impulse items than smaller households: 54.7 percent of the purchases of one-or-two person households were impulse buys, whereas 65.7 percent of the purchases for households of five were impulsive.
- 47 percent of the shoppers surveyed went to the store three or four times each week.
- Displays at the end of each aisle (end caps) produce higher impulse buys—61 percent compared to 58 percent for in-aisle displays.
- Items displayed in the checkout lane produced the highest rate of impulse buys at 64 percent.
- The more people you take shopping with you, the more impulse items you will pick up: impulse buys for one shopper were 57.1 percent but increased to 64.8 percent with multiple shoppers.
- The number of unplanned purchases increased by almost 30 percent as more aisles were visited.

Although this information was gathered in 1998, there has not been a study of this magnitude commissioned since then, and from what we've observed, their conclusions are still accurate today. The bottom line to all of this research is threefold. You'll be able to walk past items you really don't need, no matter how enticing, and purchase the items you planned to buy if you:

- become a more informed consumer,
- plan your shopping trip better,
- are aware that you are a target for product marketers and can resist their urgings for impulsive purchases.

You *can* reduce your number of impulse buys. You can shop less frequently, avoid impulse buys, and use the money you've saved to get away on vacation to some remote area where researchers never go. If you curb your impulses, you will save!

Impulse Buys in the Basket

Whenever I go to the grocery store, I put one of those hand baskets in the child seat area of my cart. As I shop I put anything I pick up that is not on my list in the basket. This way I can easily see my impulse items and evaluate them before I get to the checkout lane. There are always some things that I don't really need so . . . they get put back.

MARGARET—MT. VERNON, WA

STRATEGY 4: KNOW YOUR PRICES!

One of the mantras that Annette shares with people at conventions and other speaking engagements is, "You've got to know your prices!" How can you know if an advertised sale price is truly a good deal if you have nothing to compare it with? Years ago, Amy Dacyczyn, creator of the *Tightwad Gazette* newsletter and books, encouraged the creation of a price book. Annette did this for quite a while, and it was a great tool to help her know when a sale price was really a sale price. Here's how she set it up:

Using an old three-ring binder, Annette filled it with loose-leaf paper. She titled each page with an item we commonly purchase—her pages were arranged alphabetically and went from applesauce to vinegar. Initially, she filled it in whenever she went shopping, taking time to stand in the aisles and record the prices. She even sent Steve to a warehouse club to gather prices on a few items. Later, she simply updated it from the store ads she received each week and occasionally wrote in prices from items not usually profiled in the ads. She titled each page with the item name and then added columns headed: date, store, brand, size, price, and unit price (either pound, ounce, or per piece). She didn't use a computer, but you could easily set this up with a word processor or spreadsheet, copy the sheet on this page, or go to our website to print out more copies.

Cut Your Grocery Bill in Half with America's Cheapest Family®

Price Tracker Sheet

ITEM _____

Date	Store	Brand	Size	Price	Price per Unit

We recently updated some data from our price book page for raisins, so you can see the valuable information it provides. You can easily see that prices doubled between 2004 and 2009. We usually find that larger containers offer lower prices, but in our 2009 price comparison, we discovered that a 12-ounce container of raisins earned us the most savings. How much did it save? The highest price was $3.72 per pound and the lowest was $2.66—a difference of $1.06 per pound or 28.5 percent. Learning your prices and regularly calculating unit costs can result in significant savings. This is one of the major reasons we always shop with a calculator in hand.

ITEM: RAISINS					
DATE	STORE	BRAND	SIZE	PRICE	PRICE PER UNIT
4/10/04	Fry's/ Kroger	Dole	4 lbs.	$5.07	$1.27 lb.
5/15/06	Trader Joe's	Organic Thompson	1 lb.	$1.59	$1.59 lb.
5/15/06	Sam's Club	Sunmaid	4 lbs.	$5.19	$2.03 lb.
9/15/09	Fry's / Kroger	Kroger	24 oz. / 1.5 lbs.	$4.99	$3.32 lb.
9/15/09	Fry's / Kroger	Sunmaid	24 oz. / 1.5 lbs.	$4.49	$2.99 lb.
9/15/09	Fry's / Kroger	Sunkist	12 oz.	$2.00	$2.66 lb.
9/15/09	Fry's / Kroger	Sunmaid	15 oz.	$3.49	$3.72 lb.

Eventually you'll discover that some items are less expensive at specialty, dollar, or discount stores than at grocery stores.

Watch your confidence level soar as you become less of a consumer and more of a commodities broker—knowing when a price is great, and buying enough to feed your family for months. Eventually, you'll become as confident in your knowledge as Annette has been during several interviews when she's said, "I'm the Warren

Buffett of groceries." We'll share more about the value of stocking up and storing your bargains in Chapter 6, "Stocking Up and Organizing."

～～～

Monthly Anticipation

I keep a twelve-month calendar in a three-ring binder. Regularly I make notes of sales with dates and other finds I come across. After the first year of doing this, I started my second calendar. Now, each month I look back at the previous year in anticipation of what sales should be coming up each month. This gives me a good idea of when to shop for certain items or at certain stores.

JENNIFER—NORFOLK, VA

Hopefully by this point, you see the value of being mentally prepared when you enter the store. You'll be able to avoid impulse buys by following your plan, and you'll know when a deal is really a good deal by using your price book. Most grocery stores don't like to "play nice" or make it easy for you to compare prices so you can get the best deal. They are going to throw obstacles in your path. How well can you calculate?

Calculate This

Many grocers intentionally make shopping confusing by advertising prices of items in multiple quantities—3 for $5 or 4 for $5. By advertising items in groups of multiples they are encouraging us to buy the quantity they describe, whether we need it or not. Being able to quickly calculate the actual unit price of multiples is essential to getting a good deal at the store. Take this quiz and see how quickly you can find the unit price for each multiple deal.

Instructions: Draw a line from the Deal Price to the correct Unit Price. Prices have been rounded up to the nearest penny.

Note: The answers are not provided . . . we want you to use your head or your calculator to get it right.

	DEAL PRICE	UNIT PRICE
1	10 for $10	$1.25
2	3 for $5 Daisy Sour Cream, 16 oz.	$3.00
3	2 for $7 boxes of Splenda	$1.67
4	3 for $3	$1.00
5	2 for the price of 1 @ $5.99	$3.50
6	Buy 1, get 2 free for $5.99	$1.00
7	Buy 2 (@ $1.50 each) and get 1 free	$2.00
8	4 for $5 Fleishmann's Margarine, 1 lb.	$2.33
9	6 for $1, gift bags	$1.00
10	3 for $7, 12-packs of soda	$0.17

Be on your guard when your grocer advertises deals in multiples. Read the promotion carefully. Sometimes you only get the lower, sale price if you do buy a prescribed number of the item. Other times the promoted price—10 for $10—really means that no matter what quantity you purchase, your price is $1 each.

STRATEGY 5: READ THE SHELF TAGS

In the 1970s several consumer advocacy groups and public policy officials put pressure on the grocery industry to provide consumers with some sort of standardized unit price information in stores. Over the years most grocers and other retailers have complied, but there has been no standardized requirement for how this information should be displayed. As of 2007, eighteen states required unit pricing to be displayed for products on grocery shelves. The National Conference on Weights and Measures has tried to create an industry standard for the display unit price information, but their proposals haven't yet been implemented. Surveys we've read show that the larger the price per unit is printed, the easier it is for consumers to comparison shop. And the easier it is for us to compare prices, the quicker we'll be able to select a less expensive option. This is great for the consumer, but not for the grocer. Some grocers have made the unit pricing information so small that it's really tough to find or read, but others have created a consistent, readable, and usable system for displaying the information.

The key for us as shoppers is to use the information to find the best product for the lowest price. Being able to quickly compare product size, total price, and unit price makes selecting the right product for our budget easier.

The examples presented here are real prices from shelf tags we saw in the grocery store when comparison shopping for salad dressing. When the bottle sizes are the same (16 ounces), it's easy to figure the least expensive option by just looking at the price. But when the bottle size changes, using the price per unit box will help you calculate the best deal—as you can see in the example of the 12-ounce bottle of salad dressing. Of course, many times price isn't the only consideration; you've got to take into account flavor, quality, and other factors.

A few years back we were on a committee to plan the food for a church camping trip. We were expecting about two hundred people and, of course, we were trying to keep the cost down for the food we were buying. One of the meals was going to be hamburgers. When checking the prices, it was incredibly helpful that the grocer provided per ounce costs for the frozen burgers we were considering. If you haven't looked at burgers in a while, there are loads of options and prices. You can get 95 percent lean down to 70 percent lean; ground sirloin to just plain ground beef (beef fat is considered beef . . . right?). And the price per ounce can range from 12.4 cents to 21 cents. The nice thing about per unit shelf tags is that you don't need to be a math wizard or have a calculator to compare prices and get the best deal. If your store doesn't provide shelf tags with unit costs, ask them to, and if they do provide them, read them and save.

As long as we're talking about prices, let's wander over to the meat department and see what kind of deals we can wrangle.

STRATEGY 6:
HUNTING MEAT BARGAINS WITHIN YOUR LIMITS

Years ago, it was the man's "job" to hunt for the meat to provide for the family. All it cost was shoe leather, a few days of trudging through the forest, some bullets or arrows, time to clean and dress the meat, muscles to lug it all home, and space to store it. Today the chore isn't quite as arduous or physically taxing, but to do it economically, you still need good tracking skills, a place to store your prize catches, and the ability to know when to "pull the trigger" and buy.

No matter what type of meat we purchase, over the years we have established a per pound "buy price" for various cuts of meat. When we find items priced at or below our buy price, we stock up and freeze them. Buying meat this way can save you "oodles." Your taste and budget for meat products will, obviously, be different from ours. Please take these suggestions and apply them to the cuts your family prefers and what your budget can afford.

Note: Because prices can vary dramatically depending on where you live, do your own comparisons and learn the range of prices in your area.

Beef

London broil is great for grilling, beef and snow peas, and making beef jerky. We buy when it is $1.69 per pound or less. Recently after Passover, we came across a closeout sale for some frozen Kosher London broil priced at 99 cents per pound. We bought most of what they had.

Chuck steak makes a terrific, juicy, marinated and barbecued steak. We know some people may disagree, but hear us out. Yes, there are plenty of leaner cuts of beef that grill up great. But for our money and taste, a marinated, tenderized, fat-removed, chuck steak is delicious and costs about 75 percent less than other premium cuts of meat. A good price is 99 cents to $1.29 per pound. Trimming fat and bone makes the net price about 25 percent more.

We once hosted a picnic for several families, a potluck where we provided the meat and the others provided the side dishes, drinks, and dessert. We purchased several pounds of chuck steaks inexpensively. We trimmed and tenderized the steaks, then marinated them in teriyaki sauce and wine for a day. When we informed our guests that we were having steak, they were amazed. They could smell it cooking on the grill and waited in eager anticipation. When they tasted it, they were enraptured. And when they asked how we afforded feeding a steak dinner to twenty people, we smiled and said it was our gift to them. We told the secret to a few of our closer friends.

Another use for chuck is pot roast with potatoes, carrots, onions, and gravy—it's delicious. We also use it to make our own ground beef—this ground beef is leaner than the most expensive stuff you'll find in the store. We use it in chili, hamburgers, meat loaf, Salisbury steaks, shepherd's pie, sloppy joes, and tacos.

Round steak is used for recipes like shish kebab, stew, and beef stroganoff. We buy boneless round steak when it sells for $1.57 per pound or less.

Roast beef is a rarity at our house. It seldom goes on sale for less than $1.50 per pound, but when it does, you can bet we'll be serving it with garlic mashed potatoes and green beans. A few years ago we bought some for a church camping trip, cooked it up, sliced it, and served it as lunch meat—we only paid $1.99 per pound for it, but it was selling in the deli case for $5.99 per pound.

Corned beef goes on sale for $1.59 per pound or less—we recently saw it for 99 cents per pound after St. Patrick's Day. It makes great Reuben sandwiches.

Beef brisket is delicious, but often to get the lowest price, about $1.59, we have to buy a 10-pound slab at a warehouse store—Smart & Final. If you find a deal like this, have the butcher cut it into smaller servings you can freeze (or cut it and repackage it at home). We love to cook a brisket in a slow cooker served with a delicious mustard and onion sauce. It's a family favorite.

Pork and Ham

We eat pork chops or country ribs only when we find them for 99 cents per pound or less. Even then, we will have them only twice each month. We cook the ribs in the slow cooker, on the grill, or in the oven, slathered with barbecue sauce. Pork chops marinated and cooked on the grill or breaded and cooked in the oven are another family favorite.

We usually have ham meals twice each month. Our favorite is shank ham with the bone in. Our stock-up price range is from 79 to 99 cents per pound. We have a delicious "secret family recipe" for cooking shank ham with pineapple gravy. After the meat is sliced, we save the bone to be boiled for soup and after that, we give the bone to our large dogs—they love it.

Chicken and Turkey

This can be a touchy subject for some boneless, skinless chicken breast lovers. We simply don't buy just chicken breasts—except for the one time when a nearby mini-warehouse (Smart & Final) had a huge overstock of them for 49 cents per pound. In that instance we bought 30 pounds. There are so many less expensive ways to purchase poultry—whole chickens for 49 cents per pound or legs and thighs from 30 to 69 cents per pound.

And then there are the deals at Thanksgiving each year. That's when turkey prices plummet and we fill our freezer with inexpensive poultry. We use turkey and chicken interchangeably for all poultry recipes. Cooking the meat, saving the broth, and then cooking the carcass again for soup are some of the ways we get our birds to go the extra mile.

With a little practice, some careful scouting, and a steady trigger finger, you can bag some great deals within your limits. Leave the elk to the outdoorsmen—we love to hunt in the supermarket.

There are other ways to bag a deal on beef, and several of our website visitors have shared their suggestions below. These ideas aren't something we would do since we rarely spend over $1.50 per pound for beef and most of the time it's around $1.25 per pound. But if you normally buy more expensive cuts of beef and want to save some money, keep reading.

STRATEGY 7: BUYING IN BULK

We're fortunate to have a source for bulk cuts of meat near our house. Smart & Final's normal prices are about 10 to 15 percent less than the grocery stores, but when they have closeout prices or meat going out of code, we really clean up. A while back we picked up three, 17- to 20-pound packs of skirt steak. They had marked the meat down to $1.99 per pound (grocery store normal price is $5.99 per pound) and then dropped the price to 50 percent off because it was going out of code. We bought a little over 50 pounds, repackaged it into smaller portions, froze it, and enjoyed it for several months. Buying in bulk when the price is right is a great way to save.

If you want to really stock up, read what two of our subscribers have done to cut their meat costs.

The Big Beef Drop

One of the best things we've done to save money and time and still eat well was to buy a cow! Actually, we split a cow with another family. It is cheaper for the butcher to not have to weigh each package and maintain inventory and a better deal for the rancher to sell just one cow instead of deal dollars away for a herd. Of course, to do this properly you must have adequate storage space—we have a large upright freezer.

We found an independent butcher (not a chain or grocery store) who butchered a cow for us. He told us that he could contact a rancher directly to get the cow, or if we wanted, we could save some money and deal directly with the rancher. That's what we chose to do. The cow we purchased was about 850 pounds (gross weight after hide, hooves, and head are removed). This is basically the slab of meat after it is drained, gutted, and cleaned. We split the beef with our friends and ended up with about 425 pounds of meat. The butcher cut it into small, easily defrostable, wrapped packages. We got T-bones, rib eyes, roasts, stew meat, and about 130 pounds of high-quality ground beef as they don't add fat to make it cheaper. All told, our final cost including the cow from the rancher and the fees to the butcher was about $1,600, or $800 per family. This came out to $1.88 per pound for every cut of meat imaginable. We saved a huge amount of money and haven't had to buy beef for a year!

It goes to prove that you don't need to live in a rural area to find great savings. We live in Minneapolis and my friend lives forty miles away in a more rural area. We use the big beef drop as an excuse to get together.

Now we're looking into buying a pig as "our cow" has left some spare room in the freezer.

WENDY—MINNEAPOLIS, MN

Monthly Bulk Buy

During the last few months I've been trying to get ahold of our expenses and came across a really cool tip: buying meat in bulk on a monthly basis. I've found a butcher near our home who sells a month's worth of meat for $80. You can mix up the type and amount of meat. This has been wonderful because I feel "well stocked" and can plan or make a meal without running out for main ingredients. The money I save goes to stocking up on dry goods and frozen veggies.

LIZ—PORTLAND, ME

Having a buy price for your meat and looking for alternates to grocery stores are great ways to save, but one way we've bagged some huge discounts might just surprise the heck out of you.

STRATEGY 8: WATCH THE DATE CODES

Want to see people turn up their noses in disgust? Just mention that you often purchase meat that is going out of code. "Code" refers to the date placed by a grocer or manufacturer on a grocery item revealing its use-by, sell-by, or freeze-by date.

What's the Beef with Old Meat?

During the taping of our ABC *20/20* interview, Elizabeth Vargas viewed a video clip of Steve selecting some steeply discounted ham in a grocery store. (You can watch this entire interview on our website's "In the News" section.) She said, "You are picking up bargains on items most of us would avoid, like expiring meat. Most people don't want to buy meat that is expiring today. Why are you buying it, in fact, stocking up on it?"

What a great question. Many consumers believe that expired meat must be "no good" and disposed of immediately. They think it's unclean, inedible, and likely to make one who eats it violently ill.

We spoke with Dave, a longtime grocery employee who started in the meat department at a large grocery chain and worked his way up to assistant store manager. He said that "in the old days," butchers would unpackage the meat when it started turning a little "green," trim off the "bad parts," and then repackage it for sale. What didn't sell in the next few days, they'd cook and sell at a higher price or add to the ground-beef mix that week. Fortunately, this type of business practice doesn't occur today.

The thought of unknown-quality meat going into ground beef may turn you into a vegetarian. This is one reason we grind our own beef. But let's take a look at what the codes on meat mean.

Is Food Dating Required by Federal Law?

No. According to the U.S. Department of Agriculture (USDA), "except for infant formula and some baby food products, dating is not generally required by Federal regulations." Poultry producers must stamp the date their product is packaged, but stores affix their own sell-by or use-by dates. Furthermore, individual states have their own regulations regarding product labeling.

What Do Dating Codes Really Mean?

Here is how the USDA defines various types of dating on meat packages:

- A "sell-by" date tells the store how long to display the product, which means you should buy the product before this date passes.
- A "best-if-used-by (or -before)" date is recommended for best flavor or quality. It is not a purchase or safety date.
- A "use-by" date is the last date recommended for use of the product while at peak quality. The product manufacturer determines this date.

Is It Safe to Buy?

The USDA website shares this advice for using meat going out of code: "After the date passes, while not of best quality, the product should still be safe if handled properly and kept at 40°F or below." We immediately freeze meat that is close to going out of code to halt the loss of quality and reduce bacterial risk. Remember that a meat's sell-by date is a "guesstimate" from the packager. Have you ever seen questionably colored meat in the butcher case days before going out of code? Your eyes are your best guide to determine the quality of meat you are purchasing. We avoid the following:

- **Leakers**. Our friend Dave's term for meat awash in excess water and blood, which may contain bacteria.
- **Puffers**. When vacuumed-packed meats lose their airtight seal and become inflated. A combination of air and bacteria may cause the problem.
- **Discolored**. Meat that looks a little green or darker brown, indicating loss of quality—avoid it no matter what its code date.

Simply using your sense of sight and smell, you can choose meat going out of code that will be safe for your family to eat.

Oregon State University College of Health and Human Services publishes a food resource guide. They advise disposing of meat that exhibits any one of the following:

- **Foul odor**. They say that bad smells are usually due to microbial growth. Putrefaction can occur in protein-rich foods with an accompanying sewage-like odor
- **Surface slime**. Often, but not always, this becomes apparent when bacteria counts increase.
- **Mold**. Exceptions are old-fashioned cured ham and cheeses that are mold-ripened.

Does Packaging Make a Difference?

Meat wrapped in thin plastic wrap on a Styrofoam tray can be frozen for up to three months, but you will see some deterioration, a drying out of the meat, after that. We have stored meats such as turkeys and corned beef vacuum-sealed in heavy plastic for up to one year with no noticeable loss in quality. A study at the Center for Food and Beverage Management of Johnson & Wales University reported that vacuum sealing and freezing meat can preserve it so well that it will be as good when you cook it as the day it was packaged.

Carlos, a butcher and former navy cook, told us that it was routine to stock a ship's walk-in freezer with two years' worth of frozen turkeys prior to a one-year tour of duty. He said, "Those birds store great in that thick plastic wrapping."

Does It Really Save Money?

You bet it does. Each grocer discounts its meat differently when it gets close to going out of code. We've seen some stores that drop the price 25 to 50 percent, and others that stick $1, $2, or $3-off stickers on the packages. Each store is different, but the key is to learn what they do with meat going out of code, then look for it to be marked down.

A few months ago, as Steve stood at a meat case evaluating cuts going out of code, a butcher asked if he needed help. Steve replied, "I'd love to buy this meat, but it's not quite at my buy price yet. Is there anything you can do?" The butcher smiled, pulled out his roll of discount stickers, and knocked another two dollars off the package. You bet we bought it. This brings up another principle: always ask—especially if it's the last date for the code. You may get a really steep discount. Saving 25 percent due to a sale or advertised price reduction is great, but we really love rounding up a great deal that saves us 50 to 80 percent—we'll never beef about that!

STRATEGY 9:
LUNCH MEAT—SAVE $3 OR MORE PER POUND

If you go to the wall deli, where all the prepackaged lunch meat hangs, or to the regular deli, where they'll custom slice any amount of lunch meat you want, you're likely to spend between $3 and $9 per pound for lunch meat. When Steve was in college he worked at a YMCA camp and was told by the chef that the most expensive meal they served was a lunch with cold cuts. Any way you slice it, lunch meat is expensive. Here's how we chop the cost of cold cuts.

> **Prepackaged**. We rarely buy any prepackaged lunch meat unless it's going out of code and steeply discounted, or it's on sale and we have a killer coupon. Our buy price is between $1 and $1.89 per pound.
>
> **Deli sliced**. With prices as high as $9 per pound it's not in our budget to go to the deli counter for lunch meat.
>
> **Chubs**. We know this is a strange, unappealing name, but it refers to a large chunk of prepackaged meat. We've found some great deals on chubs of turkey ham and regular ham in the meat case of the grocery store. Lean turkey ham usually comes in 1- or 2-pound chubs and ham usually comes in 5-pound chubs. We take these chunks of meat to either the butcher or the deli and ask them to slice it for us. Most of the time it's no problem,

especially if Steve says something like, "I know it's a lot of work, but could you slice these for me?"

One day Steve had just handed a couple of turkey ham chubs to a deli person for slicing when an older couple asked him what he was doing. Steve explained how inexpensive the turkey ham was and that the deli would slice it for free. The wife thought it was a great idea and asked her husband why they couldn't do the same thing, especially because they were living on Social Security and didn't have any money to waste.

Make sure that you ask the person slicing your meat to include the "heel," which remains unsliced from the end of the chub. Often they'll throw it away, but we keep it and cut it up to use in scrambled eggs or with a chef's salad.

Once we get home we usually divide the sliced meat into smaller portions and store it in plastic zippered bags and put it in the freezer.

When we defrost a portion of sliced lunch meat, we put a paper towel into the bag with it to absorb any moisture and minimize bacteria buildup. We change the paper towel periodically to keep the meat fresher. We can usually store lunch meat this way for a week or two.

Another place we find great deals on larger chubs (10 pounds) is a mini warehouse near our home. We can often find turkey breast going out of code for $1.50/pound or less. We bring it home and slice it on our little Oster home slicer, which friends gave us when they were relocating. It's been a wonderfully useful gift.

Cook and Slice. Another option we shared earlier is to buy meat on sale, cook it, and then slice it. We've done it with roast beef—boy, was it good. We tried it with a shank ham; we had to cut the bone out, and then slice it. That was a little difficult. But be creative—try some other options and let us know what works for you.

Think Beyond Lunch Meat. One visitor to our blog wrote that she took our lunch meat concept one step further and applied it to sliced cheese. She picked up a two-pound (32-ounce) chunk of Colby cheese for $7 and took it to the deli to slice. She ended up with much more cheese than she had in the past when she bought 32 slices (21 ounces) for $6.50.

Now that we have cut the costs on buying meat, we've got to find some deals on foods to go with it. Fruits and veggies are an important part of a healthy diet, but paying too much for them can make you sick. We've got some great ways to cut your costs for produce items.

STRATEGY 10: GET PRODUCE CHEAPER

Prices are going up in every department of the grocery store. While saving with coupons and planning are excellent ways to cut your grocery bill, getting more for the money you do spend is always fun. So, how would you like to get 15 to 54 percent more for your produce dollar without clipping a single coupon? We've got a couple of strategies that will do just that.

Prepackaged Savings

You've seen beautifully stacked displays of highly polished apples, large yellow onions, and huge potatoes, right? Have you ever compared the prices of those loose produce items to the price of the same item—prebagged? Here are a few examples:

ITEM	PER POUND LOOSE	PER POUND BAGGED	% SAVED
Apples	$1.50	$1.33	11
Carrots	69¢	60¢	13
Potatoes	79¢	38¢	52
Onions	79¢	67¢	15

Obviously these prices are from one select week at a local grocer (and aren't the best sale prices we've seen), but you should be able to find similar percentage differences when you do your own comparisons. Bulk-bagged produce for most items will usually be less expensive. How about that—a savings of up to 50 percent for just purchasing something already in a bag! We always carefully check the bag for bruised or damaged items. The two possible downsides to buying the bulk-bagged items are that the fruits or vegetables are usually a little smaller than the pricier individual items, and you may end up buying more than you can use. If you have a larger family, waste is probably not an issue. If your family is smaller, then consider splitting a larger, less-expensive bag with a friend or relative. Or you could cook, can, or sometimes freeze the excess.

Save More with Overweight Bags

Once you've checked out the prebagged produce, take it one step further. Individual pieces of fruit are usually priced by the pound, but prebagged produce is priced by the unit. By law, the prebagged unit must contain at *least* the advertised weight. To avoid problems, most manufacturers will err on the side of putting a few ounces *more* in the bag. One of the best examples is carrots. We go through between 5 and 10 pounds of carrots each month. This particular week we could have purchased 5 pounds of loose carrots for $3.45 (69 cents per pound). Or we could purchase four 1-pound bags for 69 cents each. Why only four bags? Because the bags we selected contained 20 ounces of carrots each, not just 16 ounces. We got our 5 pounds of carrots in four bags and spent only $2.76—a 20-percent savings. (This was not the best price we'd ever seen, but it was the best deal for that shopping trip.) This same type of savings can be realized with any produce item that comes prepackaged and is sold by the unit rather than by the pound. To prove this, we weighed over 290 pounds of produce to check our theory. Study the following chart to see where the greatest saving occurred (indicated with *).

ITEM	BAG SIZE / OZ.	BAGGED PRICE / PER LB.	PRICE PER LB. LOOSE	BAGGED WEIGHT MAX	ACTUAL PRICE PER LB. BAGGED	% SAVED VS. LOOSE
Apples	3 lb. / 48 oz.	$3.99 / $1.33 lb.	$1.50 lb.	52 oz.	$1.23	18%
Carrots	1 lb. / 16 oz.	69¢ / 69¢ lb.	69¢ lb.	20 oz.	55¢	20%*
Carrots	2 lb. / 32 oz.	$1.59 / 80¢ lb.	69¢ lb.	39 oz.	65¢	6%
Carrots	5 lb. / 80 oz.	$2.99 / 60¢ lb.	69¢ lb.	84 oz.	57¢	17%
Potatoes	5 lb. / 80 oz.	$2.79 / 56¢ lb.	79¢ lb.	89 oz.	50¢	37%
Potatoes	10 lb. / 160 oz.	$3.79/ 38¢ lb.	79¢ lb.	167 oz.	36¢	54%*
Onions	3 lb. / 48 oz.	$2.00 / 67¢ lb.	79¢ lb.	51 oz.	65¢	20%

Our best deal on carrots was to buy 1-pound bags with 4 extra ounces in them, which saved us 20 percent in cost. As you can see, the percentage of excess weight goes down as the size of the bag goes up. Our best excess on a 5-pound bag of carrots was 4 additional ounces—the same as the excess on the 1-pound bag. But percentage wise, it is only 5 percent more compared to 20 percent extra in the 1-pound bag.

The biggest savings on potatoes was with the 10-pound bag. We netted a 54-percent savings in price compared to the loose ones, while bagged onions netted us a savings of 20 percent, and bagged apples only 15 percent. Of course, your numbers will vary depending on which season of the year it is, the sale prices in your area, and the weight differences in your bulk-bagged produce.

The bottom line is this: anytime produce is sold by the unit, weigh the item and get the heaviest unit—this can reduce your cost per pound between 10 and 25 percent.

Alternate Sources

In our area, we have a specialty store, Sprouts, which mainly sells produce. Because of their market focus, we often find their prices to be much lower than standard grocery store prices. Some dollar stores are now carrying produce and selling it for discounted prices. Other options include farmers markets, private fruit-and-vegetable stands, or co-ops. Check for alternative options in your area too. You've got to know your prices and not assume that you're getting a bargain just because it's a discount store.

The last option is to grow your own produce. Of course, you'll need to calculate how much your seeds, water, and fertilizer cost, but you'll be getting "farm fresh," tasty, and healthy homegrown veggies. Start simple, with zucchini or other squashes, and as you find success, move up to tomatoes, cucumbers, radishes, and spinach. Once you're successful at those, the sky's the limit. More about this in Chapter 11, "Gardening."

Store It to Last

If you have a smaller family or live alone, buying a bulk bag of produce can present some problems. You've got to know how long items will store: Apples and oranges will easily last one month. Carrots can grow sprouts after a few weeks, but if you wash and trim them, they'll easily last a month. Potatoes can be stored in a cool, dark box with straw or some other soft bedding (we use torn-up paper grocery bags) for a month. We store lettuce in a plastic zippered bag with a paper towel in it. The paper towel absorbs moisture and keeps the lettuce fresh longer—up to three weeks—if we change the towel a couple of times.

Is it worth all of this calculating and weighing? Over time the savings will add up, but if you don't have the time to weigh the produce, simply buying the bulk-bagged items will yield savings that can easily put 11 to 50 percent back into your pocket without using coupons. We aren't comparing apples and oranges, but we are sure that if you weigh your produce, you'll find savings similar to what we found. Are you ready to put your produce on the scale?

STRATEGY 11: SAVE WITH SEASONAL PRODUCE

Lots of money can be wasted if you simply buy whatever produce you like without considering the price and whether or not it is in season.

It's helpful if you learn when specific fruits and veggies are in season in your area, and only buy them when they are on sale. Because produce can now be easily imported from other countries or regions, you can buy apples and oranges all year long, and occasionally there will be sale prices on these imported items. But by far your lowest prices and greatest savings will be when you can buy locally grown produce in season. One of our favorite deals is the one- or two-week period in Arizona when blueberries hit their lowest price. Oh, we love blueberries—blueberry pie, blueberries on ice cream, blueberry pancakes, and blueberries in smoothies. When they finally hit their lowest price, we stock up—and stock up big—enough to last us well into next year! We buy several pounds of them, wash them, and put them right into large plastic zippered bags, where they will safely await their delicious duties in the months to come. Whatever your favorite fruit or veggie is, stock up when it's on sale and find a way to preserve it—freeze it, dry it, or can it—and enjoy it for a long, long time.

Here's an overview of some seasonal produce. Check with your produce manager or local county extension service for more exact information for your area.

Summer: melons, peaches, nectarines, apricots, plums, berries, squash, and corn
Fall: apples, grapes, pears, peppers, and potatoes
Winter: Citrus
Spring: strawberries, artichokes, asparagus

Limiting our trips to the store means that certain fruits must be eaten earlier in the month because they are more perishable. Grapes and bananas usually last a week, so once they're gone, we move on to other fruits. Pears can last up two weeks. Apples and oranges, like we said, can last a month.

We love fresh fruits so much that we've planted all kinds of fruit trees on our property and always have a garden. If you've got space or if there is a community garden you can participate in, you'll love being able to pick your own homegrown fruits and veggies.

With some creativity and some cooperation from friends and relatives, you can eat healthier and save money at the same time. Check out this tip:

Cooperative Veggies

My sister-in-law belongs to a produce co-op. With a group of friends, they take turns going to a produce warehouse that sells to restaurants and grocery stores . . . one person goes once every two weeks and spends approximately $20 per person, collected beforehand. They purchase produce by the case (so it is a good idea for the group to be six or twelve people because cases of produce are usually divisible by six or twelve). They get the wholesale price and then divide it up and deliver it to the other members of the co-op. They get tons of healthy fresh fruits and vegetables for a fraction of what they cost at the grocery store. Eating healthy is a great long-term money saver, too.

REBECCA—CHESTERTON, IN

STRATEGY 12: BUY ORGANIC FOOD SMARTER

Every time we do a grocery seminar or take phone calls during an interview on grocery savings, inevitably the question is raised, "How can I save money on organic foods?" Sometimes the question is asked out of real interest in saving money; other times it is asked in a defensive manner to protect spending habits that are out of control. If you're really interested in answers, keep reading, but if organic food is a hot button for you, you might want to skip ahead to Strategy 13.

U.S. retail organic food sales totaled $4.2 billion in 1998 and grew to $23 billion in 2008. Although organics have become more mainstream and less expensive, due to the recession total sales have waned a bit from their heady 15 to 20 percent growth per year. Experts still predict a growing market for organic foods, but at a slightly slower pace as shoppers evaluate their spending more.

Consumers are demanding healthier alternatives—some because of severe health issues, others to pursue a healthier lifestyle and thus avoid ever contracting serious health issues, and a third group buy organic just because it's in vogue. Organic products, on average, cost 50 percent more than standard foods, but you could easily end up spending 100 percent more, especially on dairy products and meat. Is there any way to get healthy, hormone- and pesticide-free food for less money? Many people we've talked to are resigned to endure a heavily increased food budget to accommodate their desire for organics. What should someone with health concerns do on a limited budget?

Here are some ways to save some money while getting healthy.

Getting Healthier

If your desire to buy organic foods is due to health issues—food allergies or sensitivities—you might want to try a tandem approach. Consider using a moderate amount of organic foods while at the same time working on strengthening your immune system. We have researched many diets from low-sugar to low-acid, and low-carb to vegan. Each one has merit and some healing effects. But we've chosen to go a different direction.

Annette's youngest sibling, Jennifer, was born with a heart defect. As Jennifer and her four older siblings were growing up, Annette's mom's mission became keeping everyone in the house sickness-free to protect Jennifer until she was old enough to have corrective surgery. As a result, whenever one child became sick, all were put on antibiotics. In light of current medical knowledge, this was definitely not a good thing, but that was back in the 1960s. Excessive use of antibiotics can have an adverse effect on overall health as the medication targets not only the bad bacteria, but also some necessary, beneficial ones in our bodies. Annette's mom eventually found a naturopathic doctor who prescribed a different way of dealing with sicknesses, and also started reading books on nutrition—specifically Adelle Davis's books.

Steve grew up in the Midwest, and his bedroom was in the finished basement of the house. The problem was that the basement flooded, and after the water was removed, the basement retained a dank, musty odor full of mold spores that Steve inhaled every day for years. He had serious allergies and some respiratory problems.

As you can see, we were not the healthiest couple when we got married. Annette went right to work researching natural ways to strengthen our immune systems and eliminate chronic sicknesses and allergies. She had watched her grandmother put leukemia into remission for over ten years through a healthy diet and a regimen of vitamins. So she started with that as our baseline and has been learning ever since.

Twelve years later, when our son Joseph was about two years old, he developed severe asthma. We went on another huge medical learning curve. We soon realized that vitamins alone would not heal his condition; we needed something more extensive. We started learning about the power of herbs while employing the guarded use of the standard medical prescription of Albuterol (a bronchodilator) and a nebulizer (electronic atomizer for inhaling the medication). At the start, Joe's asthma was severe enough to put him in the hospital, but as we strengthened his immune system, his bouts with asthma have become fewer and less intense. Today at age eighteen, he plays every sport imaginable and is as strong as an ox. About once a year he gets an upper respiratory infection—the weakest area in his body—accompanied with mild asthma. Between herbs (echinacea, lobelia, pau d'arco, and cat's claw) and hot baths, he usually gets through it in a couple of days.

We've also learned that many food allergies come as a result of a weakened immune system. Strictly using organic foods can help strengthen the immune system, but it takes a long time. In addition to vitamins and herbs, we also use many of the following food supplements: chlorophyll, aloe vera juice, spirulina, alfalfa, barley grass, garlic, lecithin, bifidus, grape seed oil, and colloidal silver, which can all strengthen your body. We have found the book *Prescription for Nutritional Healing* by Phyllis A. Balch to be an excellent resource and a starting point for researching more natural solutions to many health issues.

By strengthening your immune system, you may be able to minimize your need for organic foods.

Research Organic Sources

Because organic food is a fast-growing segment of the grocery market, prices will vary greatly from store to store. As demand and competition increase, prices will fall. Years ago, the only place to find organics was at high-end health-food stores; today it's a different story. As with most money-saving projects, researching organic sources in your area will net you great savings.

Sprouts, a smaller grocery chain in California, Arizona, Colorado, and Texas, has amazing deals on produce and meat. Their large selection of organic meat, when on sale, is very close in price to regular grocery store meat. Don't forget nationwide chains like Trader Joe's and Whole Foods. And remember that Super Walmart has a nationwide price match policy and is carrying more organic products than it did in the past.

Once you know your retail prices, venture out into your community and look for local farmers markets and food co-ops where organics might be less expensive. We met a farmer in Scottsdale who used to be what he referred to as a "chemical farmer." He now runs an organic farm on the edge of an Indian reservation that borders a Scottsdale freeway. We spent some time with farmer Ken, and the stuff he grows organically is incredible. The cool thing is, if you put in a little time at his farm, helping him weed, pick, or just simply listening to his stories, he sends you home with loads and loads of produce. So consider volunteering on a local organic farm; the sun, education, and food could be worth the effort. And when you're fully educated, you can start growing your own organic food.

The Organic Budget Buster

We don't advocate going in debt, especially for consumable items. So if your head wants everything you eat to be organic, but your budget says no, what can you do? According to a Mayo Clinic bulletin and *Consumer Reports*, some organic items really won't improve your health for the cost. They said that thick-skinned produce, such as avocados, bananas, kiwis, mangoes, onions, papayas, and pineapples, rarely allow even minuscule amounts of pesticides to penetrate through the skin. Consequently they pose little to no health risk. Additionally, they said that hardy plants like asparagus and broccoli are very pest-resistant, and, therefore, farmers use little to no pesticides in growing them. So save your organic food dollar for items like spinach, apples, peaches, nectarines, plums, milk, and meat to avoid the toxins and hormones regularly found in the nonorganic versions.

Do your rice, pasta, grains, salsa, jelly, cereal, condiments, and crackers all have to be organic too? Focus on the areas of greatest exposure and health risk for you and your family, then determine your spending priorities.

Grocery Principles Apply to Organics Too!

Many of the same principles we share for regular grocery savings apply to buying organics.

Stock up. Buy things you really need when they're on sale. Grains and beans can be bought in bulk and stored for a year or longer (we've stored hard grains like wheat for over five years in an airtight food bucket without any deterioration in quality or taste). Sale meat can be stored in the freezer. (Be sure to put extra plastic wrap on it if you're storing it for over three months.)

Menu plan sale items. Include as many sale items as possible in your weekly menu. You'll end up eating more healthy food and saving money at the same time.

Homegrown

At a recent convention where we spoke, a woman with a severe neurological disorder told Annette that she was spending $1,500 to $2,000 each month to feed two people (her husband and herself)! Annette challenged her to reevaluate her situation. She could have quit her part-time job and devoted herself to growing their own organic fruits and vegetables and come out money ahead. Her health probably would have improved with the sunshine and exercise of digging in the dirt as well as eating foods rich in nutrients. There is no doubt that growing your own food takes effort, but for Annette, spending time in the garden each day is a little slice of heaven.

No Excuses

There are so many ways to get healthy and stay healthy that no one should feel trapped into "having" to overspend on organics. Research, planning, creativity, and persistence are the keys to getting the best value for your food budget. Please don't be like some of our seminar attendees and walk out on us because we don't give them permission to spend themselves into oblivion for the sake of good health. Remember that organic products are often marketed with fear tactics. It's time to be an informed, objective "hunter"—read the signs, track down the best deals, and then bag what you really need. Living the "good life" doesn't require spending gobs and gobs of money. Physical health combined with fiscal boundaries brings the greatest benefits.

From the mail we receive, we know that organic food is a hot topic. We were thrilled to receive these helpful tips from website visitors. We hope their input encourages you to eat healthier.

~~~

Saving on Organic

I read your material on organic foods and had to write in. I am very concerned about what my children eat but want to have money for other things in life as well and so I had to write to tell you what we do.

1. **Gardening**: We have a huge garden and a large freezer. I freeze and can a lot of foods. I also have many friends who do the same and we all trade things. For example we have some grapevines that produce more than we can use and in the fall some friends come over and we spend a day making grape juice and jelly that we use all winter. It is free, organic, tastes better than anything you will find at the store, and is a ton of fun because we do it together. Another friend has ten organic apple trees and shares with all of us.

2. **Local Farms**: We use Community Supported Agriculture. In the spring I paid a local farmer $350 so I could have fresh produce all summer and fall. Every Friday I go to the farm market, hand them my bag, and they fill one to two bags full of fresh, organic, locally grown, heirloom vegetables. I have figured it out to $13 each week. It is a great deal for us as we live on fruits and veggies when they are in season.

3. **Bulk Meat**: We buy all of our meat in bulk. It comes from a local farmer and we pay about $2 to $3 per pound. Once a year we buy a whole pig or half a cow. It is pricey for ground beef but cheap for steaks and we love it—plus it supports a local farmer.

4. **Organic Salvage**: Almost everything else we buy from a salvage store that gets in a lot of organic foods.

5. **Homemade Stuff**: I also make a lot of things . . . my own peanut butter, hummus, granola, granola bars, jellies, and cleansers, etc.

We live in the country but I believe that living in more urban areas allows for other advantages that we do not have. For example, around here everything is at least half an hour away. If you start asking around you may be surprised at what you will find.

Mendy—Rock Stream, NY

Hunting for Veggies and Fruit

My husband and I were dumbfounded at how much veggies and fruit prices have increased in stores. So I went on a hunt to purchase fresh veggies and fruits from local area farmers or a co-op. I discovered a co-op that for $17 (first visit) and $15 (after first visit) provided me with a bushel basket of various veggies and another bushel basket of various fruits every two weeks. Plus if I volunteer, I get a few more little extras for free. I priced what I received from my first visit and realized that I had saved over $50! I've never been disappointed with the fruits or veggies and it seems that they last longer than what I've purchased in a store. The co-op I belong to also has organics, herbs, bread, and honey, just to name a few. Do a Google search for local farmers or food co-ops. It's amazing what you will find. The co-op we belong to is BountifulBaskets.org.

Benita—Scottsdale, AZ

STRATEGY 13: AVOID EGG-STREME PRICE INCREASES

In the fall of 2008, Steve saw an older couple standing in front of a supermarket dairy case shaking their heads. They'd come to buy eggs, but when they saw the prices, they turned and walked away empty-handed. This was at a time when egg prices had shot through the roof—they have receded a bit since then, but what we discovered at that time will still save you bucks and we're not just talking chicken feed! A dozen eggs, on sale, in early 2007 cost 79 to 99 cents. In 2008 we were lucky to see a sale price of $1.50, and regular prices jumped to almost $3.00 per dozen. Do the math, that's an increase of anywhere from 50 to 300 percent! Prices now stand at an average of about $1.40 per dozen.

Before we examine your options, here's a little egg industry overview:

According to the American Egg Board, the average American ate 248 eggs in 2010, far fewer than the 402 that folks consumed in 1945.

The United Egg Producers Association reports that there are currently sixty egg-producing companies with over one million laying hens, and twelve companies with over five million.

The total U.S. egg-producing flock shrank from 288 million in 2006 to 282 million in 2009—a 2-percent reduction. Egg production has declined 1 percent.

Steve spoke with Clint Hickman, owner of the largest commercial egg farm in the state of Arizona. The Hickman family has been selling eggs since the 1960s and has over four million laying chickens, so they know the egg business.

Clint said that egg prices are driven by demand. When the supply dwindles, prices go up. There are very few egg producers expanding their production facilities and production is down, so prices will naturally increase. Higher feed prices due to increased ethanol production and increased transportation costs also affect the retail price of eggs.

We asked Clint for tips to help consumers save money on eggs. He started by telling us that eggs are sold by weight per dozen. A large dozen must weigh at least 24 ounces. Egg producers can exceed the weight per dozen, but must not go below it. In any dozen eggs you may see some size variation from egg to egg, but overall weight is the critical measure. We tested the weight of ten cartons of large eggs and found that most of them weighed 28 ounces (4 ounces more than USDA standards). Jumbo eggs weighed an average of 32 ounces (2 ounces more than required).

USDA WEIGHT REQUIREMENTS	
SIZE	**DOZEN WEIGHT**
Jumbo	30 ounces
Extra Large	27 ounces
Large	24 ounces
Medium	21 ounces

Clint shared some insight on the value of medium eggs. Egg sizes are mostly determined by the age of the hen. A hen starts laying eggs at about twenty weeks of age and can lay for two to three years. Medium-sized eggs come from young chickens; large and extra large eggs from older hens. Hickman's family tries to have the majority of their hens mature around the largest egg-consumption holidays (times when people do lots of baking): Easter, Thanksgiving, and Christmas. At those times, with most of their chickens laying large or extra large eggs, they sometimes run short of medium eggs. Egg producers can exceed the USDA weights, so they often will substitute large eggs in the medium cartons. Savvy consumers should check the size and weight of medium eggs to get more for their money at those times of year.

Selection

When we buy eggs on our once-a-month shopping trip we usually pick up between eight and ten dozen. We open each carton and, using two fingers, move two eggs at a time to check for sticking, an indication of cracks on the bottom. And we also look for cracks on top. If we find a carton with a couple of damaged eggs in it, we'll grab some good eggs from another carton with cracked eggs to replace them. This way, the grocery store will only have one carton of unusable eggs.

Field Test

For eighteen weeks, we tracked egg volume. Each Sunday, we cook up one dozen scrambled eggs. We brown potatoes (cubed) in olive oil, add some onions, toss in some cheese, and sometimes throw in sausage or ham—it's yummy. We measured the volume of liquid (white and yolk) each week from the dozen eggs. Although the industry standard is to measure the total weight of a dozen eggs (shell and all), we thought that it would be a more accurate assessment to measure the actual amount of edible egg you get from a dozen eggs. We used various sizes of eggs: medium, large, and extra large. Below is the amount of liquid we found in the various-sized dozens:

LIQUID OUNCES FOR ONE DOZEN EGGS			
SIZE	AVERAGE	HIGH	LOW
Medium	21	24	19
Large	22	24	20
Extra Large	22.3	23	21

Field Test Conclusions

Given the small difference in average liquid volume between medium and large eggs, a sharp consumer ought to always check the price of medium eggs. If the size and weight differences are minimal, go with the smaller size. If the price difference is less than 5 cents per dozen, buy the larger size. If greater than 5 cents, buy the smaller size. If you go through a large number of eggs each month, consider buying a five-dozen package—divide the price by five for the cost per dozen. We usually keep at least ten empty egg cartons at home to redistribute the eggs from a five-dozen pack into dozens, for easier storage in the refrigerator.

Egg Storage

Commercially produced eggs are coated with a mineral sealant to prevent bacterial penetration of the shell. This allows eggs to be stored longer. According to the USDA, uncooked eggs can be stored for three to five weeks in a refrigerator at 40° Fahrenheit. This assumes they have no cracks, are not kept on the refrigerator door, and haven't been washed to remove the mineral coating. We regularly keep eggs as long as five weeks without any spoilage.

Fresh Eggs?

If you're thinking your eggs may not be fresh, here are three ways to test them.

1. **Separate**. Crack an egg into a separate bowl or cup away from other ingredients you're baking with. If it's rotten, you haven't wasted anything but one egg. (Be ready to hold your nose.)
2. **Light Test**. Hold the egg in front of a candle flame in a dark room—the center should look clear.
3. **Water Test**. A fresh egg should sink when placed in water.

Grade B Eggs Help You Save

Kroger stores nationwide (visit www.TheKrogerCo.com/ for a list of all of the different Kroger store names) have a policy of taking eggs from broken dozens and repackaging them at the store. They sell these Grade B eggs at a reduced price (between 49 cents and $1.19 per dozen at the stores in our area). But the deal gets even better when you weigh the eggs. Because the grocery store takes eggs from various dozens and combines them into their Grade B cartons, the weight of the eggs varied from carton to carton. Out of the ten dozen we purchased:

- five dozen weighed in as extra large
- three dozen weighed in as large
- two dozen weighed in as medium

Some of the eggs were plain white, others were brown, and a few were fancy signature brown eggs with the little red stamp on them (the most expensive). Check with your grocer's dairy manager and ask what they do with eggs from broken cartons. They may have a policy of reducing the price and you'll find great savings. They may not have a policy yet, and you can encourage them to establish one like Kroger's.

There you have it—an egg-stravaganza of ovoid information. Hopefully you'll be egg-cited the next time you venture into the grocery store to pick up breakfast or baking ingredients.

STRATEGY 14: KEEP YOUR EYES PEELED

Just a couple more things to remember while you're walking the aisles.

Dairy Markdowns

Watch for items going out of code in the dairy department. You can score some big savings by buying milk that's close to its sell-by date. We've found gallons of milk marked 75 percent off because the dairy manager needed to move them out before they "expired." Because we freeze our milk and then go through it quickly once it's defrosted, it doesn't go bad.

Also look for markdowns on other items like sour cream, yogurt, and cheese. These items store well for weeks after their sell-by date. Can sour cream really go bad? Think about that for a minute.

Aisle Deals

In the aisles look high and low for closeouts and markdowns. Several years back Annette called Steve on the walkie-talkies erupting with excitement. "You'll never believe what I found," she called. "It's got to be the deal of the century!" She continued, "I was looking along the top of the shelf and found these stainless steel roasting pans marked down to $2.99 each. They'd make great components for wedding presents. They've got to be worth at least $20 apiece—how many should we buy?" We bought four of them.

Donut Deals

Because we usually shop late at night, sometimes the store bakery has items that they produce each day marked down to clear out. We especially love to pick up a dozen donuts—preboxed and price reduced (especially if they have apple or cherry fritters in them). We don't do it often, but it is a fun special treat!

Check the Tags

Every store chain handles closeout pricing differently. During one TV spot in a grocery store, the manager came up to us and said, "See these orange tags? If you look for these, you'll find some great deals. We always use them to indicate a final mark-down clearance price."

Check the Back Rack

Other stores put closeout or discontinued items on a shelf or cart in the back of the store. We've found some great deals on vitamins and supplements along with other products there. Once again, don't just assume it's a good deal . . . remember . . . "You've got to know your prices."

STRATEGY 15:
FIND ALTERNATE GROCERY SOURCES

We try to keep our shopping to a minimum by planning one big shopping night each month when we purchase the bulk of our groceries, paper goods, and personal items, but the grocery store isn't the only place we pick up these items. We do take occasional trips to non-grocery-type stores we've discovered in our area, to pick up items that are greatly discounted when compared to grocery store prices. These trips usually happen when we're on an errand run in that particular part of town. Here are a few of our examples—stores in your area may be different, but we're sure you'll find similar savings.

Bread Outlets

These are a great way to save 40 to 90 percent on your bread purchases. We spoke with the district manager for a large bakery in Phoenix and he told us that their contract with distributors requires that the bread he sells at the outlet stores is at least one day old, but there are other non-retail items that are fresher. For instance they often get "over-bakes" of buns they bake for various restaurant franchises—we've picked up twenty-four hamburger buns for 99 cents and could swear that they were identical to Arby's. Day-old bread is often just as fresh as the stuff you'll find in the grocery store. We buy several loaves at a time, put pairs of them into a plastic grocery bag, tie the bag closed, and put it carefully in our freezer. When it is defrosted, it's as good as fresh. We only buy whole grain bread and have a buy price of $1.50 or less—the retail price for these loaves is usually $4 or more.

Dollar Stores

This is a relatively new find for us. When our local bread outlet was closed, we discovered that the nearest one was over thirty miles away—we were really bummed. One day Annette was in a nearby Dollar Tree store picking up some inexpensive greeting cards (two for a dollar) when she saw a Sara Lee bread rack full of packages of fresh blueberry bagels (a real favorite). She grabbed all she could and checked out. On the way out of the store an older man stopped her and asked if she had bought the whole load. She said that she had left a few. He told her that he comes there every Tuesday around 12:30 p.m. when the Sara Lee truck arrives. The next time she went, there was a line of seniors waiting for the truck with her. She picked up several loaves of multigrain Sara Lee breads for a dollar each! Dollar stores are also good for baby shampoo, baby bath, lotions, deodorant, and miscellaneous food items that they pick up on clearance or overstock. Just be careful because some manufacturers are making smaller-sized bottles and cans specifically for distribution in dollar stores. Knowing your prices and sizes will assure that you are always getting a real deal.

Drug and Discount Stores

CVS, Walgreens, Rite-Aid, and Osco. Places like these regularly distribute sales flyers advertising great deals and including coupons. We often pick up nuts, spices, mandarin oranges, cookie sprinkles, and a few personal-care items there.

Big Lots. We don't go here regularly, but have found great prices on bleach, cleaning supplies, blank CDs, tools, and some food items, music, and seasonal decorations.

Dented Can Stores

When Steve was an account exec and drove all around town for client meetings, he discovered a dented can store around the corner from one of his clients. Dented can stores buy damaged goods from grocers by the pallet or truck load—sight unseen. They sort and then merchandise the products. Some items are at "killer discounts," others can be close to retail, so you've got to know your prices. We've found some great deals on tomato paste and sauce, real maple syrup for a buck, and a couple of times some vinegar peppers marked down so low that Annette nearly danced in the aisle. You've got to be extra observant. We've found items several months or even years past the expiration date on the label. While this isn't usually a problem, watch for discoloration of the product, or if it is a canned good, look for a puffed-out top or leaks. If you are carefully observant, you can score some great savings.

Warehouse Clubs

There are some deals at the membership-fee warehouse clubs that the grocery stores just can't beat. But for the most part we stay away from these "$200 clubs." We call them that because you usually can't get out of those warehouses for less than $200. Also they are a haven for expensive impulse buying—you know what we mean—you go in for some produce and meat and come home with an air hockey table or new gazebo. Impulse buys at the grocery store may cost you $3 or $5, but at the warehouse clubs you could easily spend $10 to $300 on impulse.

While the warehouse clubs regularly stock certain items, many of their products are produced for a limited time only. This limited availability adds fuel to impulsive desires because of the fear that if you don't buy it now, you will miss a real bargain. You may think it's a good deal, but without having time to research and because you rush your decision, you'll often buy something that you don't really need, at a price that is higher than if you would have been more thorough.

Beyond the danger of impulse buys, we've come to discover that the grocery store sale prices normally beat the pants off the warehouse clubs. We researched this once for a segment we did for a local TV station and regularly present this information in our grocery seminars around the country.

ITEM	WARE-HOUSE PRICE	PRICE PER UNIT	GROCERY STORE SALE PRICE	PRICE PER UNIT	PERCENT SAVED
Heinz Ketchup	(2) 60-oz. bottles $4.69 28 oz. would cost $1.09	3.9¢ per oz.	28-oz. Heinz Ketchup 79¢	2.8¢ per oz.	27.5%
Spaghetti	6 lbs. for $2.78	46.3¢ per lb.	1 lb. 33¢	33¢ per lb.	29%
Cereal— Honey Bunches of Oats	3.25 lbs.— $6.05	$1.86 per lb.	1-lb. box $1.50 no coupon	$1.50 per lb.	19.4%
Nestle chocolate chips	60-oz. bag— $6.38 12 oz. would be $1.28	10.6¢ per oz.	12-oz. bag—$1.00	8.3¢ per oz.	31%

These are just a few examples of the differences between warehouse club prices and grocery store sale prices. Even if an item is less expensive at the warehouse club, how many times would you need to buy it and get that same savings to pay for your $40 membership fee? There are a few warehouse club items that a friend with a membership picks up for us because they are usually priced way below grocery stores: pickles in gallon jars, unsweetened applesauce in #10 cans, and nuts usually can't be beat.

Be careful if you go to a warehouse club or any of these alternate sources for groceries, paper goods, and personal-care items . . . Remember, "You've got to know your prices."

STRATEGY 16:
SAVE WITH RAIN CHECKS AND SUBSTITUTIONS

You work hard to save money on groceries. You review the food ads and plan your menu around them. You reorganize and catalog what you have in your pantry and freezer so you know what you have in stock. You plan your shopping list and figure the most efficient route to take so you can hit two or three stores in one trip. You're armed with a great plan and ready to make a killing on the food you'll purchase to feed your family.

Then you get to the store, and some of their killer loss-leader items are out of stock.

We can't tell you the number of times we've run into this situation. It's so frustrating, especially because we try to limit our trips to the store to once a month. Unfortunately, grocers aren't used to our type of shopping, so they respond to being out of stock with "We'll have more tomorrow around 9 a.m. You can come back then."

When saving money and time are your goals, coming back tomorrow at 9 a.m. doesn't sit well. We don't center our lives around going to the grocery store—much to the chagrin of store managers.

So when a store is out of stock on a specific item we want, we do one of two things:

Substitutions

If the item is something we need for the upcoming month, we ask the manager to substitute a similar item. We'll try to be sensitive and logical and ask that a store brand be substituted (if possible). We've done this with various cuts of meat, cereal, laundry detergent (asking for two smaller boxes that would equal the size of the larger box on sale).

We always explain to the manager that we don't shop every week and that we have a large, busy family and cannot come back in the morning. We usually find the manager to be very accommodating if we come to him with a logical reason and an attitude of understanding that he might not be able to help us. Managers want happy customers who return again and again, so being gentle and polite usually makes it easy for them to say yes.

Rain Checks

If the manager turns us down, we go to our next option, and that is to get a rain check. Most stores will do this, but they often put an expiration date on the rain check—sometimes only one or two weeks. Again, we tell them that we shop only once a month and that we need the rain check to have either no expiration date or one that gives us a couple of months to use. Most of the time they will give us at least one month.

We also make sure to ask for no quantity limit or that they put a huge limit on the rain check (like ten or twenty of an item) if there is no specified restriction in their store ad.

If we go to use a rain check and it is expired, we again appeal to the store manager, who almost always honors it.

This fall we wanted to buy some hams for our monthly menu (we had a couple of events planned where we would be feeding large groups), but there were no sales—the going price at the time was $1.99 per pound. We had a rain check, without an expiration date, with a price of 99 cents per pound. Annette was passing by this particular store one night and went in. She asked the manager if he would honor the rain check, and when he said yes, she promptly loaded all four of the hams that were in the case into the cart. When she got to the checkout, the checker said that she couldn't use her rain check. But the bagger said, "Check the expiration date." When the checker saw that there was no expiration, she processed the order without a problem. Talking to management and playing by the rules really helps—and so does saving a dollar per pound!

Another time, we wanted to buy some apple juice (we serve it on Sunday mornings as a special treat). We can usually find it for 99 cents for a half-gallon container. But there were no sales when we went shopping. Annette had a rain check for Old Orchard juice and decided to use it. As we walked the aisles on our monthly shopping trip, she scanned the juice section looking for Old Orchard apple juice. There were no bottles there. The only varieties of Old Orchard that they had in stock were the expensive pomegranate/blueberry flavor for $5 per half gallon or the more expensive straight pomegranate juice for $8 per half gallon. The rain check specified only Old Orchard juice for 99 cents and didn't limit us to specific flavors. Annette did feel a bit of compassion for the store and passed on the more expensive variety, but she picked up her limit of three half gallons of the pomegranate/blueberry for 99 cents each. Mmmmmm, it was delicious—and the great deal made the juice even sweeter . . . if that's possible.

If you take our advice, out-of-stock items will be less of a hassle, and you'll end up getting the deal you went in to get. Just remember to ask the manager—you may be pleasantly surprised and end up singin' in the rain (check)!

Rain Checks on Target

Here are a couple of tips for smarter shopping at Target (and other stores too). Target offers rain checks for most items that go on sale, whether the item is sold out at the moment or not. They also allow a substitution of a similar item with the same percentage off as the sale item. We use this to our advantage by obtaining a rain check on an item. Then we pick out an item that is similar but less expensive and use the discount from the rain check. Keep in mind rain checks do expire. Also, if you purchase something full price (God forbid!) and see that it has now gone on sale, you can take your receipt back to the store and get the difference back if it's been less than two weeks since the initial purchase.

Audra—Chattanooga, TN

STRATEGY 17:
DON'T CHECK OUT AT THE CHECKOUT

You're getting close to the end of your shopping sojourn. You've clipped coupons, scoured the ads, planned a menu, and even written a shopping list. Now the groceries are loaded in your cart and you're standing in the checkout line ready to see your hard work pay off with some phenomenal savings. Whew, you congratulate yourself—a job well done. It's time to relax and let the checker and bagger take over. *No, don't do it—danger lurks ahead!* It's time for you to be totally alert—eyes and ears wide-open.

We've all read articles about how accurate the Universal Product Code (UPC) scanners are at the checkout. We also know that, according to research, grocers have far fewer scanner errors than other retailers. And, of course, we know that the Federal Trade Commission has been watching and evaluating scanner accuracy for years and reports that there are errors in only about 3.35 percent of purchases—and most of those favor the consumer. Since we all know all this stuff, how come we keep catching errors and being overcharged at the checkout? How come? Because although the scanners may be very accurate, no one can calculate the cost of human error.

A few months back, Steve was checking out with a cart full of price-matched items at Walmart. Unfortunately, he happened to select a checkout lane with a newer cashier who was not very experienced at the key sequence for price-matching. After numerous tries and calls to the front-end manager, she totaled the bill for Steve. He felt frustrated knowing that he was being overcharged, but figured it would be easier to resolve it at the customer service counter than with this particular checker. He'd been charged $74 for $50 worth of groceries. In the end, the whole order had to be rescanned by a manager.

Here are six ways to keep your hard-won savings from going back to the retailer:

Group It

Group your items on the conveyer belt by type and by item. If you have several boxes of crackers, put them together. Do the same with your dairy products, your produce, and any other similar items. When you go to review your receipt, they will show up in the same groups, making it easier to check for correct quantities and to look for errors or overcharges.

Watch It

Watch the display as the cashier scans each item. You need to make sure you're getting the price you expected. If you can, ask the cashier to wait until you load all of your items onto the conveyer belt before she starts to scan them. Many stores offer a scanner accuracy guarantee—if an item scans different from the price on the shelf, you'll receive that item for free (usually limited to one item even if you are buying multiples). It pays to ask.

Beep It

Keep your ears attuned to the beep of the scanner. Why? Because today's scanners are so powerful that with a simple miscue of the wrist, an item can be rung up two or three times. When we buy multiples of items—like ten or twenty boxes of macaroni and cheese—the checker has to punch in the multiple—either by typing in a number or hitting the enter button the specific number of times. Listen, count, and watch carefully here, too—mess-ups are common. Often, after counting the multiples into the total, a cashier who carelessly lifts the rest of the items over the scanner may rescan more by mistake.

Coupon It

We don't always use coupons, but when we do, it's usually a good-sized pile of twenty or more. Most stores in our area double coupons, so it's critical to keep an eye and ear open here, too, as the coupons are scanned and the checker hits the "double" button. If you have purchased larger quantities of items on which you are using coupons, some stores set limits in the computer's programming and won't allow all coupons to be counted. Listen for the little "baarp" sound (you know the sound we're talking about . . . how would you spell it?), indicating the coupon has been rejected. Most times the cashier or manager has to manually override the system.

A couple of times we've made the mistake of forgetting to turn in the coupons . . . Arrrrrrgh! Now that's frustrating. In one case, the error wasn't discovered until we arrived home. However, since we shop at the same stores month after month and have gotten to know the staff, we made a phone call to the manager and were allowed to bring in the coupons with the receipt and received reimbursement.

Bag It

We bring our own doubled paper bags—it's a time-saving thing. Plus we really dislike those little plastic bags that hold only two or three items, cut into your hands when you lift them, and dispense their contents all over your car when you make a right turn. Bagging your own groceries usually requires that you have a second person with you—it's physically impossible to bag groceries, watch the checker, listen to beeps, and watch the computer display at the same time—even a supermom would have trouble with this task. But the key here is to bag items in groups. You're less likely to spend time when you get home wondering where that fifth box of detergent went. We group similar items together: all frozen stuff, all produce, etc. Another reason we like to bag our own groceries is that we don't have to worry about what we'll find on top of the bananas when a young or inexperienced courtesy clerk tries to bag our mega-sized order. And we can keep the bags more uniform in weight—we've had some checkers try to cram ten to fifteen items into one paper bag!

Rescan It

After you've paid for your groceries and the cart is loaded, take about three steps and turn to visually scan the area. Check the loading area where your groceries come off of the conveyer waiting to be bagged. Check the floor just in case the courtesy clerk put a bag down there, and check the bottom of your cart. Also check the area where you set your purse or wallet while writing your check, dispensing cash, or swiping your debit card. Leaving keys, your wallet, your cell phone, coupon holder, or any of the groceries you've purchased costs you time. And while you're scanning things, scan your receipt for accuracy. Even with a diligent eye during the checkout process, you might find an error.

Daydreaming at the end of a shopping trip can cost you dearly. So stay focused and don't check out at the checkout. On our once-a-month shopping nights, one of our favorite things to do is to "check out" at home over a small cup of ice cream or some other treat we have a hankering for.

———⌒———

Receipts—Check 'em and Save

I carefully check my receipts before I leave the store. In the last six trips, I've found errors on four occasions. This meant that I received the mischarged item for free.

ANN—PITTSBURGH, PA

BACK HOME—ENJOYING THE SAVINGS

Some people question the sanity of our once-a-month shopping idea. Yes, it's a lot of work, but so is going to the store three or four times each week in our opinion. Because we only do this twelve times each year, it somehow seems more manageable—especially in light of how little we spend. Once we get home after a four-or five-hour shopping trip, we put away only the perishable items—dairy, produce, and meat. It's usually late and we're too tired to put everything away, plus the kids love to forage through the bags looking for "surprises." The next morning, all of us work together to put away the dry goods.

If we get a great deal, but what we buy goes bad or gets lost, it's not really a great deal. We'll share more in Chapter 6, "Stocking Up and Organizing," about how we store and keep track of all of the food we bring home.

If our shopping method seems overwhelming to you, remember that we've been doing it since 1985. You won't start off doing exactly what we do. Simply use these seventeen strategies as a catalyst to question if what you are doing is as efficient or effective as you'd like it to be. Evaluate the time involved and the potential return for each strategy and give some of them a try. Can you make some changes and implement a couple of these ideas? Sure you can! If you ask people who have run a long-distance race, they'll tell you that they didn't start off running marathons. They started with short distances and slowly built up from there. You can do the same thing, so get your running shoes on and get started!

WHAT YOU CAN DO NOW ABOUT SHOPPING

Timid Mouse

1. Take your one-week menu and make a shopping list.
2. Commit to going to the store only once . . . *no matter what.*
3. The next time your grocer is out of stock on an item you came in for, ask for a substitution or get a rain check.
4. The next time you go grocery shopping, put a hand basket in your cart and use it to track how many impulse items you pick up.

Wise Owl

1. Make a plan to go shopping twice each month and stick to it.
2. Set aside some extra money so you can stock up on sale items.
3. Research buying a stand-alone freezer and find the space to put it.
4. Research alternate grocery sources. Check out dollar stores, bread outlets, or dented can stores and decide if they are worth the effort.
5. Start a price book. Pick five (or more) items to begin tracking. When they hit rock-bottom prices, stock up!

Amazing Ant

1. Try shopping even less, once every three weeks or once a month.
2. Buy only seasonal produce and encourage your family to grab fruit whenever they want a snack.
3. Research and join a food co-op.
4. As you walk the aisles, look high and low for discontinued or marked-down items.
5. Try buying a chub of lunch meat fom the meat section, and ask the butcher or deli person to slice it for you.

4

Couponing—One of Many Ways to Save

Have you ever been in line at the checkout of the grocery store *behind* a coupon queen? You know, the person who has two carts of items to purchase and a stack of coupons that is 4 inches tall? It takes the checker ten minutes to go through her order. Then they start scanning her coupons—which takes another ten minutes. In the end, the total bill is reduced from $225 down to 50 cents. Meanwhile the people in line behind her have fallen asleep, or are enthralled with her couponing prowess, or are ready to scream because they just came to the store to pick up a head of lettuce.

Yes, coupons can save you a boodle, but at what cost? We'll be totally honest with you. We do use coupons . . . most of the time. But there are times when life is so crazy that we really don't have time to clip, sort, purge "expireds," and use coupons. That's why we wrote the other chapters in this book. We advocate a balanced view of couponing, one in which family time and healthy eating are as important as saving money. If you have time to clip coupons and want to increase your savings, keep reading. We'll also discuss some of the fee-based coupon programs to help you evaluate if they're worth the cost. But if you have several young children at home and are barely keeping up with the laundry, life, and getting a few hours of sleep at night, come back to this chapter when your kids are a little older and life has slowed down a bit. The time you spend with your kids is worth more than all of the coupons in the world, plus there are other less time-consuming ways for you to save on your grocery bill.

But before we dive into coupons, let's test your coupon history knowledge.

Which company is regarded as the innovator of the coupon? Here are some clues:

- The first coupon debuted in 1887.
- The company that invented the coupon is still in existence today.
- The coupon was for a free product sample.
- The inventor of this product was a pharmacist.

Any idea? If you haven't figured it out yet, just take a trip to the grocery store and go to the beverage aisle. You'll recognize the company's trademarked script logo and their dominant red-and-white packaging. Yes, we're talking about Coca-Cola. And *yes*, Dr. John Pemberton invented the soda fountain drink in 1886. His first year of promoting the drink resulted in sales of 25 gallons of his syrupy concentrate—enough for about 3,200 servings. The official Coca-Cola website gives no statistics on the effectiveness of the coupons Dr. Pemberton distributed in his second year of promoting his drink, but they must have helped, because over 125 years later, not only is Coca-Cola still around, but coupons are still a huge part of product promotions for companies around the globe.

HOW BIG IS THE COUPON BUSINESS?

You'll be amazed.

For many years, Steve was involved with designing and producing millions of grocery and commissary coupons. He worked with NCH, a coupon clearinghouse, to establish coupon codes and to have them test his coupons before printing. NCH is owned by Valassis, the company that distributes the Red Plum coupon insert that appears in your Sunday newspaper. They *know* the coupon business. Steve recently talked with their vice president of marketing, Charlie Brown (yes, that's his real name), about the popularity of coupons today. We learned that in 2009 coupon distribution was up 11 percent from the previous year, but that consumers redeemed *23 percent more* coupons in that same time period.[3] The use of coupons is definitely increasing as consumers work to stretch their budgets.

Of the 281 billion coupons distributed in 2008, only 2.6 billion (about 1 percent) were redeemed. In the U.S. over 311 billion coupons were distributed in 2009 (over 1,000 for every man, woman, and child in the U.S.), with about 3.2 billion (1 percent) of those coupons actually being redeemed (about 11 per person). That's roughly $3.5 billion in cash, given directly to shoppers from various manufacturers. With that much money being given away, you've got to wonder if you're getting your fair share. What do these statistics mean to you? It means that if you have the time and inclination to use coupons to get what you really want or really need, you can save some big bucks.

COUPON DEFINITIONS

There are several different types of coupons, and it is important that you know the difference so that you can play by the rules and save lots of money legitimately.

- **FSI**—color-printed coupons delivered in the Sunday or other newspaper.
- **Magazine**—printed on the page or "tipped-in."
- **Direct mail**—coupons delivered via mail to your home. Usually for local restaurants and home services.
- **Newspaper**—printed on the page of a newspaper. Could be grocery, tires, department stores, or arts and craft stores.
- **Peelies**—instantly redeemable coupons attached to the packaging of a product. These coupons have one of the highest redemption rates and offer some of the greatest discounts.

- **Checkout coupons**—earned based on your purchases and printed at the checkout. These coupons can't be used on your current purchase and usually can't be doubled. Sometimes the coupons are for dollars off your next purchase. Many of these coupons have relatively short expiration dates and expire before we can use them the following month. But most stores will allow us to hold back a few items to create a second purchase, and use the coupon then. Just ask!
- **Store coupons**—usually included in a store ad or mailed to your home. These coupons are created by a grocer, not a manufacturer, however, there are a couple of important distinctions to watch for:

  Store brand product—coupons for specific store brands won't be honored by other stores (unless they have a competitor's coupon policy), and they usually won't be doubled.

  Brand-name product—manufacturer coupons are sometimes printed with the store logo on them. You can tell if it is a manufacturer's coupon by reading the fine print or dealer copy. If they have a mailing address and promise the retailer 7 or 8 cents plus the face value of the coupon, it's a manufacturer's coupon. These coupons will be honored by other merchants (regardless of the store logo) and may be doubled.

- **In-aisle coupon machines**—sometimes called "blinkies" because of the blinking red light used to catch your attention. These dispensers hang on the shelf and "pop" out coupons. These coupons usually can't be doubled.
- **Internet**—downloaded or printed from manufacturer or coupon vendor websites, or loaded to your store loyalty card or cell phone.

MEETING THE COUPON QUEEN

Many years ago we were out "garage-saling." About two miles from our house we came upon a sale where a woman had all kinds of grocery products lined up on tables to sell. She had cereal, sponges, toothpaste, canned goods, and tons of other stuff piled high on her tables. We struck up a conversation and asked where it all came from. She smiled furtively and simply said, "It came from the store." We pressed her to give us more details. She explained that she was selling off a small portion of what she had received for free (or very little) by using coupons; the rest was inside her house. She took us inside and showed us an entire room (about 12 by 15 feet) lined with shelves, filled floor to ceiling, with grocery products—and with tons of stuff piled on the floor too. We asked her how many kids she had and she told us that there were just two in her family—her husband and her. Then she explained that she loved the challenge of getting things inexpensively. On any given week, she'd buy twelve Sunday newspapers—just for the coupons. Then she'd spend several hours planning her shopping strategy, going from store to store to match coupons with sale prices, sometimes going in and out of one store five or six times so that she could exceed limits placed on individual purchases by the stores. We didn't say much to her then, but as we drove away Annette looked at Steve and the kids and said, "There has to be more to life than that."

Yes, you can get stuff for free or next to nothing, but if getting the stuff consumes your life, is it really worth it? Not for us. But if coupons can really save you money, how do you do it without spending your entire life at the grocery store? Here's what we do.

ARE WE COUPON CRAZY?

Many people assume that the way we keep our grocery bill so low is through the unbridled use of coupons. Nothing could be further from the truth. We do use coupons, but not on every shopping trip and certainly not on every product. Using coupons is just one of many ways we've cut our grocery bill in half.

As with any of our strategies, couponing takes some time and organization to make it effective. How we organize and use coupons is certainly not the only way to use them, but we're hoping that as we describe our methods (and those of others), it will help you create a system that works for you.

Remember, not everyone has to use coupons to save on groceries. There are seasons of life when couponing simply won't fit with your lifestyle. A single mom raising several kids will be lucky to just get to the store with a list, let alone coupons. But that's okay. A working couple with several active kids and limited time for shopping may also opt out of using coupons. And that's okay too. There are many months when our schedule is so hectic that coupons remain unclipped and unused, and for sanity's sake, we know that that's okay.

Even when we do use coupons, we don't advocate the "coupon queen" approach of having multiple newspaper subscriptions, spending days and days clipping and sorting coupons, spending hours planning a strategy, and then going to multiple stores each day, so you can come home with hundreds of dollars of products for just a few pennies. We've decided to take a more moderate approach to couponing *and* to life. Here's how we use coupons.

The Coupon Caddy

Annette's first coupon container was a little nylon zippered pouch. It was okay for a novice, but as her couponing expertise increased, so did the size of her coupon container. She graduated to a shoe box with discarded business-sized envelopes filled with sorted coupons. Later, Steve built a larger, sturdier container that she still uses today. It's built out of ¼-inch PVC plastic, discarded from a photo lab near his office, and designed to fit perfectly in the seat area of a grocery cart. She still uses old envelopes to sort her categories, but now she can tote thousands of coupons to the store and is prepared for any type of sale.

You don't need to have a custom-made box to help you coupon better. Look around for a container that works for you—a cardboard or plastic shoe box or storage container, an expandable file, or some other container that fits your couponing style.

Which Stores

When we were first married, Annette had no clue how to play the grocery shopping game and win. She thought loss leaders were grocery store managers who wandered off a hiking trail, and cherry pickers were people who climbed cherry trees. And she shopped once each week at the grocery store near our apartment. She didn't compare prices between all of the grocery stores or go to a couple of them to save money.

We live in an area where many grocery chains—including health-food stores and warehouse clubs—compete for market share. There are always great deals as the stores battle for customers. Some regularly offer double, triple, or even quadruple coupons to lure shoppers into their stores.

As we described in the shopping chapter, Annette makes a list based on the grocery ads of all of the loss leaders from every store in our area. Then she determines which two or three stores we will shop at for that month. When the price is right, Annette matches her coupons with the sales to stock up on things like deodorant, feminine products, shampoo, BBQ sauce, cold cereal, salsa, and other staple items. We'll cover more coupon strategies in a little bit.

If a particular store is running a triple-coupon promotion, we may shop there just to use coupons on their loss leaders and a few other coupon-related products, then do the balance of our shopping at another store that is known for having better prices overall.

To use coupons effectively, you need to know the strengths and weaknesses, and coupon policies, of the stores in your area. Some have more liberal coupon policies, others have lower prices on more items, and still others may have lower prices on produce or better quality cuts of meat. Get to know all of the stores in your area so that you can get maximum value out of your couponing efforts.

The Coupon Categories

Steve sorts his coupons into multiple subcategories. For instance, his dairy coupons are micro-sorted into cheese, yogurt, sour cream/cottage cheese, margarine/butter, and miscellaneous dairy. He can do this because his area of the store, the outer loop—dairy, meat, and produce—has fewer coupons distributed than the shelf areas. Annette likes to work with as few categories as possible—a necessity for her—because she's dealing with so many different product types on the inner aisles of the store. We'll share a few other coupon sorting styles to help you determine which might work best for you.

Originally Annette only had five coupon categories: dairy case, personal care, cleaning products, frozen foods, and shelf items. As her coupon collection increased, so did her categories. Now her categories include the four previously listed (Steve took over the dairy section) plus cereal, snack foods (granola bars, crackers, chips, candy, and cookies), pet supplies, and paper products (which also includes batteries and games). We know this sounds strange, but the paper products envelope had the fewest coupons in it and had room for some miscellaneous coupons.

The coupons in each envelope are grouped by item to make them easier to find. For instance, the "cereal" envelope contains groupings for General Mills, Quaker, Post, Kellogg's, and other products. Within each manufacturer she organizes the coupons by product. These groupings make finding a specific coupon a snap.

The largest coupon category Annette has is "Shelf Items." It's huge. She organizes her coupons within this envelope based on the aisles of the grocery store where she first shopped. The coupons are organized in the following order: peanut butter; jelly; ketchup, mustard, and mayo; pickles; olives; vinegar; salad dressings; sauces; canned fruits and veggies; canned meals; meats; soups; rice; pasta and Italian products; Mexican products; chocolate drink mixes and syrups; baking supplies—sugar, oil, evaporated milk, cake mixes, chocolate chips; tea, coffee, juice, and soda.

You may be thinking, *Wow, I couldn't ever do that and keep everything straight.* Just realize that there is no right or wrong way to sort or file coupons. Everyone will do it differently. If you've never purposefully used coupons before, start by clipping coupons for products you already use and organize them in used envelopes. If that works for you, and you're using the coupons you've clipped, grow your system from there. If couponing becomes a workable money-saving tool for you, your sorting and storing methods will grow and improve. Remember that successful couponing depends less on a fancy container and more on your consistency. Consider some of the following options:

~~~

ABC—Alpha . . . Betical Coupons

I have a different way to keep my coupons. Of course, everyone thinks it is way different, but it works for me. I file the coupons alphabetically—then when I shop, I just look for the product by name (e.g., Palmolive dish liquid). I look under P and find it.

Barbara—Wilmerding, PA

Categories by Organizer

Annette and her best friend from grade school, Dianne, stay in touch regularly. Besides catching up on the latest family news and life in general, they always talk about their great grocery deals. They are a dynamic duo of discounts. Dianne is single and has the time and organizational skills to really make a killing with coupons. She does such a good job using her coupons that she'll often send her extra coupons to Annette in the mail.

We asked Dianne how she organizes her coupons. Her coupon organizer has thirteen dividers, and as a result she has thirteen categories:

1. Rain checks and store coupons
2. Meat and frozen food
3. Beverages
4. Breakfast foods and bread
5. Dairy, cookies, and candy
6. Baking
7. Spices, pasta, potato, rice, canned fruit and veggies
8. Paper goods
9. Cleaning supplies
10. Hygiene, makeup, and medications
11. Battery, bug spray, and miscellaneous store product coupons
12. Fast food/restaurants
13. Entertainment and miscellaneous service coupons (car wash, health club, prescription transfer)

Within each category, Dianne organizes the coupons alphabetically, so she can find them in a snap.

We posed the coupon sorting question to people on our America's Cheapest Family Facebook Fan page and received a variety of other responses, including using a photo album with plastic sleeves or a binder with baseball card plastic sleeves to keep coupons divided. Another person used business envelopes and kept them in an envelope box.

It seems that most people are going to use whatever they have available to sort their coupons. There is no need to spend a lot of money to purchase a specific coupon sorting tool.

Coupon Club Sorting

If you join a website coupon club like CouponMom.com, GroceryGame.com or some others that we'll discuss later, you'll be encouraged to file your unclipped FSI coupon flyers in a three-ring binder by the date they were distributed. Then each week you'll be told which FSIs contain coupons you should clip so you can get maximum savings at the grocery store.

GETTING MORE BANG FOR YOUR COUPON BUCK

Coupons are an enticement to try a product. It's a mini ad, promising you something better: better savings, a better life, or a happier tummy. Without a plan for how you use coupons, you could fall prey to a marketer's plan and end up buying things you don't really need. We don't just buy something because we have a coupon. Coupons are used strategically to buy products we normally use and to allow as little money to seep from our bank account as possible (unless we're having a serious ice cream craving). Following are a few ways that we expand the value of most of the coupons that we use.

Get Small, Save Big

Combining a coupon with a sale-priced item is good, but an even better deal is when you use that same coupon on a smaller-size package to get it for free or for just a couple of cents. A while back, ketchup went on sale at 79 cents for a 28-ounce bottle. That's a good price, but when Annette combined the sale price with a 25-cent-off coupon (doubled to 50 cents), she was able to buy that catsup for just 29 cents per bottle. Using every coupon she had, she was able to stock our pantry for the next six months for a couple of dollars.

For us, the value of couponing is buying the things we regularly use while spending the least amount. Even though a smaller item may initially cost more per ounce than a larger package, after a coupon is applied, it ends up being much less expensive.

Multiplied Values, Multiplied Savings

In many parts of the country where grocery competition is fierce, grocery chains will use double, triple, or even quadruple coupon promotions to lure customers through their doors. The grocer essentially pays you to use your manufacturer's coupons. In our area, double coupons have become a standard offer for a few chains. They offer to double a manufacturer's coupon up to a maximum of $1. In other words, a 25-cent coupon is now worth 50 cents, but a 60-cent coupon is only increased to $1. When stores offer to quadruple coupons, they still set the dollar maximum, so that's the time to use up all of your 10- to 25-cent coupons. You should see the cashier's face when Annette pulls out a twenty-year-old, 20-cents-off, pre-bar code coupon with no expiration date. They simply don't know what to do if they can't scan it. It usually requires a manager's override. One grocery chain in our area won't even accept them—that's sad!

If you're not sure whether the grocers in your area multiply coupon values, just call them or check their weekly ad. If they do offer to multiply a coupon's value, that's the time to get your coupons super organized and match them up with sale items.

Buy One, Get One Free

Ask your store manager how their computers calculate the savings on "Buy One Get One Free" offers. If they charge half price for each item, you are usually allowed to use two manufacturer coupons—one for each item. If they charge full price for the first item and nothing for the second item, you'll only be allowed to use one coupon. It pays to ask.

Stacked Coupons, Greater Deals

Another great way to save is called coupon stacking—using a manufacturer's coupon with a store coupon. You can't use two manufacturer's coupons to purchase a single item, but many grocery chains and drugstores produce their own discount coupons—either online, in the newspaper, in a color circular, or through special printers at the checkout. Most stores will honor the use of a manufacturer's coupon with a store coupon. However they won't multiply their own store coupons.

If you're not sure that your coupon strategy will work, ask someone in customer service or the store manager. They're generally well informed as to their coupon policies. We've done this a number of times and not only does it build rapport with the workers in the store, but it helps us move quicker through the checkout because we've already confirmed the usage of a particular coupon with the manager.

Closeouts

This is about the greatest way to get a deal. Most grocers have an area in each department where they display discontinued or closeout items. Usually the prices are handwritten on the package and the bar code is crossed out. The discounted price is usually good, but imagine if you had a coupon to go with it. We've walked out with yogurt, lunch meat, steak, deodorant, vitamins, and a slew of other products for pennies or completely free by using coupons on closeouts.

Honesty Pays

One of the most important coupon strategies is to be organized with your coupons. Make sure that you don't try to redeem expired coupons or have more coupons than products purchased. Being honest and playing by the rules will always benefit you, especially if there is ever a question about your order.

Expired Exceptions

Over the years we've learned some cool things about using expired coupons.

Grace period. The expiration dates on coupons have some flexibility. The retailer accepts the coupon and has to process it through their accounting department. They bundle all of the coupons and send them to one clearinghouse for sorting and redemption. The face value of the coupon plus a handling fee (around 8 cents) is paid for each coupon. Each manufacturer sets a deadline for when the coupons must be processed. According to Charlie Brown, at NCH, some manufacturers allow two weeks after expiration for coupons to be turned in, others several months. Because the manufacturers give the stores a minimum of two weeks to get the coupons turned in, some stores will accept coupons that are expired a few days, but less than a week; others won't accept expired coupons at all. Every store will be different, so ask—especially if it's a killer deal.

Store coupons. Managers have even more discretion with their own store coupons. We have a chain in our area that will accept their own store coupons and rain checks even if they are expired. They can do this because they control the redemption of the coupon—they don't have to send it to an outside clearinghouse.

Expired for the military. Overseas military commissaries are given additional time to send their coupons to a clearinghouse. As a result, commissaries will accept coupons up to six months after their expiration date. There is an organization called the Overseas Coupon Program and their website, www.OCPnet.org, lists the bases around the world, along with addresses and names of the volunteer coordinators where you can send your expired coupons. They also provide instructions on how to package the coupons and properly fill out the customs forms. At this time they don't accept Internet or store coupons, just manufacturer's coupons. About $10 million worth of coupons are sent to military bases each year. It's a great way to rally around our military families and help them stretch their paychecks.

SAVING WITH STORE BRANDS

When Steve was working for a small graphic design studio, they did a project for the company that marketed Brillo soap pads. His job was to design a package for a generic version of Brillo to be sold at Kmart stores. They had boxes of original Brillo and the generic soap pad in the office. The soap pads were manufactured by the same company and looked identical. The only difference was that they would be packaged in a different-colored box (the box was the same size as the original). Repackaged national-branded products are often called private label or store brands. The stores love them because they can buy them for much less, have their logo on them, and sell them for a greater profit.

Private labeling is a big business. In 2009, store brand sales of basic food category items such as flour, pasta, grains, salad dressings, and mayonnaise enjoyed 20 to 30 percent growth over the previous year. Look at the shelves the next time you're at the store and you'll see it for yourself. Many stores are producing two or three types of private-labeled goods, from budget priced to gourmet.

Keep your eyes open because you're going to be seeing coupons produced for these store brands too. These will be store coupons, not manufacturer's, and most likely won't be able to be multiplied or used at other stores.

In February 2009 we were taping a TV spot in a grocery store for the *Dr. Phil* show. Steve was talking to a PR representative from the store about how the overall grocery market was really hurting at the time. Rob told Steve that his chain was going to focus on putting more private-labeled products on the shelves because consumers were looking to save money and they could sell the private-labeled products for less than the national brands and still make a greater profit.

WHERE TO FIND COUPONS

Newspaper Free Standing Inserts (FSIs) represent over 86 percent of all of the coupons distributed and redeemed. Magazine and direct-mail coupons comprise about 6 percent of distribution, with newspaper, on-pack, military, and Internet coupons making up the rest. Internet coupon distribution is the fastest growing segment, up about 75 percent in 2009 (less than 1 percent of coupons distributed are from the Internet). There are coupons all around you, so where you find your coupons will depend on the amount of time you have to spend and how hard you want to look.

Our main source for coupons has been and continues to be the newspaper FSIs found in our Sunday, statewide newspaper and in a free local weekly newspaper. Annette has created a coupon-swapping network of friends and relatives (you could add coworkers if you find some thrift-minded buddies). We throw our unused coupons in a grocery bag and pass them to another family. Because each family has different tastes, there are always coupons left that entice the next person going through the bag. The advantage of this system is that you can easily end up with multiple copies of coupons for products you love. The disadvantages are that some of the good coupons will be already taken and by the time the coupon bag gets to the last person, some of the coupons could be expired.

Many people who get the newspaper don't want to "mess with" coupons. If you know people like this, just ask them to throw their coupons into a plastic grocery bag and give them to you every couple of weeks.

Internet sources for coupon distribution are growing. Two of the more popular sites are SmartSource.com and Coupons.com. SmartSource requires you to download a special computer file that allows you to print their coupons. They also limit you to printing two copies of any one coupon. The website www.GroceryCouponGuide.com is a great source for finding links to other sites where you can download coupons directly from the manufacturers. They have lots of current information on grocery deals and the best ways to leverage coupons with sales. Or you can visit Ashley Nuzzio's website, www.FrugalCouponLiving.com. We met Ashley when we were on the *Dr. Phil* show. She has a real heart to help families save money with coupons. She also encourages them to share any excess coupon items they get with those in need.

Coupon technology is always changing. There are now iPhone apps for downloading coupons from Coupons.com and some stores are now allowing you to load your store loyalty card with coupons from various websites. Keep your eyes peeled—we're expecting that eventually you'll be able to set up a user account with specific coupon preferences for products you like and they'll automatically load to your loyalty card or be e-mailed to you, but that hasn't happened yet. Give it time: less expensive distribution of coupons is going to be expanding.

~

Grateful for Coupons

I write or e-mail the companies that make some of my favorite items to compliment them on their products. In response, the companies usually send me coupons, oftentimes it's a $1 off or "free" item coupon. This gives me another outlet for collecting coupons while letting the companies know how good their products are.

SUSAN—JACKSON, TN

COUPON FRAUD

According to industry experts, the use of fraudulent coupons costs retailers (not manufacturers) over $500 million each year. It's a big business and unfortunately, it hurts honest consumers like us as manufacturers put more restrictions on the use of their coupons.

We became acquainted with fraud in May of 2009 when a relative forwarded an e-mail to us that contained two coupons for free products: Velveeta cheese and Reynolds Wrap aluminum foil. Because of Steve's years of experience in designing and printing grocery coupons, he immediately thought something was fishy. If these were legitimate coupons, the manufacturer would have little control. There wasn't an expiration date on either of them, so the cost to the manufacturer would have been exorbitant. Steve checked it out on two websites: Snopes.com and Cents-Off.com (the website for the Coupon Information Corporation). Both sites identified these coupons as scams. They also said that the manufacturers wouldn't honor the coupons and warned that anyone distributing, printing, or attempting to redeem them could be subject to prosecution. Trying to redeem a fraudulent coupon is the same as stealing. There are so many legitimate ways to save money; it's not even worth the time to think about cheating. If you want to see a current list of fraudulent coupons go to: www.Cents-Off.com/body_coupon _counterfeiters.cfm.

Coupon fraud is a major concern for manufacturers. Charlie from NCH told us that the two types of bar codes that are currently in use on coupons (UPCA and EAN128) will be phased out by January 2011 and be replaced with GS1 Databar. The change will allow manufacturers to put more information into the bar code, including multiple manufacturers, expiration date, product identification, serial numbers, lot numbers, and coupon offer code. By using a more complex bar code they are hoping to speed up the redemption process and minimize fraud.

Because of the misuse of Internet-generated coupons, distributors have had to develop complex technology to control the printing and proliferation of their coupons. If you receive a coupon offer that seems too good to be true, please check it out on the websites above and stop the distribution of it.

COUPON CLIPPING

Annette sometimes clips, organizes, or weeds out expired coupons in places where most people wouldn't expect: Abbey's dance practice, Joe's baseball practices, after dinner while we sit at the table and talk, or while Steve reads a chapter book to the kids. We always bring something to do when we're sitting and waiting for the kids or at the doctor's office. There are unending opportunities to organize coupons if you simply look for them.

Other times she'll gather the kids around the kitchen table and have a coupon clip-fest. As the kids got older, she taught them to weed out expired coupons. Abbey, our youngest, became very proficient at it when she was only eight years old.

Once the coupons are clipped, they are stacked in piles by categories, then filed into the envelopes.

USING COUPONS

When Annette is planning her menu or shopping list, she will often pull out coupons to be matched with a sale item and put them in a separate envelope to be used at the store. As we walk the aisles, we keep our eyes peeled for manager markdowns, closeouts, and other unadvertised sales. When we find these special deals, we whip out our coupons to see if we have coupons to match with them. If we do and it ends up being a killer deal, we pull out the walkie-talkies and give a whoop of triumph! We're not just buying products because we have coupons; our goal is to get the best-quality products for the least amount of money.

The coolest part about coupon shopping is standing at the checkout and seeing the retail price of your grocery order, then handing a huge wad of coupons to the checker and watching the total plummet. Ahhh, the sweet taste of victory!

The only thing that can tarnish your victory is forgetting to give the checker your coupons. Like we said earlier, we've done this a couple of times, but were able to resolve the situation by going back to the store with our receipt and turning in the coupons. Yes, it was extra work, but wouldn't *you* go back if you left $50 at the store?

If you only have a couple of grocery stores in your area, it's likely that couponing won't be your best way to save. If you have several young children at home, don't stress over doing coupons—time with your kids is more important. But if your kids are older and able to help or your spouse is willing, enlist their help in your coupon crusade. Working together as a family to stretch your budget builds tremendous unity, teaches important life skills and consumer habits, and can be a lot of fun too.

One last awesome benefit of being a savvy coupon shopper has nothing to do with your coupons, savings, or the total bill. We love watching the face of the person in line behind us as our final bill plummets and our grocery bags stack up. They have their eight retail-priced items on the conveyor belt and their jaw on the floor—they usually start asking us questions about how we do what we do—it's like a mini-seminar in the checkout lane. Now that's really crazy!

Here's a perfect example of a family working together as a team to use coupons:

Clip Coupons for Free Flights

I wanted to share a money-making idea for children—as well as a money-saving idea for the family budget! I have been price matching at Walmart for several months and have realized a savings of about $35 per week. This helps tremendously, trying to feed ten of us—including five boys who are teenaged athletes!

I am not fond of the coupon hunt but my fourteen-year-old son is. So, he does all the clipping and sorting, and I split the savings with him each week. He has earned quite a bit of money doing this, that's for sure! It took a little "training" on my part to make sure the coupons he cut for me weren't all junk food! He still slips one in occasionally. I even reward his hard work and buy that treat for everyone! In a very short time, he saved enough money to fly to California and spend a weekend with his grandma. He was thrilled and so were we!

ELIZABETH—MESA, AZ

If our way of using coupons is too overwhelming to you, you might want to consider a different approach to using coupons.

~

Do Coupons Make Sense?

I recently joined an online coupon program in Arizona called Coupon$ense, which costs me $14 each month. So far in the last month I have saved over 40 percent off my grocery bills (and it does help eliminate the time I was spending doing the coupon clipping and price comparison myself). Being pretty frugal myself I am sure I saved at least 30 percent off my normal bill prior to joining them, so I pretty much joined it for the time it would save me doing the "work" myself.

BONNIE—SCOTTSDALE, AZ

GROCERY GAMES

We have been asked numerous times about the value of money-saving grocery coupons clubs. We evaluated a couple of these coupon-matching website services, comparing annual cost, time involved, and potential savings with the way we shop. And we asked, how much work is involved to achieve the savings they publicize? We'll review the concept, the cost, and the value.

TheGroceryGame.com

Teri Gault, coupon-clipping super shopper from California, founded this international website in 2000. She perfected her method of matching coupons with loss leaders, and decided to "package" the concept. Her site reviews stores all over the U.S. and provides a weekly list of great sales at selected stores. She claims that many of her subscribers are saving 67 percent each week on their grocery bill. Some of the zip codes we checked have very few stores listed, and in our area they were missing two major grocers and several smaller stores. So it's possible that TheGroceryGame won't give you information on every store chain in your area. You can check your area by typing in your zip code. The website also lists several international versions of TheGroceryGame.com. We checked out these sites and they don't yet offer the same specific store sales/coupon information. They only contain shopping tips and articles along with ads for different products.

If you are a beginning couponer or wanting to take your couponing to a higher level, there are some positive and negative aspects to Teri Gault's program that you should know about.

+ Positives

1. **Selection**. She "cherry picks"—purchasing only loss-leader items from a particular store and trying to match coupons with them for the greatest savings.

2. **Stocking up**. She advocates stocking up on items when they reach rock-bottom prices.

3. **Cycles**. Recognizing the cycles in the grocery-marketing game, Teri recommends buying enough of an item to last until the next big price reduction.

4. **Colors**. She identifies three categories of deals by colors:

    a. **Black**: Good deals, but only buy if you really need them—better prices are coming.

    b. **Blue**: Great savings. These prices are rock-bottom, based on their database of pricing for your area. It's time to stock up at these prices.

    c. **Green**: These items will be completely free (unless tax is charged) when you use a coupon.

5. **Matching**. She helps you match coupons from FSIs with sales for maximum savings.

6. **Geography**. The website says that it reviews stores all across America.

—Negatives

1. **The cost**. They offer a free four-week trial of Teri's shopping list. Afterward it costs $10 for eight weeks of information on one store. If you want

more stores included you'll pay an additional $5 per store for eight weeks. Example: You have three stores in your area where you shop. The cost for you would be $20 every eight weeks, or $2.50 per week or $130 per year.

2. **Newspaper Subscription**. TheGroceryGame assumes that you save and file each week's FSIs. To do that you've got to have a newspaper subscription or pick up a paper on Sunday only. If you assume a cost of $2 per week for the paper or $104 per year, your annual cost for the game is now $234.

3. **Stores may be limited**. Not every store in your area may be included in her listing. If that's the case, you'll have to manually review the ads in your area to make sure you're getting the best prices.

4. **Time**. Her system advocates going to the store each week. We advocate reducing your trips. The fewer trips to the store, the less you spend. You'll also have to go to her website each week to review sales, make your shopping list, and clip your coupons. It all takes more of your time.

CouponMom.com

Stephanie Nelson's CouponMom website is similar to the TheGroceryGame in how it surveys the stores' sales and helps you match the FSI coupons to the sales. Where it differs is that she charges no fee. Here are the positives and negatives.

+ Positives

1. **Deals**. She helps you identify the best deals from local ads in your state.

2. **No fee**. There is no monthly charge.

3. **Coupons**. She has an affiliation with Coupons.com so you can print coupons right from her site.

4. **Tips**. She provides lots of shopping tips and info on the site and has a forum and blog you can participate in.

5. **Generosity**. In 2000 Stephanie started a program called Cut Out Hunger where she encourages smart shoppers to donate their excess bargains to food banks.

—Negatives

1. **Newspaper**. You've got to have a subscription or at least get a Sunday paper; otherwise you won't be able to match coupons to the listed sale items.
2. **Stores may be limited**. In our state she listed only one chain and we have at least eight to choose from.
3. **Filing**. You've got to file all of the FSIs versus just clipping and filing the coupons you want to use.
4. **Time**. Her system advocates going to the store and visiting her website each week.

If you want to give one website a try, we'd recommend starting here. It's free and you can see if using a system of matching FSI to store ads each week is something you have the time and inclination to do on a regular basis. If you find it helpful, use it. If you want more specific store information, sign up for the GroceryGame service.

These two websites are nice if you want someone to do some of the work for you or if you are just starting out with coupons and need help establishing a system. But if you're pressed for time, this type of couponing probably isn't going to work for you. The biggest drawback for *us* is that they encourage going to the store each week—so you don't miss a great deal—rather than planning better and reducing the number of trips. You can probably achieve the same amount of savings by swapping coupons with friends and reviewing the ads yourself.

If you plan a menu and a shopping list, watch for loss leaders, use coupons moderately, and go to the store less often, you'll save as much as these websites advertise. Remember, there's more to life than hunting down bargains so you can walk out of the store several times each week with armloads of free items. This is a battle—not just to save money, but to give you more time to do the things that really matter to you!

Here's what happened to one mom who let couponing change her family's diet too much.

I Was a Coupon Mom

Several years ago Annette met a mom at our daughter Abbey's dance class. Melody was standing in front of an eight-foot-long table that was covered with coupons. She was a member of a coupon club in Arizona called CouponSense.com (similar to TheGroceryGame). She said that this club and their system saved her tons of money. We called her recently to check up on her couponing habits—here's what she said.

I was part of the CouponSense program for three years. I paid a monthly membership fee plus had six Sunday newspapers delivered each week. CouponSense gave me a discount on the newspaper, so my monthly cost was only about $20.

Before I started the program I spent $120 each week on groceries to feed our family of seven. After I became proficient, I cut our weekly bill to $60. I was spending the same amount of time shopping that I previously had, but ended up having much more food in the house. There was a real "high" associated with walking out of the store with so much free stuff.

Eventually I realized that I was spending more and more time getting the deals and the "high." I'd go to seven stores almost every week and pick up many of the deals the website proposed. There were times I'd log on to the website to check the status of bargains at my nearby store only to find out that some other member had already been there and cleared the shelf.

I began to focus less on what I needed to feed my family, and more on how much I could get and how little I could spend. I finally came to the realization that I had more candy, chips, beverages, shampoo, toothpaste, deodorant, mustard, and relish than I could reasonably use or store. I also noticed that we were eating more prepared foods, but I justified it by saying that it was cheaper than eating out. The program simply was not adding to our quality of life. I didn't want to be eating this way—fast and easy wasn't my goal—I wanted to feed my family healthy food. I got really frustrated when junk food ended up being cheaper than fresh, healthy stuff.

I don't participate in the program anymore. Our kids are older now and eating more, so now we spend about $140 each week, but we're eating less prepared food and I feel better about our choices.

As Steve talked to Melody, he picked up her frustration with the way she was sucked into the unending quest for getting a deal. She didn't blame the coupon club or its members; she blamed herself for letting it get out of control. Online communities can be a great source of encouragement, but if we don't set personal boundaries, it's easy to lose focus and end up living a life that doesn't satisfy. There *is* much more to life than simply saving money.

COUPONS AND GOOD HEALTH

Some bloggers and many people reacting to news stories about our money-saving habits have criticized us for using coupons, saying that we couldn't possibly be buying or eating healthy food. One of the things they don't realize is that when we take a TV crew shopping with us, they have control of what they edit out and what they leave in. A two-hour shopping trip will usually be condensed into one or two minutes of airtime. Whether shopping alone or with a person from the media, we always make a point of including fruits and veggies in what we purchase. And we buy only a few items that are processed/convenience foods. By growing some of our own food and getting adequate amounts of exercise and rest, we stay pretty healthy. Coupons aren't the culprit for poor health—*poor choices are*. We choose to use coupons for items that we would normally purchase—and we choose to buy only a few foods that are processed.

If you want to eat fewer processed foods and save money, you can do it. It is going to require different thinking and a little more work. But over time as you develop new systems and habits, the work will become easier, you'll find new sources, and you'll be able to save more money. This whole book is designed to educate you so that you can make the choices that are right for your family. Sometimes those choices will cost you a little bit more out of your grocery budget to save you money in other areas. Choose wisely and choose life!

Saving My Conscience

Sometimes the desire to save money and the desire to do the right thing collide. We've started shopping for groceries monthly. Should I shop at

Walmart (twenty miles away) or at the store in the small town near home (nine miles away)? Of course, groceries are more expensive at the small store, but the owner has said the store can't survive if people just stop by to pick up the occasional item. Is saving money more important than supporting the local economy? I think I've answered my own question. I'm going to shop at the local store on the day they give a 10 percent discount to seniors. That way I can save money *and* not feel guilty doing so.

JANICE—OZAWKIE, KS (POP. 500)

And before we finish this chapter on coupons, here's one more way to save. While this isn't truly a coupon strategy, it does save money and help the environment—and that's a great combination

Savings Are in the Bag!

Bring your own bags to the grocery store and most stores will give you a 3-cent to 5-cent credit for each one.

DOREEN—PHOENIX, AZ

Coupons are big business for manufacturers and a great bonus for us as consumers . . . if we keep them in perspective. If they become too important, we'll buy products we don't need, or we'll try to use coupons in ways that weren't intended. We've also got to strike a balance between the time and effort we put into saving money and using our time to build stronger families or stronger relationships with others. Don't believe for a minute that becoming a coupon queen is a lofty goal worth sacrificing more important things for—it's okay to settle for being a coupon princess instead.

WHAT YOU CAN DO NOW ABOUT COUPONS

Timid Mouse

If you're new to couponing try these three tips:

1. Determine if you really have the time and gumption to do more with coupons.
2. Start collecting coupons from your Sunday newspaper FSIs and creating a filing system that works for you.
3. When you're reviewing the grocery ads and planning your next shopping trip, try to match coupons to sale items.

Wise Owl

If you want to kick your coupon savings up a notch, try these ideas:

1. Start a coupon swap with friends at church, work, or in your neighborhood.
2. Get a bigger container for your coupons and keep them sorted.
3. Start scouring your favorite grocery store ads for their store coupons and start coupon stacking.
4. If you have the time and inclination, try CouponMom.com or the GroceryGame.com.

Amazing Ant

1. Get on your local stores' e-mail lists, especially if they send out special coupons to list members only.
2. If you've got an abundance of food items in your house as a result of brilliant couponing, help someone else in your neighborhood or church who needs food or donate some of your excess to a food bank.
3. Send your expired coupons to our troops through the Overseas Coupon Program at www.OCPnet.org.
4. If you've really got some extra time, teach someone else how to get the savings you get—heck, maybe you can even start your own website or blog!

5

Cooking That Will Save You Time, Money, and Sanity

In 1955 the fast-food industry was in its infancy—McDonald's only had nine locations nationwide. Restaurant meals were reserved for special occasions, and most girls were required to take a home economics class before they graduated high school. Mom (and sometimes even Grandma) was at home cooking up delicious meals from scratch. Cooking was a necessity, but it was also a source of family pride, social interaction, tradition, and nutrition. Over time, as our family sizes have shrunk and work or recreational activities have increased, the time and desire to cook at home have all but disappeared. This lack of culinary interest has been nurtured as restaurant carry-out services have abounded, grocers have increased the number of prepared meals they sell, and several new business models have developed to help the harried homemaker to prepare "homemade" meals easier. These market segments have flourished, at least until recently, when the economic crunch woke many of us up from a convenience-driven stupor. So now cooking at home has suddenly become trendy again. The unfortunate thing is that in the past fifty years, a great deal of cooking knowledge has been lost.

Here's an example of how far we've declined in cooking basics. In 2006 Oprah Winfrey aired a series of shows called the *Debt Diet*. She had several personal finance experts (David Bach, Glinda Bridgeforth, and Jean Chatzky) interface with real families who were struggling with debt. Oprah profiled each family, their kids, their homes, their debt, and their lifestyles. At one point, Lisa and Steven Bradley (one of the families, who were struggling with over $100,000 worth of debt) were talking with Jean Chatzky about how often they ate meals out of the house. Lisa said that they usually picked up three meals a day from restaurants. Jean calculated that they were spending in excess of $20,000 annually eating out. At dinnertime Lisa would typically drive around to two or three drive-thru restaurants to pick up dinner. The family (Lisa, Steven, and their two daughters) took their meals into different rooms of the house to eat in front of various televisions or computers. When Jean Chatzky showed them how much they were spending eating meals out and told them that they couldn't afford to continue, she suggested that Lisa cook some meals at home. Later in the show we saw Jean and Lisa in the kitchen. Jean was reading from a cookbook and looked up at Lisa and said, "You need to slice up an onion." Lisa stood there with a bewildered look on her face. She froze in the middle of the kitchen with an onion in one hand and a paring knife in the other and said, "Uh, Jean . . . how do you slice an onion?" Her response, unfortunately, is typical of many young moms today. They don't know how to cook because they have never been taught. If you're one of these moms, don't feel condemned or live in despair, just realize that you can learn—one skill at a time.

Then there are those who know how to cook, but because of successful careers (their own or their husbands') choose not to cook—preferring to pick up carryout rather than shop and prepare meals from scratch. Living in Scottsdale, Arizona, we have often been in homes where owners have installed a beautifully equipped kitchen with really expensive appliances that are seldom used. If your budget can afford it, and your family approves, then don't worry about cooking and just skip this chapter. If you're struggling with debt or health issues (or both), or you have kids at home who may not aspire to or ever achieve your earning potential, then you may need to examine this habit.

We've also heard from many singles and seniors who find cooking for themselves to be too much trouble or something they simply don't feel like doing. Steve was at a doctor's visit with his eighty-year-old dad a few years ago. The doctor asked him about his diet. Dad said, "Well, I just don't eat that much, a muffin and coffee in the morning and then snack the rest of the day." The doctor replied, "Oh, you're a tea and toaster—that's something you'll need to work on." Meaning that when you live alone, cooking becomes less important and you can end up starving yourself nutritionally. If you can pick up a few tips here, you may end up eating healthier *and* saving some money.

Whether you don't know how to cook or choose not to, we're not advocating "cold turkey" changes. It is completely unrealistic to think that you can just decide one day to start cooking and be instantly transformed into Rachael Ray. You don't need a total culinary makeover, you just need to decide to take the next step. So, wherever you are in the cooking continuum, just start by doing *one thing*. This chapter isn't going to cover basic cooking skills—there are plenty of cookbooks and websites that do that. Annette's mom used to tell her, "If you can read, you can cook." We're going to give you ten different strategies or methods to make your time in the kitchen easier and more efficient. From bulk cooking to double or quadruple batch cooking and even some tips for sharing the kitchen with friends, you'll be armed with all kinds of new ideas to try.

HOW WE STARTED

Remember that Annette started our marriage as a culinary-challenged chef. But she made it her aim to not just learn to cook, but to become excellent in the kitchen. First she would call her mom every day to get her help in preparing that night's dinner. After a while those calls only came when she was trying a new recipe. With some basic kitchen skills under her belt, she was able to glean new ideas from cookbooks, friends, and magazines. We're not saying that we now eat gourmet, seven-course meals every day and that Annette spends every waking hour dreaming about or preparing sumptuous meals—she simply doesn't have the time to devote to this! What we are saying is that you can learn, like Annette did, to work efficiently and feed your family nutritious and delicious meals without spending all of your time or money doing it.

According to the USDA, dining out has increased from 16 percent of all meals in 1978 to over 30 percent today. The trend is declining as families have to tighten their budgets and as more women choose to either leave the workplace or work from home. This is good news for the family budget, but bad news for restaurants. If you apply some of the things we share, you'll find that you'll have more free time and more available money to go to a restaurant once in a while. But chances are you won't want to go out to eat because you'll have so many delicious meals waiting for you at home that you'll want to eat there and save the restaurant for a real celebration.

There was a night, several years back, when we were tempted to go to a restaurant *after* one of Annette's meals went terribly wrong. Even the best cooks, no matter how experienced, have an off night once in a while. This was one of those meals that became a family legend—it started off as garbage soup, but ended up as a disaster we called Tapioca Soup (you'll have to go to our website to read the grisly details).

As you become more proficient in the kitchen, you will have fewer failures, but please don't have the unrealistic expectation that you'll never make a mistake. Simply make it your goal to learn as much as you can—the mistakes will take care of themselves and add fascinating chapters to *your* book of family legends.

Before we talk about the cooking system we use to prepare a large number of meals in one day, we need to share some basic things we do, as a matter of course, to save time and money, while reducing our exposure to sickness.

We referred earlier to grinding our own beef on cooking day. It might sound like a lot of work, but the savings and health benefits are worth the effort.

STRATEGY 1: BECOME A GRINDER—MOOOVE OVER, MR. BUTCHER

No matter where you live, you've likely noticed a rise in beef prices in the past few years. Some credit Dr. Atkins and his low-carb diet, while others point to problems associated with mad cow disease, E. coli poisonings, and higher transportation or grain costs. Regardless of the reason, prices *have* risen, and in order to keep our food budget in line, we've had to be more careful and creative in our purchasing habits.

One thing we've done for many years is to grind our own beef. It started out of concern for our health, but it has turned out to be a money saver too.

Health. We believe that most meat processing plants have high standards of cleanliness. But in 2007 when we read that the Topps Meat Company, one of the largest manufacturers of frozen hamburger patties, was the subject of a huge product recall (22 million pounds) and was shutting down after the USDA had suspected it in spreading E. coli bacteria through its ground beef products, we were alarmed. This was the second large recall we'd heard of in a year. According to beef industry experts, the problem could have come from the beef being infected prior to processing or it may have been inadequate testing and cleanliness in the processing plant—either way, this story confirmed the decision we had made several years prior to minimize our use of store-bought ground beef. In 2003, we'd read a *Consumer Reports* article about contaminated beef, where they pointed out that there was a higher likelihood of contamination with meat that is ground than that which is sliced. The reasons behind their caution were multiple:

- Despite the best sanitation efforts of plant workers, pieces of contaminated beef could be stuck in the grinding equipment, evade cleaning, and contaminate future batches of meat.
- Because ground beef is comprised of some meat scraps taken from various cows, it is possible that one piece from a particular cow could be contaminated and as a result of mixing, contaminate the whole batch.
- The USDA does random checks of various batches for E. coli and salmonella, but does not check every batch. As a result some contaminated beef could sneak through.
- Meat that is sliced (rather than ground) comes into far less contact with potentially contaminated machinery.

We've had friends who were butchers suggest that we rinse all beef and thoroughly cook it (150-degree internal temperature) to minimize exposure to, or kill any bacteria. And they further suggested minimizing the purchase of ground beef products.

As a result of this information, we have stopped buying the cheapest ground beef in 5-pound chubs and started looking for inexpensive cuts of beef that we could grind at home.

We purchased a meat grinding attachment that was designed to fit on our heavy-duty KitchenAid mixer and set out to learn the finer points of making ground beef. Initially, we trimmed all the fat off the meat, but we found that 99 percent fat-free meat was so lean that it burned easier, had a different taste (more "gamey"), and didn't stick together well for meatballs and meat loaf. Now we intentionally leave some fat, but our finished product looks similar to the super-lean ground beef that sells for $5 to $6 per pound in the grocery store.

In order to minimize the possibility that we could spread bacteria when we're handling our meat, we rinse the uncut meat under running water, then slice it on a plastic cutting mat. When we're done grinding the meat, we disassemble the grinder attachment and wash it along with the knife and cutting mat in hot soapy water with bleach added to it. Being safe takes a little extra effort, but the peace of mind is worth it.

Cost. The money savings for grinding your own beef are substantial, especially if you are able to stock up on meat when it is on sale. But to do an actual cost comparison, we had to take into account the waste—fat and bone—to see if we were really saving money.

The inexpensive ground beef we previously purchased was reported to contain 20 percent fat. And we were paying approximately 99 cents per pound for it—actual cost of the meat, less the fat, would be $1.19. These days, the lowest prices we see for the "fatty" ground beef is about $1.49 per pound. In order to achieve a real savings, we set our target cost at $1.50 per pound for the finished product.

Here are a few actual figures from the past two years.

CUT OF MEAT	PRICE PER LB.	%WASTE	FINAL PRICE PER LB.
Chuck roast—bone-in	99¢ (sale price)	25%	$1.24
Chuck steak—boneless	99¢ (sale price)	0	99¢
Top round purchased bulk from a restaurant supply warehouse	$1.00 purchased with a coupon. 27 lb. slab	15%	$1.15

We've found that purchasing boneless cuts, on sale, provides the lowest cost and least waste. On the other hand, purchasing bone-in chuck provides wonderful bones for boiling and making beef broth. And once boiled, they make wonderful treats for our large dogs.

We've done several cost comparisons of our home-ground beef versus the store brand super lean, premium-priced ground beef. Whew, talk about savings. For ground beef with a fat content of 5 percent or less, you can expect to pay $3.49 to $5.99 per pound. At $1.50 per pound, we achieve a savings of 60 to 80 percent! Unfortunately, since we *never* purchase such expensive meat, the savings are just on paper. However, as with so many other economizing strategies, we are enjoying a higher-quality product without the associated cost.

A couple of downsides to grinding your own beef are that it takes some extra time and it can be messy. To minimize the mess, we tape a piece of waxed paper to hang loosely over the opening where the ground beef comes out to prevent splattering on the kitchen counters.

But for the health benefit and the cost savings we think that grinding our own beef is worth the time. And so do the kids. When they were younger, they used to fight over who got to operate the meat grinder on cooking day (don't worry, the attachment is kid-safe). To minimize conflict, we kept track of it on the kitchen calendar.

We hope that this concept has encouraged you to stop beefing over higher hamburger prices and start looking for udder ways to save more mooooolah.

STRATEGY 2: BUY IN BULK

Here are three quick ideas from visitors to our website with other ways to save money and time when using beef in your recipes.

Bulk Burgers and Meatballs

Early in our marriage we had six children, and I worked outside of our home. To feed our large family, we would buy a load of meat (usually a side of beef) from the butcher. Of course, we received some less than desirable cuts of meat, so we'd get creative. For example, we'd take several pounds of ground beef and make two or three large meat loaves to freeze raw. We'd also make large batches of meatballs (about eighty at one time) and freeze those too. Then we mounted a hamburger press on a board and let the kids take the rest of the ground beef to make loads of hamburgers—we separated them with waxed paper to keep them from sticking together. Buying in bulk and working together fed us well and saved us lots of money.

MARCI—PHOENIX, AZ

Broiled Beef Is Better

Here's how I save on lean ground beef. I watch for bulk lean or extra lean ground beef at a good price and buy a lot of it. Then I break it up and bake all of it in a broiler pan in the oven so that the fat drips below. Bake at 350 for about ½ hour. After cooling a bit, I separate it into quart-sized freezer bags—approximately one bag for each pound of pre-cooked meat. I freeze them and when I need a pound of ground beef for a recipe I just put a bag in the microwave or submerge it in water to defrost. This saves a great deal of time and mess when I am in a hurry to put a meal on the table. And I have lean ground beef for the price of regular ground because I bought it in bulk!

LINDA—BOTHELL, WA

Meatballs Are in the Bag!

My goal is to double and freeze one meal on my menu per week. I can take five pounds of ground meat, make one meat loaf for dinner, prepare a second meat loaf to freeze, and use the rest of the meat for meatballs. I freeze the meatballs on a tray overnight (covered with wax paper) and then pop them in a bread bag in the morning. They freeze well, but I don't like to put raw meat into my zipper bags. That's why I use an old bread bag to put the meatballs in first, according to family portions and company portions. Then I put them into the zippered bag to store in the freezer. The meatballs are versatile, because you can cook them with a BBQ sauce, sweet and sour sauce, or use them with spaghetti.

DEBBIE—CORTLAND, NE

No matter what kind of meat you buy, you're most likely not going to eat it without some seasonings or spices to enhance the flavor. Knowing how to buy spices, store them, and use them is a great way to make your food more enjoyable and to save money.

STRATEGY 3: SPICE IT UP!

It is said that variety is the spice of life, so it must follow that spices will add variety *to* life. It's not a subject often discussed or considered, except when trying a new recipe. You go to the cupboard to discover that you don't have that one spice needed to finish your dish. You run to the store and stand in front of the spice display and gasp at the prices. Having a full assortment of the spices you most commonly use is a time and money saver.

Sure, spices can turn an ordinary dish into something so full of flavor that it becomes a mouthwatering family favorite. But they can also be so expensive that buying them might be prohibitive or just not worth the effort. Every family is going to have their favorite types of foods, and with them go a number of commonly used spices that you should have in stock. We purchase many of our spices at Walgreens, price match others at Walmart, and even find some deals at the dollar store. For larger containers of spices we often shop at Smart & Final, a retail restaurant-supply warehouse near our home that has a surprising selection of spices at great prices. We even have some friends who purchase bulk spices from distributors they have found online—see the list at the end of this section.

Over the years as Annette has learned to cook her repertoire of over one hundred meals, her use of spices and understanding of which to use has increased. She says she isn't a spice guru—or a Spice Girl, for that matter—but she has learned quite a bit about using spices and has compiled a list of the basic spices we have in our house and their uses. (We'll assume that everyone has salt and pepper, so we've left them out of the chart.)

SPICE	USED IN
ALLSPICE	Sausages, cakes, desserts, fruit pies, jerky, chicken, fish, breakfast breads, stews, split pea soup, rice pilaf
ANISE	Licorice flavor for cakes, breads, cookies, fruit, root vegetables

BASIL	Pesto, great with tomatoes, herb breads like Focaccia, spaghetti sauce, poultry, lamb, fish and seafood, and a must for Italian dishes of any kind
BAY LEAF	Stew, soup, stock, marinades, pickles, beans, tomatoes
CARAWAY SEED	Rye bread, crackers, sausage, cabbage, soups, stews, pork
CARDAMOM	Sweet and savory, pastries, pudding, ice cream, breads, hamburgers, meat loaf, fruits
CELERY SEED	Soups, stews, stir-fry, salad dressing (crushed seeds), breads
CHILI POWDER	Peps-up bland dishes, Mexican dishes, and, of course, chili
CHIVES	Raw in salads, yogurt sauce, and as a baked potato topping
CILANTRO	Soups, stir-fry, Mexican dishes, rice, potatoes, fava beans, clams
CINNAMON	Desserts, spice breads and cakes, Middle Eastern dishes, coffee, chutneys, mulled wine, pumpkin bread or pie, baked apples, apple pie
CLOVES	Ham glaze, spiced breads, desserts, syrups, preserves, mulling cider
CORIANDER	Curry powder, vegetables, baked apples, pies, marinades, fish, soup stock
CUMIN	Greek shish kebab, breads, chutneys, meats, vegetable stew
CURRY	Indian cooking, meat stews, lentils, vegetarian dishes
DILL	Fish, seafood, root vegetables, potato salad, green salads, salad dressings, and pickling. Annette uses a little dill in her dough for shepherd's pie.
FENNEL	Fish, Italian breads, pickles, soups, roast pork, beans, vegetables
GARLIC	Chicken, lamb, Italian dishes, soups, Greek dishes, stir-fry
GINGER	Oriental dishes, works well with garlic, great with fruit
LEMON PEEL	Cookies, cake, breads, muffins, Oriental dishes

MARJORAM	Salads, egg dishes, mushroom sauces, fish, poultry
MINT	Chicken, pork, lamb, grilled fish, fruit salad, fruit punch, lemonade
MUSTARD	BBQ sauces, root vegetables (especially potatoes), pork, shrimp
NUTMEG	Lamb, fruit desserts, cakes, egg and cheese dishes, pumpkin pie, pumpkin bread
ONION POWDER	Great with meats, veggies, pasta, rice, potatoes
ORANGE PEEL	Cookies, cakes, breads, Oriental dishes
OREGANO	Italian and Greek cooking (our common bond), beans, stews, soups
PAPRIKA	Adds spice and color to Hungarian cooking, potatoes, rice, noodles, fish, chicken, egg dishes, soups
PARSLEY	Fresh in green salads, soups, spaghetti sauce, meat loaf, meatballs
PEPPERCORN	Add if you want to increase the heat of a recipe—can be ground
POPPY SEEDS	Breads, bagels, pretzels, cakes, salad dressing, vegetables—just don't eat any before a drug test.
ROSEMARY	Focaccia and other breads, stews, vegetables with olive oil, lamb, beef, poultry, shish kebab, crackers
SAGE	Pork, poultry, stuffings, sausage, stew, focaccia bread
SESAME	Breads, cookies, Asian cooking, noodles
TARRAGON	Fish, poultry, egg dishes, marinades for game meat, herb vinegars, mustards, flavored butters—Annette uses this in turkey gravy.
THYME	Clam chowder, marinade for pork and game meat
TURMERIC	Colors sauces yellow, beans, lentils, soup, rice, pickles, relishes
VANILLA	Dessert baking, fruit, pancakes, cookies, ice cream, custard, cakes, syrups
WHITE PEPPER	Less potent than black pepper—used to add zip

Bulk Spices

Here are a few sources for bulk or discounted spices:

Sahuaro Spice Company

3611 N. 34th Avenue, Phoenix, AZ 85017

Phone: 602-272-8557

Web: SahuaroSpiceCo.com

This company has been mixing and selling spices since 1930 and is owned by
   the Bowlus family.

Call for exact shipping prices.

Atlantic Spice Company

2 Shore Rd., North Truro, MA 02652

Phone: 1-800-316-7965

Web: AtlanticSpice.com

Shipping adds 20 to 25 percent.

San Francisco Herb Company

250 14th Street, San Francisco, CA 94103

Phone: 1-800-227-4530

Web: SFHerb.com

Shipping adds 18 to 23 percent.

How often have you been invited into a friend's kitchen to cook? Not too often, we bet. Well, we're inviting you to come into our kitchen, but we've got to warn you that what we're going to show you might change your life just like it did Annette's. We've got a way to cook a lot of meals in a short amount of time. Keep reading and let us know what you think once *you've* given it a try. Are you ready? Let's get cookin'!

STRATEGY 4: COOK LESS: SAVE TIME, MONEY, AND SANITY WITH ONCE-A-MONTH COOKING

Saving money isn't always the main motivation for doing the things we do. As we've aged, we've come to discover that time is an ever more precious commodity. We are constantly juggling kids' schedules, errands, work, chores, and, if we're lucky, some recreation activities.

One way we've found to earn back several hours each week is once-a-month cooking. We know it sounds crazy, overwhelming, and maybe even ridiculous, but it really does work.

Years ago, when Steve spent long hours driving to and from work and appointments, he heard a radio program extolling the wonders of cooking many meals in one day—once-a-month-cooking (OAMC). Mimi Wilson and Mary Beth Lagerborg, the authors of the OAMC book, were being interviewed. They told some humorous stories and many of the wonderful benefits they derived from bulk cooking. Of course, like any devoted husband, he immediately came home and presented this great idea as something Annette ought to consider.

At that time, we had just two children, two and four years old. Annette was struggling to care for their needs, keep up with the house, and cook a decent dinner each night. So when Steve presented the idea, Annette's initial reaction was to balk and feel totally inadequate and stressed at this huge undertaking. But after some time thinking and considering the possibilities, she decided to buy the book and give it a try.

She *was* completely overwhelmed during her first attempts at following the instructions contained in the OAMC book. The most important thing to remember when trying something new is to stick with it. It's never going to work perfectly for you the first time. And the things that work for us might not work exactly the same for you. This is exactly what Annette discovered. Many of the recipes that Mimi and Mary Beth included in the book didn't work for our family. But Annette saw the value of the system, so she worked to customize it to our lifestyle. Now that she has modified it to fit our family's tastes and schedule, she just wouldn't live without it.

The basic premise of OAMC is that you can save time and energy through economy of scale. To cook one meal you may need to pull out some meat, veggies, spices, a cutting board, knife, frying pan, and pot. You chop the veggies and slice the meat, then cook the items, adding ingredients as you go. When dinner is finished, you have to clean the pot, pan, knife, and cutting board. The cycle is repeated every night. Once-a-month cooking utilizes efficiency to save time and effort. Instead of chopping up a couple of carrots for one recipe, you calculate how many of the recipes on OAMC day use carrots and cut them up all at once. The same is done with other items, such as browning ground beef, chopping onions, or cooking chickens. Ingredients for multiple recipes are prepared together, then separated into the individual meals. Even though the day you cook all of the meals is busy and there is a lot to clean up, you are saving time by eliminating the repetition that is involved in so many meals by doing it all at once.

How much time can OAMC save you? It's hard to give you an exact number of hours, but for argument sake Steve created the following calculation (individual savings will vary depending on diet, family size, cooking style, and whether you live in New Jersey where most activities are prohibited by law—of course, we're just kidding about New Jersey).

ACTIVITY	TIME SPENT
Annette's involvement: OAMC cooking day—preparing seventeen meals. Time spent preparing, cooking, and cleaning up.	6 hours
Family involvement: Usually at least one of the kids will help Annette the entire day, and as other family members are available, they'll pitch in too. So the approximate number of "man" hours would be 6 plus another 5 (for the intermittent helpers).	11 hours
Meal preparation: Daily warming of the meal and preparing side dishes. 30 minutes per meal.	8.5 hours
Total hours spent preparing seventeen meals	25.5 hours

Conventional meal preparation: Assuming cooking from scratch and cleaning up 17 meals at an average of 2 ½ hours per meal (some take less time, and some take more).	42.5 hours
Total time saved	17 hours per month

We know that we save *at least* thirteen hours each month, and many of our friends have said the same thing—OAMC saves huge amounts of meal preparation time.

Annette has had various friends accompany her on OAMC day, and they go from having the typical "deer in the headlight" look to being amazed at how much can be accomplished when things are organized. Are you ready?

Here's how we do it.

Planning

We plan the menu for the month based on the family's schedule and what cuts of meat we already have in the freezer (refer to Chapter 2, "The Power of the Plan"). Normally, Annette will have somewhere between twelve and seventeen meals to prepare on cooking day. "Wait a minute," you say, "I thought you were cooking for a full month, like thirty-one days." You're right, but stay with us. The menu for the other days of the month consists of roasts, chops, leftovers, and other meals that are prepared on the day they are eaten. Some meals don't lend themselves to being cooked in advance and frozen. Her menu list usually consists of five beef dishes, six chicken or turkey, two or three pork or ham, and three miscellaneous, such as lentil vegetable soup or calzones.

The Night Before

Cooking day really starts the night before, when Annette pulls out a large slow cooker and throws in a beef brisket, corned beef, or a couple of chickens. This is done, according to the OAMC book, so that you start your day off with a meal already completed. When beef brisket costs 99 cents a pound or less, we stock up. These make a wonderful meal of shredded beef with mustard and onion sauce, served over rice, pasta, or baked potatoes. Corned beef is defatted and sliced for use in Reuben sandwiches later on in the month. The chickens are deboned and used in recipes like chicken enchiladas or BBQ chicken.

The Pans

The morning of cooking day, we clear the kitchen table and cover it with many large glass baking dishes (13 x 9-inch size) and large storage containers. Each container is labeled using a piece of masking tape with the name of the meal scrawled in black marker. Steve likes to be creative and sometimes the labels are a little difficult to figure out—"Messy Joseph" for sloppy jocs, "Chicken Farmer John" for chicken Parmesan, and many others. The kids have caught on to the scheme and now that they are older, come up with their own clever meal names.

Some proponents of OAMC advocate storing the meals in plastic zippered bags or plastic containers. We prefer to use glass containers because of their versatility. They can go in the microwave or the oven, and there is no concern about chemicals such as bisphenol A (BPA) and phthalates or other contaminants being transferred to our food when it is cooked. Concerns over BPA food contamination have been investigated by groups such as the U.S. Center for Disease Control, *Consumer Reports*, and the Good Housekeeping Institute. Conclusions vary, with some experts saying there is no danger, while others proclaim the need to avoid certain types of plastic containers. We don't know the answer, but we do know that glass containers have never been suspected of contaminating food.

We use a lot of plastic zippered bags, but not for storing OAMC meals because sometimes these bags can "unzip" or tear, usually at a most inopportune time, leaving you with wasted food and a big mess to clean up. But if you are cooking smaller quantities you might find that 9 x 9-inch glass baking dishes, casserole dishes, or some other smaller ceramic containers will work best for you.

The Task List

Next Annette makes a list of tasks, such as peeling and chopping onions, washing and slicing celery, grinding beef, deboning chicken, dicing chicken or turkey, or making shepherd's pie crust. All the kids who are helping choose tasks they would like to work on throughout the day—age appropriate, of course. She calculates how many recipes will use chopped onions, carrots, or celery and cuts up enough for all of the recipes. This is where OAMC becomes super-efficient. Remember, if your family is smaller, your tasks will be smaller also. But if your family is larger, you've got to enlist help, either from your kids, your spouse, or a friend.

Cookin' Time

Fire up the burners and let the cooking begin! Aprons on and knives at the ready, we dig in with a passion. This is the approximate order in which we tackle the tasks.

1. **Veggies**. First, the veggies to be used in several recipes are washed and chopped.
2. **Meat**. Next we start browning sausages for pasta sauce, or boiling a ham. These take some time, so they're started early. We also debone and cut up or grind beef for recipes that call for it.
3. **Poultry**. In the winter months, there is no need to debone chicken because the poultry meat is already cooked. We usually cook one turkey—of the several purchased at Thanksgiving time—every four to six weeks during the cooler months of the year. The meat is first used for a sit-down turkey meal, then the remaining meat is frozen in plastic storage bags. On cooking day we defrost it and cut it into smaller pieces for use in various recipes. In the summer months, we cook chickens in the slow cooker overnight, outside, so that the meat is ready to debone the next morning.
4. **Simmering meals**. Next Annette starts to assemble meals that take a long time to simmer and cook. These include soups, stews, and her famous multigenerational pasta sauce—Ragu, eat your heart out!

When our kids were younger, Annette rarely ever got to eat a warm meal. You know the drill—you finally get everyone seated at the table, the meal is served, and then Mom starts the ritual of cutting up the meat for the youngest kids. By the time you're done, your meal feels more like something out of the last ice age than the hot, delicious meal you envisioned.

This situation was especially daunting for Annette on nights when Steve worked late and didn't make it home for the start of dinner.

Annette combated this problem by modifying many of her once-a-month cooking recipes to use diced or cubed chicken, ham, turkey, and also ground beef. Because the meat is already cut into bite-sized pieces, the kids could eat right away and Annette could enjoy her meal too. It was a simple change that moved her from the ice age to the modern era.

5. **Assembly**. Once all the ingredients are chopped, sliced, cooked, and sitting in their appropriate baking dishes or pots, the final assembly begins. BBQ turkey or turkey Parmesan are put together. Sauces are mixed for sesame chicken, ham and scalloped potatoes, or sweet-and-sour chicken and poured over the meat in a baking dish.

6. **Storage crew**. Steve's job is to seal each dish with plastic wrap or close up the plastic container and carefully store the meals in the freezer. We stack the 13 x 9-inch baking dishes with a piece of Plexiglas or cardboard between them to make removal from the freezer easier. We also make sure to leave the labeled ends of the baking dishes facing out so they can be easily read.

7. **Cleaning crew**. Finally everyone pitches in to wash and put away all the pots, pans, and other utensils used that day.

The night of cooking day, we will usually go to a fast-food restaurant or grocery deli, order a carryout meal and bring it home. We try to keep the cost under $15. After cooking all day, the last thing you want to do is plan another meal, plus, since we don't frequent fast-food restaurants, it is a special treat.

We know that this process may seem overwhelming to you. Please take it slowly. First try planning for one week's worth of dinners—somewhere between four to six meals. Then try cooking them in one day. Give this a few tries before you attempt to cook for more days. If you're successful, expand your planning to two or more weeks. Lack of freezer space may limit the scope of your cooking day, so you'll have to be creative with how much you cook and how you store it. Even if you can manage only a few meals in one day, you'll save loads of time during the week, especially if you have small children or Mom works outside the home.

———~———

Once-a-Month Stress Reduction

We are a military family in D.C. Most military families hate coming here because of the financial pressures—it's very costly to live in D.C. We have been able to take some stress out of our lives by using the once-a-month-cooking concept. Although I haven't been able to get my shopping down to once-a-month, I am able to make it last between three and four weeks—that's pretty close! With rising gas prices and considering how far away from the base (where the commissary is) we had to live to be able to find affordable housing, this is fantastic. I also can't say thank you enough for what you write. I've learned a lot. I was not very good at economizing before and your tips have helped so much.

CHARLA—HERNDON, VA

Seasons of Life

No matter what your season in life, this concept can be beneficial. When our kids were under six years old, Steve's job was to take them out of the house for the morning to play at the park. They would come home, take naps, and we would finish up cooking together. As the kids have grown, they have become an invaluable part of the cooking team. Now, Steve will work on house projects and "borrow" one of the boys to work with him while the other kids are helping with the cooking tasks. Yes, we think that it is important for boys to have basic cooking skills too.

Sharing with Others

If you're a single or a senior, a 13 x 9-inch pan full of anything could last for months. Consider making smaller portions or sharing a cooking day with a friend and then splitting what you have made. Working with someone else is always more fun, and you may just discover some exciting new recipes (we'll share a few stories about how some friends have done this). Another advantage to having prepared meals in the freezer is being able to pull one out on a moment's notice to help a family in need. We've done this several times upon the arrival of a new baby or when a family friend has been dealing with an illness or a tragedy. Meals in the freezer can also be a lifesaver when you have unexpected guests.

Advanced Cooking Saves "Face"

About once each month we have a party for the students we teach at the English Corner here in China. Most people here are thrilled to be invited to an "American" home to eat American food. For one party we were expecting about fifteen people to attend. You can imagine my surprise when *forty* people showed up. I had dinner already prepared and knew there wouldn't be enough food. As the guests kept arriving and eating, I began to panic. In the Chinese culture it is considered incredibly rude to run out of food. Also since several of our friends had invited more people than they had originally communicated, they would have felt unbelievably embarrassed for putting me in an awkward position. I quickly ran into the kitchen and opened the freezer. Fortunately when I had done my once-a-month cooking, I had precooked and frozen the same meal I was serving that night. I microwaved the packages of frozen meats and transferred the contents to the slow cookers already on the table—nobody was the wiser. As is appropriate for the custom, I had plenty left over and no one lost face!! Thanks for the impact you have had on our lives. You are influencing Asia now!!!

Kristi—Chengdu, China

Be Flexible

Our cooking days have changed over the years. In the past we always did cooking day on the last Saturday of the month, a couple of days after our once-a-month shopping night. As the kids' activities and schedules have changed, so have our cooking days. Sometimes we have to schedule them for a weekday when everyone is available.

No matter the day or how many meals you make, we're convinced that the time savings you'll enjoy will far outweigh the effort you put forth. It takes a while to master OAMC and to modify your favorite recipes to be freezer compatible. Here are a few things we've discovered:

- Pasta shouldn't be fully cooked before being frozen, or it will turn to mush when thawed.
- Potatoes *must* be thoroughly cooked before being frozen or they'll turn black—we've learned the hard way.
- Eggplant turns rubbery and watery when defrosted and reheated.
- Gravy tends to separate and needs to be recombined when thawed.
- Mayonnaise by itself doesn't freeze well, but when combined in a recipe it does fine.

Mistakes are inevitable, but once you've mastered this concept, you'll wonder how you ever lived without it.

Most nights when we pull out a meal from the freezer, dinner preparation takes about half an hour. Since the main dish is already prepared, all that needs to be added are veggies or salad along with pasta, potatoes, or rice.

And the best part of the deal is that on those really crazy days, when Annette is still running errands late in the day or picking up kids from activities, with a simple phone call to Steve or one of the kids at home, dinner can be ready and waiting when she gets there. Pass the pasta, and let's eat!

Cheers for Once-a-Month Cooking

I just did our first once-a-month cooking with our family. It was fun and also met my goal of sending all my kids out into the world with the ability to cook. I had also thought it wasn't for me because I love to cook. But what I am finding this week is that having the meals in the freezer is so freeing that I am more cheerful at dinner and often have time to make a dessert.

CRYSTAL—KEMPTON, PA

Below is a sample of two months' worth of menu ideas that Annette created. Each month the menu is different depending on what we have either stocked in the freezer or what we bought on sale. The chart is also divided up by the type of meat or meatless meal it is.

SAMPLE ONCE-A-MONTH
COOKING DAY MEAL PLANS

	MONTH 1		MONTH 2
BEEF	1. Stuffed grape leaves 2. Tagliarini 3. Sloppy joes 4. Stew 5. Shepherd's pie	BEEF	1. Reuben sandwiches 2. Hash 3. Hamburgers 4. Tacos 5. Shepherd's pie
CHICKEN	1. Chicken pot pie 2. Nacho chicken 3. Orange chicken 4. BBQ chicken 5. Sesame chicken	CHICKEN	1. Lemon chicken 2. Chicken Parmesan 3. Nacho chicken 4. Chicken fajitas 5. Chicken enchiladas
HAM / PORK	1. Sweet & sour ham 2. Split pea soup 3. Ham & scalloped potatoes	HAM / PORK	1. Orange ham 2. BBQ ham
MISC.	1. Vegetable bean soup 2. Calzones	MISC.	1. Cream of broccoli soup 2. Vegetable lentil soup 3. Eggplant Parmesan

STRATEGY 5: DIVIDE AND CONQUER WITH TEAMWORK

Here are some ideas from friends who are part of AmericasCheapestFamily.com and have tried our method or other approaches to bulk cooking. Remember the old saying, "There's more than one way to fry a fish." Try our way, their way, or invent your own, but do something!

~

Teamwork and Creativity Conquer Intimidation

I was intimidated by the idea of trying to cook a month's worth of meals all at once, especially considering I never really learned how to cook. But my husband and I decided to try a week's worth and thought surely we could expand from there. Our kitchen is small so we split the task with me inside at the stove and him outside at the grill.

I start by browning several pounds of ground beef (bought in bulk for savings), with some finely chopped onion and some Cavender's Greek Seasoning on some of the ground beef (a good all-purpose mix). He works outside, grilling several pounds of chicken breasts, bratwursts, and steaks—basically whatever we bought on sale. Then we divide the meat up into meal-sized portions and either refrigerate or freeze it depending on the schedule. We use the ground beef as a base for stroganoff, spaghetti, soft tacos, taco salad, or a variety of casseroles. The chicken is cut up into bite-sized pieces for chicken Caesar salad, fajitas (steak can be used here too), casseroles, or combined with cut-up smoked sausage or brats for jambalaya. I still do quite a bit of cooking out of boxes and cans (mixes and sauces) but it is still a family meal and not fast food. The great part is that dinner is ready in thirty minutes or so, and takes the stress out of trying to figure out what to prepare after working all day. My husband and I take leftovers for lunch, and our teenage daughter does too—which also saves money.

We now are planning and cooking up to two weeks' worth of meals. Eventually, I hope to work my way up to a month's worth of meals, but none of this even would have happened if I hadn't started bulk cooking! Thanks Annette and Steve, for giving us your knowledge and tips and the tools and encouragement to use them!

DENA—FAYETTEVILLE, AR

Working together as a team, whether you're a married couple, single parent, or solo, always produces a better return. If you don't have a "team," start looking for ways to create one in your home or with some friends.

STRATEGY 6: MULTIPLY YOUR PORTIONS

Cooking multiple portions of a single recipe is the easiest and fastest way to get ahead of the meal preparation curve. It doesn't take twice as long to make a double, triple, or quadruple batch, so you really do save time. Experiment with recipes and find out which ones you can double and which you can't. Freeze the excess and plan it into your menu. You'll be surprised at how quickly your freezer is full and your time is more available to do other things.

Cookin' Double Saves Time

I love to cook, but don't always have the time to make a great meal each day. I've started to cook double portions when I do cook. Then I freeze half of what I make. This way we can always have homemade meals.

LINDA—LELAND, IL

STRATEGY 7: BE CREATIVE

Some of you are going to look at your kitchen or the kitchen tools you have and throw up your hands in surrender. Limits promote creativity, not crises. You can spend less time cooking by making larger batches and thinking ahead. You just have to think outside of the "pot."

<hr />

One-Pot Bulk Cooking

Your website is exactly what I needed right now. I am working slowly into once-a-month cooking. It's kind of hard living in a foreign country when you only have one pot, two burners, and limited containers. But it is going well and I am loving it. Two days ago I made sauce that will be used for multiple meals: spaghetti sauce, pizza, or chili. I also cooked some ground beef that can be added to the sauce or used for tacos or stuffed peppers or whatever. Today I cooked beans for chili or burritos. I am also experimenting with my pizza dough. I usually make it and use it right away, but this time I put some in the fridge and some in the freezer to see what that will do. We are so glad to have been influenced by you during the early years of our marriage.

KRISTI—CHENGDU, CHINA

When Annette visited several older single women, she discovered empty refrigerators. As they talked, she heard the same story, that cooking for one person isn't worth the effort. But, on a fixed income, eating out for every meal isn't realistic either. Just as the old-time quilting bees and barn raisings were great social and constructive get-togethers, getting a few friends together to cook can be just as rewarding and delicious too.

STRATEGY 8: SHARE THE LOAD—THE MEAL SWAP CLUB

Our thrifty friend Becky from Indiana shared another approach to bulk cooking. She and some friends have a Meal Swap Club. Don't turn the page yet; we don't mean trading a baloney sandwich for a PB&J in the grade school cafeteria. Here's what they do.

Five friends who have similar-sized families get together once every six to eight weeks to plan a series of meals to cook and share. Each person comes with three to five recipes to present to the group. They discuss the meals and settle on a menu.

Once the menu is approved, each member purchases ingredients and prepares three different meals in large enough portions to be divided equally among the families—serving four to six people per family. Six to eight weeks later they get together to distribute the frozen meals and plan the next set of recipes. The dinners are packaged in zippered bags or disposable containers. They bring in their receipts, the expenses are totaled and averaged, and then they exchange money to even out the costs—or each person can handle their own costs.

This arrangement encourages variety, new recipes, trying new foods, creativity, and helping others. Becky says, "It hasn't happened yet, but if the group decides on a meal I know my family won't like, I'll freeze it to give to a family who needs an extra meal."

One drawback is a lack of control of the cost of meals. The members commit to be as thrifty as possible—although that means different things to different people. "If I know that another member is making something for the next session, and I spot a great deal on an ingredient she will be using, I'll give her a call," says Becky.

If you know you have meals in the freezer, you're less likely to buy fast food or expensive convenience foods on busy days. The best part is that each participant prepares only three extra-large portion meals and walks away with fifteen meals for her family.

This creative concept is not only for large families. Singles and retirees can benefit from it too!

SAMPLE MEAL SWAP CLUB MENU

- Terri—country-style ribs, meatballs, and honey pork chops.
- Becky—tangy rump roast, potato broccoli cheese soup, and cheese-stuffed shells.
- Tris—poppy Swiss sandwiches, beef enchiladas, and spaghetti pie.
- Cheryl—chicken salad casserole, mystery chicken, and wild rice chicken.
- Mary Ann—Fajita kits, citrus pork roast, and calzones.

STRATEGY 9: MAKE HASTE TO NOT WASTE

According to a research study conducted by the Discovery Channel and distributed on DiscoveryNews.com, almost 30 percent of all of the food produced ends up in the trash—wasted (only about 14 percent of what we bring home is wasted). The waste is as a result of several things: simply buying too much; serving portions that are too large and go uneaten; the undesirability of eating leftovers; and attempting to store food either improperly or for too long (yes, we've had those fuzzy green "science experiments" in our refrigerator on occasion). Another cause of wasted food comes from farmers who may overproduce vegetables due to better farming methods, but aren't able to sell all that they have produced. All of these factors contribute to wasted food, wasted water to grow the food, and wasted fossil fuels used to harvest the food and refrigerate it at home. If we can learn to buy more carefully, store what we buy, and use what we store, we can actually save money and help the environment at the same time.

Try some of these ideas to keep from wasting what you have grown or purchased.

Cool as a . . . Banana

I have heard many people say they freeze bananas for future use in banana bread, etc., but I was never sure how to prepare the bananas for freezing. One woman told me she puts the whole banana (peel and all) in the freezer and then thaws it later when ready to use. I am one who doesn't want to wait for the thaw. Therefore, we peel the bananas, wrap each in plastic wrap, and then put them in a freezer bag for easy storage. Frozen bananas that have been prepared this way are easy to mash for banana bread, make the perfect frozen ingredient for a smoothie in the blender, or are great as frozen popsicles in the summer. To serve this cold treat without a stick, peel back the plastic and wrap a folded paper towel around the "handle" part. Cut in half, these banana popsicles were some of our children's favorite teething coolers.

RUTH—SCOTTSDALE, AZ

Blend Your Crummy Crusts

I save the crusts and end pieces of my loaves of bread in a zippered plastic bag in the refrigerator. When it's full, I make my own bread crumbs in the food processor. I add whatever spices I want, such as Italian seasoning. Then I use these bread crumbs to coat chicken and my family loves it. They are much more flavorful than the canned bread crumbs and way less expensive.

SUE—SCOTTSDALE, AZ

Great Broth—No Bones About It

Whenever we eat bone-in chicken, I freeze the leftover bones until I have a soup-kettle full. I fill the kettle with the bones, a carrot, an onion, celery tops, a turnip, a couple of bay leaves, peppercorns, salt, 1/2 cup of white wine (which will help pull calcium from the bones; 1 tablespoon of vinegar does this also), and water. I simmer this brew for four to five hours, then strain it through cheesecloth and freeze in various-sized plastic containers. This broth is very potent, and I can dilute it by at least half for any recipes calling for chicken broth.

I love to try new recipes, and there is hardly the unsuccessful dinner dish I cannot transform into delicious soup with the help of my home-made chicken broth, assorted vegetables, and maybe a can of minestrone or beans.

INGER—KELSEYVILLE, CA

Cheap Stock from Cast-Off Veggies

No more store bought cans of chicken stock. I use stock in all sorts of recipes but have found the price going up steadily over the past few years. So I switched to making vegetable stock at home. At first I just used a carrot, a couple stalks of celery, and an onion, then I realized how much I was throwing into the compost pile that was usable from my daily cooking. I started saving my carrot peelings, outer layers of onions, tops and bottoms of celery, and other various vegetable "cut-offs" in a resealable container. Once I accumulate enough to make a batch of stock (several handfuls worth), I roast the vegetables in the oven for about thirty minutes, add some bulk dried herbs and a few quarts of water, and bring to a boil. After the stock boils and looks about the color of weak tea, I add some salt to taste. "Rinsings" from canned tomatoes add some wonderful flavor to stock as well. I use the stock in homemade soups or any other recipes that call for cooking liquid. Freeze the finished stock in resealable containers, allowing a little head room for expansion.

JILL—SALEM, OR

~

Cool Broth

I freeze all of my chicken, beef, and vegetable broth in ice cube trays. Once they are frozen, I store them in freezer bags or plastic containers. When I'm ready to use them, I just pull them out one or two cubes at a time depending on the recipe.

JOANNE—BELMONT, NC

Here are a few other ways we minimize waste:

- **Jelly or jam**. When the jar is empty, swish a little water in it to rinse out and pour the contents into a smoothie or pancake batter.
- **Ketchup**. Pour what remains in one bottle into another by standing the two bottles mouth to mouth for an hour. Or use a little bit of water to rinse out the bottle and pour the remains into another bottle of ketchup. You can do the same with store-bought salad dressing and pancake syrup.
- **Refreeze**. If there is a large amount of a meal left over (like turkey or ham), we layer the sliced pieces in a glass baking dish, along with any leftover gravy, cover with plastic wrap, label it, and put it in the freezer for another meal later in the month. If it is left in the fridge, some of it would be eaten as a leftover meal, but there is a possibility that it could be forgotten and go bad.

With a little attention to the remains of a meal or a container, we can actually make it go farther than before.

STRATEGY 10: STRETCHING THE RESULTS

Having an attitude of wasting little to nothing will open new horizons for your menu planning. Instead of just serving leftovers, think in terms of converting what's left into another meal. We do this with roasted chicken. We save the back and rib portion of the chicken, which has very little meat on it, and freeze it. When we have three or four chicken backs, Annette uses them to start a pot of chicken soup. Here are a few other ideas to help you transform one meal into more.

1 Chicken, 3 Meals?

Our dear, economizing friend and neighbor Ruth Ann shared how she gets three meals out of one chicken.

- Boil or roast a large chicken—include onions, celery, and other spices.
- Debone and skin the chicken.
- Divide the meat into two piles.

Meal #1: Use the first pile of meat to make chicken salad sandwiches.

Meal #2: Use the second pile of meat for chicken stir-fry or chicken stew.

Meal #3: Put the bones, with a little meat still on them, in a pot of water. Add onion, celery, carrot, and other veggies you have handy. Throw in rice or pasta and you have chicken soup or broth.

You may find different ways to stretch the usefulness of a chicken, but the key is to think and plan and waste not.

Don't be chicken!

Garbage Soup

That's right, Garbage Soup. It doesn't sound very appetizing, but in reality it can be. Several years ago, Annette read about the concept of saving small portions of leftovers in a glass jar kept in the freezer, to make soup. After some consideration she decided to incorporate this practice into her money-saving cooking habits. Whenever she had one serving or less of green beans, corn, mixed veggies, beets, or any other vegetable, she'd pour them into the one-gallon glass jar and save it for use later. Gravy, small pieces of meat, and single servings of rice or beans were also added. When the jar was full, she would allow the mixture to thaw, pour it into an eight-quart pot, add a few fresh ingredients to balance out the "recipe," and cook it up.

The Garbage Soup concept isn't as bad as it sounds; as a matter of fact, the soup has received rave reviews not only from our kids, but even from a family with whom we shared a meal when their mom was sick. Later the mother of the family said to Annette, "We really enjoyed the soup; it was delicious. Could I have the recipe?" "Th- the recipe?" Annette stammered, "Well, it's, it's an old family recipe, and it's kind of a secret," she muttered. So with the family enthusiastic and friends raving about the flavor, Garbage Soup made its way into our lives on a regular basis.

This is yet another way to creatively convert one meal into several.

<hr/>

Get Stewed

Here's another way to stretch a meal. One night I'll make beef stew and the next night I'll put the remainder of the stew into a pie crust to make a beef pot pie. Sometimes if I make a large enough pot of beef stew I can make four pot pies out of it and then freeze them. Most people cut the beef for stew beef into large chunks. If you dice them up smaller there is an appearance of more because there are more little pieces of beef in each bite.

JENNIFER—BLACK CANYON CITY, AZ

As you cook more and more, you'll discover greater efficiencies and ways to reuse food to reduce waste. Your creativity will produce powerful savings. And if you ever have the opportunity to talk to a professional chef or someone who lived through the Great Depression, ask for some tips. You'll be amazed at what you learn.

These last couple of tips didn't fit in any one category, but we just had to include them because they're so different and creative.

That's Italian

A wedge of real Parmesan cheese is expensive. The "rind" is not coated with wax as many may think but it is salt hardened. Do like the real Italians do and place the rind in the soup pot towards the end of cooking. You'll like the flavor and there is no waste.

KATHY—SEATTLE, WA

Presoaked Bulk Beans

I read in a bean and legume cookbook that you can soak large amounts of beans at one time and freeze what you don't use in portion sizes for later use. It saves me loads of time and takes care of a big, time consuming task all at once. It really makes it easier and faster to use dry beans in recipes because I have eliminated the soaking step by doing it earlier.

DEBBIE—GREYBULL, WY

Cooking is a skill that takes time to learn, but provides a lifetime of enjoyment. Annette always tells people at our seminars, "If I can learn to cook, so can you." You'll be amazed at how much joy it brings you and how much money you'll save. You may not become a famous chef or TV celebrity, but you can provide your family with memories of great meals, and if you teach your kids how to cook, you can equip them with a great skill set to provide for their *own* families.

WHAT CAN YOU DO NOW ABOUT COOKING?

 Timid Mouse

If cooking is a foreign language to you:

1. Get a couple of beginner cookbooks. We like the *Good Housekeeping Illustrated* and *Betty Crocker* cookbooks best.
2. When you do cook a meal, cook a double portion and freeze the excess for a future meal.
3. Learn to use a slow cooker.
4. Have a recipe swap with some friends to expand your cooking horizons.

 Wise Owl

If you know how to cook, but need some encouragement:

1. If you know someone who is especially adept in the kitchen, ask if you could prepare a meal together so you can learn a new recipe (and hopefully some time-saving tricks).
2. Find a friend or friends who would be willing to participate in a meal swap or bulk cooking day (one or two weeks' worth of meals).
3. Take stock of your kitchen tools and storage containers. If you are in need of more or better items, start looking at garage sales and thrift stores or put some of the items on your Christmas list.
4. Review your spices and make sure you are fully stocked.

 Amazing Ant

1 Plan and attempt to cook two weeks' worth of meals in a weekend.
2. Start grinding your own beef.
3. Keep track of the amount of food that you are throwing away and make it a goal to minimize the waste by shopping smarter, serving less, or storing it better.

6

Stocking Up and Organizing—Store It, Find It, Use It

We view our pantry and freezer as two of our most effective tools for helping us save money. Because of these tools we can stock up on low-priced food items and save them to be eaten for months to come.

Our goal in this chapter is to arm you with enough information so that you can maximize the use of your stored foods and minimize wasting time and money because of disorganization or spoilage. We'll also cover which foods freeze well and which ones don't and how we organize our refrigerator and freezer for maximum efficiency. If you follow our advice in the previous chapters, you'll have your menus and shopping organized to the point where you are spending much less total time and money than you did previously on them. With extra money in hand and the knowledge of when a sale is truly a great deal, you're ready to stock up and save even more.

STOCK YOUR PANTRY AND MAKE A KILLING

If you look through kitchen remodeling catalogs you can find all kinds of fancy devices for storing canned foods and soda. You can also find all kinds of convenient pull-out shelves and special tip-out drawers. All of these things sound nice, but they come with a price—a hefty price. And most of them are not essential to your food storage needs. Since buying our first home in 1985, we have worked to develop as much storage space as we could, for the least cost possible. In our first house Steve built floor-to-ceiling pantry shelves out of particleboard for about $15. In our current home we have a room where the previous owners stored their horse equipment (a tack room). We've converted it to be our pantry room. This is where our 25-cubic-foot chest freezer is. The wall facing the freezer was 12 feet long and totally empty. Steve found a deal on metal shelving that was only 12 inches deep—Saks Fifth Avenue was moving one of their Phoenix locations, and he bought about 50 linear feet of 8-foot-tall, metal, back-room shelving from their liquidator for $200—that was a real deal! Some of those shelves now line our pantry room and the rest are used for non-food storage in the garage. You've got to have a place to store the food you stock up on, and sometimes that place will need to be created in unusual ways with unusual materials.

Many women have asked Annette for a list of items they should stock up on, thinking that if they replicated our list, they would be able to spend what we spend. We'll list the basic items that we stock and why. What you stock will differ based on your family size and food preferences, but the principles you use will be the same.

As our pantry has become well supplied with the items we use regularly, our shopping habits have changed. We used to purchase things to consume the following week or month. Now we mostly shop for sale-priced items to keep our pantry stocked with goods that we regularly use. We've already talked about setting a "buy price" for most items and stocking up when we find them at this price or close to it. Honestly, on occasion we do run out of a particular item while waiting for a sale. In that case, we look for the best price at the time and buy a small quantity to get us through until the next sale. The menu plan is made more from what we have in stock in our pantry and freezer than what we will be purchasing from the store.

Doing this well and inexpensively may take some time, so make your list and keep your eyes peeled for deals.

Here are a few guidelines we use for determining what we should stock up on:

1. **Stock up on nonperishables**. For the most part, we stock our pantry with things that aren't perishable. This may seem basic, but stocking up is counterproductive if you end up throwing away items that have gone bad. The only exceptions are things that can be stored in the freezer (meats, frozen veggies, nuts and fruits, etc.).

2. **Don't overstock for new recipes**. We don't stock up on things that we haven't used before or that we are trying for the first time. Just because canned, pickled pork rinds are on sale doesn't mean we need to buy ten jars. If we don't normally eat the item or don't like it after we open it, it's a waste of money. So, just because we mention an item doesn't mean you should run out and buy it—unless, of course, it is something you use regularly.

3. **Track usage**. Every family will go though items at a different rate. So you should know your family's pace. If you use one jar of jelly every three months, having four jars on hand would last you a year. A good way to determine this would be to number and date (with the month and year) the items you purchase in quantities. For example, the jelly jars would be labeled 1 of 4—7/12; 2 of 4—7/12; 3 of 4—7/12; 4 of 4—7/12. If you finish off your last jar of jelly in September 2012, you would know that it took you two months to use four jars. You would be safe to stock up on twelve for a six-month supply.

4. **Know the shelf life**. A while back we found a great deal on mayonnaise, so we bought six jars. We don't use a lot of mayo, so by the time we got to the last jar, it had turned from creamy white to a gross, brownish orange color and the oil had separated. Of course, it got pitched! Most items have expiration dates on them. Pay attention to them and do like the grocery stores do—pull your oldest items to the front and put the newest in the back. Let your eyes and nose be your guide when it comes to older items you have in your pantry. Later in this chapter we'll describe what to look for.

If you do a Google search for "food storage" or "food shelf life" you can find plenty of guidelines. The most extensive one we've seen, which covers refrigerated, frozen, and pantry foods is located here: http://www .HowDoYouCook.com/search/label/Food%20Storage%20Chart.

5. **Buy loss leaders**. Items in a grocery ad that are at rock-bottom prices are considered loss leaders. These items are used to lure shoppers into the store to purchase other full-priced items. We stock up on many of the loss leaders.

Here's what we typically stock in our pantry:

ITEM & DESCRIPTION	QTY IN STOCK
Applesauce We buy a nonsweetened brand from a warehouse club in a #10 can. Used at the end of the month to supplement our fruit intake. Must be eaten quickly or it will spoil in the refrigerator, so we schedule it two or three times in one week once opened. Smaller family units may be better off buying 32-ounce jars or smaller, to minimize spoilage.	3 or 4 cans
Asparagus, canned We keep this in stock to eat when asparagus is out of season. It also helps to stretch our menu at the end of the month when our fresh veggie supply is waning and adds variety to our diet.	3 to 6 cans
Baking soda Used in baking, as a pool chemical, in laundry, and for brushing our teeth (sure, it sounds gross, but our dentist is amazed at how clean our teeth are). Purchased in 10-pound bags from a warehouse club.	20 pounds
Beets, canned Kept in stock to eat at the end of the month when our fresh veggie supply is waning. Adds variety to our diet.	3 to 6 cans
Black olives Used in pasta salads, green salads, tacos, and relish trays for potlucks and parties.	6 to 12 cans
Bouillon cubes We buy these in 1-pound containers and always keep chicken and beef on hand—127 cubes in each box. Used for adding flavor to many recipes and gravy.	1 pound of each

Cocoa powder We've found the best prices to be Kroger's generic brand. It is expensive, but used sparingly for Annette's killer gooey brownies and no-bake oatmeal cookies.	1 tin
Cold cereal We regularly reach our buy price of $1.50 or less per box with either a sale or by combining a sale with coupons—even for some really expensive types of cereal. We mark the box tops with the purchase month and year, then store them in the pantry. This helps us to use the oldest boxes first. We schedule cereal on our breakfast menu twice each week. It can easily be stored for eight months to one year. The rule at our house is to combine a "sweet" cereal with a "healthy" one. The kids go along with this rule and readily share it with any friends who happen to be visiting on a day when we have cold cereal. We consider cereals like cornflakes, Rice Krispies, and Raisin Bran to be "healthy" types. And cereals like Froot Loops, Cap'n Crunch, Apple Jacks, or Golden Crisp are "sweets." We add fresh fruit whenever possible.	10 to 20 boxes
Cream of chicken/mushroom soup We use a couple of cans of each per month in various recipes.	4 to 8 cans
Extra virgin olive oil Used regularly for making hash browns on Sunday morning, pizza dough, and in salad dressings. We usually find the best deals on gallons, but you'll sometimes find better pricing on quarts.	1 gallon
Gelatin dessert We always keep several boxes on hand to whip up for a quick refreshing summer dessert. Brand names don't matter; just go for price. It's not very nutritious, but adding fruit does help—and a little whipped cream makes it a real treat!	10 to 15 boxes
Honey Used for cooking and baking. We usually purchase in a 1-gallon bucket from a local honey distributor. Over time it can crystallize. Just set it on the stove when cooking something in the oven (like a turkey) to melt it down.	1 gallon
Hot cereal During the colder months we cook this up twice each week from scratch. It only takes about twenty minutes to cook eight cups. There are usually some leftovers that our "bottomless pit" teenage boys love to devour after they finish working out at night. We stock up on oatmeal and farina—sometimes purchased in bulk and stored in plastic containers. We also purchase the instant type when it is on sale for $1 per box or less. We use this when we travel or when life is hectic—although we don't like to make it a habit.	3 to 5 pounds / Instant 1 or 2 boxes

Hot cocoa / hot cider We drink this in the wintertime and stock up when it goes on sale. We usually buy cocoa and cider in boxes with individual packets when it's on sale. We've also bought hot cocoa in larger, bulk containers.	3 boxes of each
Jelly or jam PB&J sandwiches are a staple at our house. We also use jelly on toast and in smoothies.	6 to 12 jars
Ketchup Best prices are found during the summer barbecue season—especially Memorial Day, Fourth of July, and Labor Day. Used on hot dogs, hamburgers, meat loaf, and in some salad dressings. Sometimes we buy it in gallon cans and transfer into smaller squeeze bottles.	6 to 12 bottles
Legumes We keep several varieties on hand: split peas, navy beans, pinto beans, chickpeas, and lima beans. Split peas are used in ham and split pea soup. Often when Annette makes a pot of turkey soup, she'll add one cup of mixed beans (soaked in water to reduce gassiness) for additional protein. Legumes get harder as they age, so older ones will have to be soaked in water longer before cooking. We like cooking them in a slow cooker.	1 to 2 pounds of each
Maple syrup We rarely purchase the real stuff. It's a special treat if we find it on sale. We eat pancakes (whole grain) once or twice each week. We know syrup can be made from scratch, but we prefer to purchase 1-gallon containers of Mrs. Butterworth's or something similar at a warehouse-type store.	2 gallons
Mayonnaise Best sale time is during the summer. Don't stock up on too much, as it can go rancid. We use it for tuna fish and cold-cut sandwiches, potato salad, macaroni salad, etc.	6 jars
Mustard We purchase this by the gallon and then transfer it into smaller squeeze bottles, or in small bottles (for pennies) using a coupon.	1 gallon
Nuts We keep four varieties in stock: peanuts, walnuts, pecans, and almonds. Lately these have become very expensive— probably due to the South Beach or Atkins diets. We use them sparingly in our baking. Steve likes to snack on walnuts—it helps him avoid sugary stuff; Annette prefers peanuts. Store in the freezer in zippered bags to avoid them going rancid.	2 pounds of each
Peanut butter We buy the all-natural stuff—just peanuts and salt. The oil separates from the peanuts and must be mixed in (we use our mixer to do this). All opened jars are stored in the refrigerator. We keep no more than six 32-ounce jars on hand. If stored too long they can go rancid.	6 jars (32 ounces)

Pickles We buy spears by the gallon. Vlasic is our favorite brand. We eat them at lunch or on pizza nights. Joe loves to snack on pickles.	2 gallons
Pineapple chunks We buy these in #10 cans and use them to supplement our fruit intake when we run low on fresh fruit. We'll go through one can in about two days. They can be spooned into a plastic container for school or work lunches. Be careful, they can start to ferment if stored too long in the refrigerator . . . *hic!*	3 cans
Pudding We love warm chocolate pudding cooked on the stove—instant is taboo in our house. The best prices are found around Thanksgiving.	10 boxes
Relish Mostly used in tuna fish sandwiches and on hot dogs. Bought in gallon containers and then transferred to reused peanut butter jars.	1 gallon
Rice, brown and white We prefer to use brown rice as a side dish for health reasons, but we always have white rice on hand for times when dinner needs to be thrown together quickly. Brown rice cooks in 40 to 50 minutes, white in 20 minutes. Brown rice can go rancid after 6 months if stored at room temperature.	5 to 10 pounds
Salad dressing We make this from scratch if we have the time (Italian, oriental, and honey French), or we stock up when it is on sale.	6 to 12 bottles
Sauerkraut We use one can per month for Reuben sandwiches and sometimes on hot dogs.	4 to 6 cans
Shortening We know this is controversial, but pie crusts and certain cookie recipes just require it. One can lasts us two years. *Used sparingly in your diet it shouldn't be an issue.*	One #10 can
Spaghetti and other pasta It makes a great side dish or main dish. When it hits our buy price, we stock up on 10 to 16 pounds as we go through about 1 ½ pounds in one meal—with a little left over for lunches.	10 to 16 pounds
Stuffing Most of the time Annette makes this from scratch (remember we cook one turkey almost every month during the winter/cooler months). If she can pick up a box for pennies, with coupons, she'll keep them on hand to prepare as a side dish— this can be served at times other than Thanksgiving.	1 to 3 boxes

Sugar Since we do a lot of baking from scratch, we keep quite a bit of sugar on hand. We realize that sugar is not the best thing to eat, so if you have health issues, minimizing sugar consumption is a good idea. It stores well, so we stock up only when it's on sale. It can be stored in plastic storage buckets to prevent moisture damage.	10 to 25 pounds
Tomato paste Used for making our traditional family recipe spaghetti sauce and sloppy joes. We buy the 4-ounce cans when they hit our buy price; otherwise we purchase the large #10 can at a warehouse club and spoon it into small plastic storage containers to freeze.	20 cans
Tomato sauce Another ingredient in our spaghetti sauce as well as in meat loaf and in another family favorite, tagliarini (ground beef and noodle casserole). We buy #10 cans and divide into two plastic storage containers to freeze once the can is opened.	2 cans
Tomato soup We know this can be made from scratch, but when it's on sale, we stock the pantry. It's always a great accompaniment with grilled cheese sandwiches.	6 to 10 cans
Tomatoes, diced Used for spaghetti sauce and in other recipes. We buy #10 cans (approximately 6 pounds) from a warehouse club.	4 cans
Tuna We buy 3-ounce cans of dark meat in water when they are on sale. We avoid Bumble Bee brand, no matter what the price, because the tuna is more shredded than chunked.	12 to 24 cans
Vegetable oil We actually prefer peanut oil or canola oil, but if we can't find it on sale, we go with vegetable oil. Used sparingly in pancakes and quick breads. Very seldom do we fry anything.	2 gallons max
White flour Used sparingly, often mixing it with some whole wheat. Mostly used for baking cookies, brownies, cakes, pancakes, pizza dough, banana bread, and sweet bread. Store in the freezer to prevent bugs.	10 to 15 pounds
Whole wheat flour We keep whole grain wheat in 5-gallon storage buckets. It stores well for years this way. We purchased a good-quality wheat grinder and grind up enough grain to fill two or three smaller containers at a time—which are then stored in the freezer. We mix whole wheat flour in almost everything we bake. Dessert-type recipes have more white flour than wheat in them.	
Yeast Purchased in bulk through a warehouse club in a 1-pound package. Store in a glass jar in the refrigerator—this keeps the yeast from losing its potency. Two teaspoons equal one packet of yeast.	1 pound

The location of your stash of food is important also. The cooler and drier the location, the longer your food stores will last. If your home is small and space is limited, you'll have to get creative with where you store food. The first pantry shelves Steve built were on a wall of our laundry room where there was a 4-inch setback from the entryway into the kitchen. Four inches wasn't much space, but on a 6-foot wall with floor-to-ceiling shelves we were able to stock lots of canned goods and other small items. Other options include storing food in plastic containers under beds, in closets, or under a circular or square piece of wood with a tablecloth on top—it can become an instant end table. If you're creative and organized, you will find the space you need. If you need more information about food storage, contact, a food co-op or the USDA's Food and Nutrition Information Center (http://fnic .nal.usda.gov).

Stocking up on low-priced items is one of the most effective ways to control your grocery costs. You'll love "shopping" in your pantry as you recall the great deals you've gotten on each item. As you learn to play the market and buy only when prices are low, you'll become more like a commodities broker than a consumer. Just be careful and try to contain your emotions when you've cornered the market—we've been overheard in the supermarket letting out a war whoop of success as we've discovered another killer deal. It's not a good idea to let the grocers know we're having that much fun—they might raise their prices!

CANNED FOOD STORAGE AND USAGE

The USDA has set some guidelines for the storage and usage of canned foods. As always, don't just rely on the label to tell you if the food is safe to eat; you need to use your eyes and nose to be your final guide.

Storage Guidelines

High-acid foods—such as tomatoes, fruit, and fruit juice—can be stored for up to eighteen months. Low-acid foods—such as vegetables and meat—can be stored for two to five years.

Examine the can carefully. Don't buy canned products that are dented, leaking, or bulging. Look specifically at the top or bottom lid for swelling. Multiplying bacteria in the food will cause it to expand and make the can bulge. A dent in the can could mean that the interior coating could be cracked, allowing the food juices to come in contact with the bare metal and cause it to rust.

At home, store canned food in a cool, dry place. Don't store it in cabinets over the stove, under the sink, or in a damp basement or garage. Some people store cans on their sides in a gravity-fed rack, with the oldest cans in the front. As the oldest cans are removed, the newer cans roll to the front.

When preparing to eat canned food, check the expiration date on the label and reexamine the can. We always wash the top of the container before we open it. If the container spurts liquid or foam when opened or if the food has a foul odor, don't eat it.

Here are some other tips for storing food:

The Fast-Food Pantry

We live twenty miles from the nearest fast-food restaurant, so I have devised my own fast-food menu. I keep my pantry stocked for a few easy meal nights. When 4 p.m. hits, and I don't feel like cooking, or have not pulled anything out to defrost, I look at my pantry.

I always keep taco fixings on hand (and usually have cooked ground meat in the freezer to zap in the microwave), spaghetti or other pasta, and tortillas. Tortillas can be used as a quick individual pizza crust, roll ups (with whatever leftovers we happen to have), scrambled egg burritos (which also freeze well), or we just melt cheese in a folded tortilla and dip in salsa.

DEBBIE—CORTLAND, NE

Stock Up on Sales and Save

I'm always watching the papers for sales. When I see a storable food item at a steeply discounted price I don't just buy one or two, I stock up on as many as I have coupons for. Oftentimes I pay pennies for dollar items. I always keep in mind how much storage space I have and the shelf life of the item.

DIANNE—MIDLOTHIAN, VA

ORGANIZATION: DO THE KITCHEN DANCE

Organizing your kitchen is much like choreographing a dance. All the elements must work in perfect accord to create a seemingly effortless, elegant, and efficient performance.

If you have the wrong tools, or they're in the wrong places, your kitchen dance will be stuttering and herky-jerky—not at all pleasant. It's taken us years to get the right things in the right places.

Our family and our kitchen are both large. If yours are smaller, use this as a starting point and adjust our suggestions to fit your needs. Several years ago we redesigned our kitchen and replaced the cabinets and appliances. We worked with a designer to determine the best layout to help us work efficiently in the kitchen. Because our kitchen is a galley type—longer and narrow—we weren't able to get the optimal triangular working area between the stove, sink, and refrigerator, but we did definitely improve on what we had before. You may not have the luxury of redesigning your kitchen, but you can evaluate where you have things stored and move them to make your working space more efficient. You can also do a Google search for efficient kitchen layouts and find some expert ideas that might help you.

Near the Sink

We keep all items associated with washing dishes as close to the sink as possible. On top of our sink we always have a scrubbing sponge, steel wool pad (stored on a dry sponge to help it dry and not rust), and a bottle of dish soap. In the cabinet under the sink we store dishwasher detergent, dish soap, a fire extinguisher, empty cans for grease, a shoe box full of new sponges, steel wool pads, a gallon bottle of bleach (for use in our wash water—just a "glug"), and our water filtration unit. We used to have a reverse osmosis system, but removed it because it took up too much storage space (the tank was huge) and wasted water. We now have a great two-stage filter system that takes up much less space, costs much less (on eBay), and produces great tasting water. Because this is a potentially "wet" cabinet, we lined the bottom with a heavy-duty plastic tarp (cut to fit exactly) and put some thick cardboard on top of that to absorb any random leaks. Keeping all of these items neatly stacked and in one place makes taking inventory easy and quick.

Pots and Pans

We store these close to the oven/stove in two locations. Our largest pots are stored on a lazy Susan in a corner cabinet, along with pot and pan lids and glass mixing bowls. Frying pans are stacked in a pull-out drawer under the island where most of the food preparation is done. To keep nonstick frying pans from getting scratched while being stored, we place a sheet of butcher paper between each pan. You could use waxed paper or a dish towel too. To optimize our space, we nest smaller pots or pans inside larger ones.

Storage Containers

We have an entire lower cabinet dedicated to plastic storage containers. About half of the containers and lids are ones we have purchased. The rest are leftover margarine, ice cream, and other miscellaneous containers. The key here is to stack them based on size and type (squares in one stack, rounds in another) and keep them as organized as possible. A cardboard box holds larger lids that aren't stored in the drawer above. This cabinet is under the island/food preparation counter and is easily accessed when putting a meal away and storing leftovers.

We call it the "Tupperware" cabinet, but it contains every make of plastic container. Abbey is gifted in organization and loves to keep this cabinet neat and tidy. Unfortunately, there are times when others in the family (who will remain anonymous) have differing ideas on how things ought to be stacked—maybe we need a photo or chart . . . but that might be taking it a bit too far!

In a drawer adjacent to the Tupperware cabinet we keep our recycled plastic zippered bags and reusable aluminum foil. The zippered bags are stored inside another plastic bag of the same size. When washing the bags, we check for holes and toss any that "won't hold water." The foil is folded up and kept in a cardboard shoe box to keep it neat.

Cooking Utensils

We keep spatulas, scrapers, metal and wooden spoons, and a host of other often-used cooking utensils on the counter near the stove in three large crocks. They are sorted by material with metal items in one crock, wooden in another, and plastic and rubber in the third. The key for us is to keep them readily available and easy to find—there's nothing worse than needing a spatula in a hurry and having to dig through a drawer of utensils all jumbled together, or trying to open the drawer only to have some long-handled item wedged up against the cabinet, effectively locking the drawer closed.

Knives

In this same general area of the kitchen we have a drawer dedicated to sharp knives. Years ago we had a knife block on the counter, but we didn't like displaying the knives and giving up precious counter space, so when we redesigned the kitchen, we started using the drawer. For safety's sake, we only keep knives in this drawer, so when we open it, we know to be careful.

Spices and Baking Supplies

We have three upper cabinets (two for spices and one for baking supplies) to the side of our stove where we store all of these items. We know that many experts say that you should keep spices in cool, dry areas, not near the stove, but over the years we've not noticed any deterioration in the quality of our spices. To make the space more efficient and the small spice containers easier to reach, we store almost all of them on 10-inch plastic turntables. The spices are kept in alphabetical groupings to make finding them easier. This all may sound like overkill, but most of our systems evolved over time and out of a desire to simplify and streamline our work.

We buy some baking supplies and spices in large quantities and store them in smaller containers—usually from previously purchased spices. We soak the label off and label it with the new contents. Years ago, Steve used his graphics background and our computer to design custom labels for all of the different recycled containers we were using. Now our cabinets have a more consistent look.

Dish Towels, Aprons, and Pot Holders

These are also kept in the "working area" of the kitchen near the stove, spices, and knives. Having quick access to towels when a spill happens is critical, and so is being able to quickly whip out a pot holder when grabbing something from the stove.

Casserole and Baking Dishes

We keep these useful items in two different upper cabinets on the far side of our kitchen. Ceramic and glass casserole dishes are used for cooking vegetables and reheating leftovers. In a lower cabinet we have a large stack of 13 x 9-inch and larger glass baking dishes. We use these to freeze the meals that we make on our once-a-month cooking day. Because they aren't used as often, they can be stored in a less accessible location.

Dishwasher

We do have one and use it regularly—it's located to the left of our sink. Maybe when the kids are all grown and gone we'll wash our dishes by hand. We have the dishwasher divided into three areas (top rack, bottom rack, and silverware) and the kids take turns unloading the various areas. The job is usually done in five minutes

Kitchen Organization with Kids in Mind

We do a couple of things here that might be considered strange, but we've done it so that the kids could help in the kitchen from a young age.

We all use plastic cups for meals (and you only get one cup per day—this saves room in the dishwasher). We wanted all of the kids to help with setting and clearing the table, but didn't want to have to worry about broken glasses. We also use unbreakable plates—we chose Corelle plates made by Corning Ware. They can be dropped and usually don't break, and they look better and last longer than plastic. We know kids are going to drop things—it's a given—so we wanted to minimize our concerns and their anxiety.

Second, we put the dishes, glasses, and silverware where the kids (and elderly relatives) can easily reach them. Dishes and water cups are stored on a shelf in our floor to ceiling pantry closet in the kitchen, and silverware is kept in a drawer by the dishwasher. These may not be the most efficient locations, but they have allowed the kids to be totally involved in dinner preparation and kitchen cleanup—and in our minds that's more important.

Keeping your kitchen organized is a serious matter. Disorganization costs you precious minutes each day and hours each year in inefficient searches for "lost" items. Well organized and maintained, you'll waltz through your culinary tasks and have time outside the kitchen for other people or projects.

Now for our confession: Writing about organizing our kitchen has shown us how much cleaning and *reorganizing* we need to do—honestly, why do we still have watercolors and sidewalk chalk in a kitchen drawer? It indicates to us that we've been busy raising our kids and that it's time to do some cleaning, evaluating, and passing some of these wonderful but unneeded things on to other families. And so, the kitchen dance goes on . . . are you in step?

TIPS FOR CABINET ORGANIZATION

Take a tip from us—don't wait eight years (when your kids are almost grown) to re-evaluate your cabinets. Do it every couple of years or before you have a garage sale.

- **Place by use**. Put items near the area where they're used. Spices near the counter where you prepare meals. Storage containers near the area where you put away leftovers. Pots and pans near the stove.

- **Place by user**. Put kids' dishes and cups at their level. If you have arthritis or can't reach higher shelves, put your daily-use items in lower, easy-to-reach spots.
- **Place by frequency**. Put more frequently used items in easier-to-reach places. Seldom-used items can be on higher shelves or in cabinets away from the main work area.

Organizing the Pantry Shelves

Keeping our floor-to-ceiling pantry shelves neat and organized is critical to being able to use what we have in stock. Here are a few things we do with these shelves:

- **Think like a grocer**. We keep similar items together. Things like canned veggies, canned fruit, fruit juices, pasta, oils, and cereal all have specific shelves where they are kept. On each shelf we try to be like a grocery store and "front" the items so the label is readable and all of the same items are together.
- **Cardboard**. We use cardboard boxes, cut down to size, so we can see the cans or other items to keep groupings together. Sometimes we use cardboard pieces as extra shelf dividers to keep things neat or to allow stacking of items so that lower cans can be taken out without moving the top cans.
- **High and low**. We place items that are accessed more often at eye level or lower; those items used less often will be up higher. The only exception to this rule is placing heavier items like our food storage buckets on the floor or on the lowest shelves.

No matter how much storage space you have, keeping similar items together and neatly organized will help you keep a more accurate inventory and you'll be able to more easily access what you need.

If you need more shelving, check the classified ads, CraigsList.org, or FreeCycle.org.

Investing some time and a little bit of money to increase your pantry storage capacity will allow you to start seeing your food cache swell and your grocery bill shrink.

ORGANIZE YOUR FRIDGE TO AVOID SCIENCE EXPERIMENTS

When Steve was in high school, he spent a summer working in the food service of a gymnastics camp in trade for a whole summer of free coaching and gymnastics workouts. Not only did it earn him a college scholarship, but it also taught him the value of planning, organizing, and working efficiently in the kitchen. Earl was a retired chef who loved to come to this camp each summer in northern Michigan. He enjoyed working with the high school kids on his kitchen staff and taught them to serve up phenomenal meals for the five hundred campers who were there for two weeks at a time. One of his greatest strengths was how he managed the kitchen to minimize waste. Unserved meat, left over from a roast beef dinner, was "recycled" into a beef stew later in the week. Uneaten bread ends were saved and allowed to dry out to be used in stuffing for a special turkey dinner at the end of the camp session. The only thing he didn't recycle was leftover oatmeal . . . and we're sure if he put enough thought into it, he could have come up with a plan for that too—a substitute for cement maybe?

The camp had a large walk-in cooler (refrigerator). This was another area where Earl knew his stuff. He had several thermometers in the cooler to monitor the temperature at different shelf heights. He knew that whenever the door was opened, some cold air would leak out and warmer air from the kitchen would replace it. The back of the cooler was always the coldest and most temperature-stable area. Here are some tips Steve learned from Earl about storing things in our home refrigerator.

Top Shelves

Knowing that the top shelves of the walk-in cooler would be subjected to slightly warmer temperatures, Earl stored items that didn't need to be kept as cold, things like margarine and cooked meats that were going to be served in the next few days.

At home, don't store things like milk, eggs, or mayonnaise on the door or the top shelf where temperatures can rise well above the recommended and safe 40 degrees necessary to keep food fresh longer. You can store things like fruit juices, wheat germ, bran, sesame seeds, icing, butter, margarine, pickles, salad dressings, and other condiments with high vinegar or sugar content on the doors and top shelves. These items are much more shelf stable and less vulnerable to spoilage due to warmer temperatures. We do store one dozen eggs on the door of our kitchen refrigerator—but that is because we go through them so quickly (in two or three days).

Raw Meat

Earl kept raw meat products in the back of the cooler (in the coldest section), separated from ready-to-eat foods to avoid possible contamination from leaking juices.

At home you should minimize the storage of raw meat in your refrigerator. If we keep any in our fridge, it's only there because we are going to eat it the next day, or because we're marinating beef jerky (we keep that in a zippered bag for a day or two).

Keep your raw meats in the coldest part of your refrigerator, on the lowest shelf by the back wall or in a meat drawer. Store the meat on a tray with a lip that will minimize raw juices from dripping into other parts of your fridge. You'll avoid possible contamination and a time-consuming mess to clean up.

Produce

At camp, to avoid possible frost damage, we never put produce boxes in the coldest area of the cooler. At home you should avoid putting fruits and veggies near the back wall of your fridge. This is the coldest area of most refrigerators due to the location of the cooling coils. Because of this it can get cold enough to freeze and ruin frost-sensitive items—especially lettuce, spinach, and celery.

Label It

Earl practiced the FIFO (first in, first out) principle. A food service truck delivered groceries a couple of times each week. The kitchen staff was responsible for sorting, labeling, and storing all of the food that came in. All boxes and containers were clearly labeled with the contents and the date they were put in the cooler. We always moved any older items still in the cooler to the front of the shelf so they would be the next things used. This practice helped everyone to find things quicker and ensured that we wouldn't have any "science experiments" festering unused in the back of the freezer.

At home we have labeled the shelves on the door of our fridge for medications and herbs (a high shelf), dressings and sauces, and condiments. But labeling leftovers in the fridge just doesn't always happen. We keep a waterproof marker and labels in a drawer in our island, near the spot where we pack up leftovers, and sometimes we do succeed at this, but it really depends on how rushed we are after dinner and who is packing up the leftovers. If there is one piece of steak left over, we know it won't last long, so we usually don't need to worry about it going bad.

Clean It Out

About the middle of the summer, Earl had the kitchen staff take inventory of the contents of the cooler, just to be sure that we were using everything he had ordered. If we discovered any food items that were "left over," or unused, especially if it was something especially good like steak, it was served to the kitchen staff at a special dinner.

At home it's a good idea to have a regularly scheduled time to clean out the fridge. Some experts say it should be done every week. But let's get real! If you're a busy family, you'll be lucky to get to it once a month. We do this once a week when we eat leftovers, but we also do a more thorough clean-out in conjunction with our once-a-month cooking. Regularly inventorying your fridge helps you remember what you have stored so you can use it up before it goes bad.

Your fridge is an important weapon in your money-saving arsenal, but it has to be maintained to give you the best return on your investment. So start your own experiment to create a waste-free zone of cool food. Stock it up, use it up, and clean it out!

Here are a few other storage ideas to make your refrigerated groceries last longer:

~~~

Long-Term Veggie Storage

I've found that cutting up veggies, like carrots, celery, or cauliflower and then putting them in storage bags along with a moist (not dripping) paper towel helps the veggies not to get dried out. Another benefit is that they last longer too.

L.M.—LIVERPOOL, NY

~~~

Worry-Free Containers

Save your empty margarine tubs and other plastic containers so when you send leftovers home with friends and family you don't have to worry about getting "Aunt Tillie's" antique casserole dish back.

BEVERLY—PEMBROKE PINES, FL

~~~

Store Lettuce and Herbs Longer

To keep our lettuce and things like basil and mint fresh longer, I gently wash and then shake them dry. Then I put a paper towel in a plastic zippered bag and put in the lettuce or herbs. The paper towel absorbs any excess moisture and keeps the veggies crisper. If the towel gets too wet, I exchange it for a dry one. I can keep a head of lettuce fresh for two weeks or more this way.

CAROL—SCOTTSDALE, AZ

Having a well-stocked pantry, an organized kitchen, and an efficient refrigerator are great tools in your arsenal of defense against rising food prices. Next we're going to share how we manage the *coolest* weapon in our frugality cache.

FREEZE IT—STORE IT—ENJOY IT!

One of our greatest tools for saving on groceries is our freezer. Over the years, as our family has grown, so has the size of our freezer. Like we said earlier, we started with a used 9-cubic-foot chest freezer, then five years later purchased a used 21-cubic-foot upright. Now we have a 25-cubic-foot chest freezer that we purchased at a steep discount when our local Montgomery Wards went out of business.

A mainstay of our money-saving philosophy is buying storable food on sale—stockpiling as much as we can safely store—and slowly depleting that supply over several months. We trust that another great sale will come along by the time our stockpile is depleted. Our goal is to always eat food purchased at its lowest price. Our ancestors had to rely on smoking meat, root cellars, and canning to preserve their food so they could survive from harvest to harvest. Ours is not a battle for survival, but a fight to keep our food expenses low. We're often asked, "What can you freeze?" Our answer is, "Just about anything—if you know how." Below is a compilation of foods we have frozen successfully (and a few unsuccessfully). Later in the chapter we'll talk about how we keep our freezer organized so we can quickly find what we have stored.

Before we jump into our list, you need to know the four keys to successful freezing:

1. **Eliminate air**. Air dries out food, giving it that unpleasant "freezer burn" flavor. Using multiple layers of plastic wrap, zippered plastic bags, or a vacuum sealer prevents this. Frozen, vacuum-sealed food can be stored for at least a year. Annette's mom loves her vacuum sealer and saves money by washing and reusing the plastic bags. Another friend of ours likes zippered plastic bags, and uses a drinking straw to suck the air out as she zips up the bag. Getting the air out keeps the freshness in.

2. **Minimize moisture**. Moisture forms ice crystals that, when thawed, can turn absorbent foods soggy. This is especially true with breads and muffins. Cool them completely before freezing and double bag whenever possible. When defrosting, add a paper towel inside the bag to absorb moisture.

3. **Use sturdy containers**. Beyond plastic wrap, we employ a variety of plastic containers. Try to fill the container as much as possible to minimize air, but still allow for expansion when the liquid in the food freezes. Use sturdy containers, because margarine tubs or other thin plastic containers may crack or get crushed in the freezer. Plastic containers are fine for short-term storage (one to two months). Square containers fit more efficiently in a freezer.

4. **Blanch fruits and veggies**. Most vegetables and some fruits will not freeze well unless they are cooked first. Blanching is the process of lightly cooking

by boiling for a brief period of time (two to five minutes). Most basic cookbooks describe this process. If you overcook and then freeze, the veggies will be very mushy when defrosted.

ITEM	SPECIAL INSTRUCTIONS
EASY TO FREEZE	
Baking chocolate/ coconut	Keep it wrapped up airtight.
Bananas	Freeze old bananas, in the skin or out, in a zippered bag for use later in banana bread, smoothies, or pancakes. If you fully defrost a frozen banana in the skin, it's hard to peel it because it is so mushy.
Berries	Strawberries, raspberries, brambleberries, blueberries, blackberries, and other miscellaneous berries all freeze well. Rinse and store in zippered bags in small quantities.
Birthday cake	If you make too much, freeze it for later.
Bread, bagels, and muffins	The goal here is to minimize condensation. Double-bagging and removing as much air as possible are the keys. We pack two or three loaves to a plastic grocery bag, tie the top, and set it gently in the freezer. Once frozen, it can be located elsewhere in the freezer. Try not to crush it by placing under heavier items. We predominantly buy whole wheat bread—it's denser than white bread, contains less moisture, and has fewer problems when defrosting.
Cheese	We freeze mostly shredded cheese, but, on occasion, solid chunks. Chunk cheese will crumble when thawed out. Ricotta cheese freezes okay; when defrosted, water may separate and need to be mixed back in or dumped out.
Drinks	Fruit juice, lemonade, tea, and coffee all freeze well. Allow expansion room.
Eggs	Scramble raw eggs and freeze in small containers. Be sure to label how many eggs are in the container.

Flour, cornmeal, brown rice, sunflower and flax seeds	Freezing keeps these items from getting buggy or becoming rancid.
Fruit	We've frozen sliced peaches and nectarines without any cooking preparation. Use later in smoothies. Apples need to be cooked first, then frozen.
Green onions	We buy several bunches at a time and chop into small pieces, then store in a zippered bag. Cilantro and parsley can also be stored this way.
Lemons	We juice our lemons and freeze in ice cube trays, then remove from the tray and store in zippered bags. We haven't had any luck with freezing juiced oranges or grapefruits; the juice separates from the pulp and tends to get bitter when thawed.
Lunch meat	We find great bargains when items are a couple of days from going "out of code." Can be stored for months. Hot dogs also fit in this category.
Margarine/butter	Freeze as is—but don't drop it on your toes when it's frozen!
Meat	Be sure it is wrapped well—no ripped plastic. If you're going to store for longer than a few months, double wrap. Beef, pork, chicken, lamb, fish—all freeze well. Our best deals have been on meat that is close to code. According to experts, fish doesn't freeze well for long periods of time.
Milk	Tap off about 1 cup from a gallon jug to allow for expansion when it's frozen. To defrost in the winter, we place it in the sink overnight. In the summer, we place it in the sink, then shake it every hour and place in refrigerator when half-defrosted. For quick thawing, microwave for seven minutes or less; shake using a pot holder (the milk in the handle of a 1-gallon container can get hot). Repeat the previous step if necessary. Shake before serving to mix in separated fat.
Nuts	Store in sealed plastic bag or container. Keeps them from going rancid on the shelf. Test before including in recipes if stored for over six months.
Snickers bars	Frozen is the *only* way to eat 'em.

| Turkeys | Since frozen ones come vacuum-sealed, they can be stored easily for a year and possibly longer. |

FREEZE AFTER COOKING

Mushrooms	If they're on sale, we buy several pounds, clean, slice, and cook in a wine and butter sauce. Then we store in smaller containers for later use.
Pasta	Must be undercooked. Store in zippered bag or plastic container.
Potatoes	Must be thoroughly cooked or else they'll turn black—we learned this the hard way.
Rice	Cooked, but not overcooked. Store in zippered bag or plastic container.
Soups	Cook it up, cool it down, ladle into a container, and leave some space for expansion.
Spaghetti sauce	Cook it up, cool it down, ladle into a container, and leave some space for expansion.
Veggies	Unless buying flash-frozen from the store, these must all be cooked first (i.e., blanched). Beets, broccoli, carrots, cauliflower, celery, corn, green beans, spinach, and Swiss chard all freeze well.

WON'T FREEZE WELL

Cream cheese	Doesn't freeze well because it gets lumpy, crumbly, and watery. You can reconstitute it by using a mixer, but it still won't be as good as fresh stuff.
Eggplant	Turns rubbery and leaks water even after it is cooked.
Melons	Don't know how they do it in the frozen food section (it must be flash frozen); it just hasn't worked for us.
Salad vegetables	Lettuce, cucumbers, radishes, and cabbage. Water in the cells of the vegetables expands when frozen and bursts the cell walls. When the food is thawed, the liquid seeps out and the food becomes limp. We've read of some people taking wilted lettuce and using it in a soup recipe.
Whipping cream	It gets grainy and won't whip up smooth after being frozen. Can be used in cooking recipes, but not for frosting and other whipped applications. If you must store, whip it first, then freeze in small quantities.

Because every family eats different types of foods, you'll probably want to try to freeze other things. Just remember to minimize air and moisture. If you're not sure how well an item will freeze, start with a small amount and test it. As you master the use of this tool, you'll not only enjoy eating food from your deep freeze, but you'll also revel in the cold, hard cash you're able to sock away.

A REAL COOL TOOL

Our freezer is like the secure vault at the bank. It allows us to safely store and protect our frozen treasures. Truly, a freezer is one of the best investments (and not an expensive one) that you can make. If you follow our advice, it will easily pay for itself in the first year of use. Remember that our first freezer was really tiny— only 9 cubic feet, but it was big enough for our family of three to start accumulating some significant savings. Even though our apartment was small, we made space for it in our dining area and used the top of it as extended counter space.

The Cost of a Freezer

We bought our massive chest freezer with a discount coupon for about $400. You can find them for less by buying them used or getting a smaller size. But regardless of what you buy, you will still have to pay for the electricity to run it.

Does it pay to have a big freezer, or will the cost to run it eat up your savings? According to the EnergyStar.gov website, the annual cost to run a freezer is somewhere between $43 to $115 depending on size, age, and usage. We pulled out our freezer documentation and our latest utility bill to calculate our costs. According to Frigidaire, our 24.9-cubic-foot freezer uses 629 kilowatts hours of electricity per year. Based on our electric rate, we've calculated that we spend $62.90 per year, or $5.24 per month to run that freezer. And we know that we have easily saved not only the cost for the electricity it uses each year, but probably paid for the freezer several times over since we bought it. A freezer can truly be a moneymaker for your household.

Organizing Your Frozen Assets

If you have a freezer but it isn't well organized, you'll waste time and money as you search for items you think you have stored, or buy duplicates of items you forgot you had. Our system works for us, and perhaps it will motivate you to create one that works for you.

Years ago, our storage method really paid off. We had just moved into our first house and had a home warranty. A service person came to repair our air conditioning system. He did his job and left. Three days later, we opened the freezer—located in our laundry room—and discovered that the technician had turned off the circuit breaker that controlled it. Three days without power in the middle of an Arizona summer can spell disaster. But very little had been ruined or even thawed. Here's why:

We don't open the freezer every day. We try to plan a single trip to the freezer to take out what we need all at once. So if we're going into the freezer for meat, we check to see if we need to grab milk, bread, margarine, or cheese. Not opening the freezer keeps the cold in and saves money.

We keep the freezer in the house. Since our freezer was indoors, the damage was minimized. Plus, the extreme temperatures of a garage or back patio cause a freezer to work harder and cost more money to run.

We bag it. We organize all freezer food by category in double paper grocery bags. Long ago we abandoned the wire baskets that slid inside the freezer. They simply didn't use the space efficiently. With the grocery bag method, we can stack the bags two deep in vertical alignment. We never have to reach to the very bottom of the freezer; all we do is grasp the top of a bag to retrieve items we want. This is especially helpful if you are height-challenged, like Annette. After all, who wants to tumble headfirst into a chest freezer?

Besides organization and access, we learned that storing food in grocery bags had an added bonus: insulation. Because the food items in the bags were tightly packed and touching one another, thawing was kept to a minimum. The only items that became totally defrosted during our "power outage" were a couple of inexpensive, store-bought pizzas and a package of pork chops. These had been laid on top of the bags inside the freezer. Everything else remained perfectly frozen.

We organize it. Your categories may be different, but here's how we group the food in our freezer:

Turkeys. Our cache of inexpensive birds purchased prior to Thanksgiving line a large portion of the bottom of the freezer.

Meat. Each kind has its own bag—beef, chicken, pork—while hot dogs and lunch meat share one bag.

Cheese. Most of the cheese used in cooking is purchased shredded from a warehouse store (it's less expensive than chunk cheese and easier to use in many of our recipes), then divided into smaller storage containers. These containers are stacked and put into a grocery bag. Other solid cheeses are stored there also. If you do freeze chunks of cheese, you discover when it is thawed that it will be crumbly and very difficult to slice. However, we received an e-mail from a website visitor in Switzerland who claimed that if you let the frozen cheese sit out on your counter for a day, covered with a moist towel, and allow it to come to room temperature it will re-gel and not crumble when sliced.

Frozen veggies. We normally have two or three bags full of frozen veggies. We sort them by type and put two varieties in each bag: green beans and corn, Brussels sprouts and mixed veggies, etc.

Baking supplies. Carob powder, nuts, coconut, white and wheat flour, and chocolate squares.

Milk. We store up to five gallons on the bottom of the freezer—this will last us one month. Most health experts recommend that we drink eight glasses of water daily—we encourage everyone in our family to do this. Our kids can have one glass of milk daily; the rest is used for cooking, baking, and with cold cereal for breakfast. To store milk we pour off a couple of inches from each gallon to allow for expansion when it freezes.

Bread. After our periodic bread-outlet or Dollar Tree store run, we'll have three or four bags full of bread. These include hamburger and hot dog buns, and rye bread for Reuben sandwiches—one of our favorites. We seal our bread in another plastic bag to reduce the amount of condensation that builds up as it freezes. Then we carefully set it in the freezer to avoid crushing and creating grotesquely misshapen loaves.

Bagels and English muffins.

Margarine and butter.

Using paper bags isn't the only way to organize a freezer—read what this frugal friend did.

___

Freezer Pleazer!

I just reorganized my freezer using plastic bins. It's great and really easy to find what I need. I marked them "Beef," "Chicken," and "Pork." This has really helped me to know what I already have in the freezer so I can shop more carefully.

Leslie—Jacksonville, FL

Taking Stock

Another advantage of storing in grocery bags is that it makes taking inventory much easier. Once a month, when Annette is planning her menu and shopping trip,

Steve will take a complete inventory of the contents of the freezer. He can pull out a bag and assess an entire category. As we mentioned in the shopping chapter, taking an inventory of the contents of our freezer is a monthly ritual and an important part of making sure that we use the items we have stocked up on.

Upright vs. Chest Freezers

Prior to our huge chest freezer, we had a 21-cubic-foot upright freezer. We still applied the category-type storage method. But instead of grocery bags, we used a few cardboard boxes and some cardboard dividers that were cut to size. Each shelf held one or two categories of food. We stacked meat on its side, similar to a library book, rather than in piles that could easily slide and fall. Frozen veggies were stacked in groups of similar kinds. From an organizational point of view, we found the upright to be easier to access and quicker to retrieve things. However, it didn't hold as much, and was much more difficult to defrost. Additionally, whenever we opened the door, we could feel the cold air "falling out" on our feet.

If space is limited, you can't go wrong with an upright freezer. But if you have the room, you'll get more storage space and use less energy with a chest freezer.

Frost-Free vs. Manual Defrost

There are two types of freezers out there, and the opinion is split as to which is best. We have only had manual defrost freezers and with Arizona's low humidity only have to defrost it once each year. Frost-free freezers have a timer that cycles every six to eight hours and heats up the freezer coils just slightly. It's enough to eliminate the icy buildup on the coils. The upside of frost-free freezers is that you don't have to defrost them. The downside is that they use slightly more electricity and tend to dry out food because of the constant temperature changing. Our refrigerator-freezer is frost-free and in addition to the cycling of the coils, it also has a fan to keep the air moving—which can also dry out food. Several people we've talked to say that their food regularly gets a freezer-burned taste from their frost-free freezer.

Our advice is to go with a manual defrost freezer; it works great for us. If you choose to go with frost-free, it would be a good idea to invest in a vacuum-seal device to protect your meat and other perishable foods from freezer burn.

If you are in the market for a new or used freezer, you should read "Don't Get Soaked Buying Used Appliances" in Chapter 7, "Economizing Equipment." You can find a great deal with a little research and a few of our shopping tips.

Other Freezer Tips

From the City of Mesa, Arizona, website:

Did you know that a refrigerator or freezer in the garage or outside can be a real energy hog? High temperatures make your refrigerator or freezer use much more energy. Consider disconnecting them at least for the summer, or moving them to an air-conditioned area.

From an electricity provider website:

Avoid placing a refrigerator or freezer in your garage or on your patio. During the summer, a refrigerator in your garage or on your patio can cost $15 to $20 a month.

From the Amana website:

Refrigerators and freezers are sensitive to the surrounding air temperature. When the room temperature falls below 55° F, the compressor may not run long enough to maintain proper temperatures in the refrigerator and freezer sections. The freezer compartment will increase to the ambient room temperature, which will affect food preservation. Self-defrost models exposed to freezing temperatures will encounter defrost-drain and drain-pan freeze up.

We do not recommend refrigerators or freezers be kept in areas that reach temperatures below 55° Fahrenheit or above 110° Fahrenheit.

Keeping your pantry, kitchen, and freezer organized, will give you better tools for building the meals you love, save you loads of time, and help you keep the savings you've earned.

WHAT CAN YOU DO ABOUT STORAGE
AND ORGANIZATION NOW?

 Timid Mouse

1. Evaluate your food storage spaces/pantry. Do some research and figure out how to make your current space more efficient and the food more easily accessible.
2. Take stock of what you have in your pantry and organize it by type of food item.
3. The next time you go food shopping, look for a loss-leader item that you can stock up on.

 Wise Owl

1. If you have a freezer, organize it by food type in bags, plastic containers, or cardboard boxes. If you don't have a freezer, start saving money to buy one and begin your research.
2. Start tracking your food usage. If you have some items already stocked up in your pantry, label them with the date and 1 of X, 2 of X, etc.
3. If you have kids who are old enough to help in the kitchen, move some of the dishes, cups, and silver to a place where they can easily access them. Consider using unbreakable plates and glasses.

 Amazing Ant

1. Evaluate your kitchen cabinets for efficiency and move items that are in the wrong places.
2. Reorganize your refrigerator to make better use of the space and the coldest areas.
3. Look for an out-of-the-way place in your home where you could build shelves to store more food.

7

Economizing Equipment—
Powerful Money-Saving Tools

Being thrifty and having nice things aren't mutually exclusive propositions. Our philosophy is to buy the best-quality items we can afford at the lowest price we can find. We aren't into having the latest fashions in clothes, cars, or kitchen gadgets. Nor are we into having lots of different tools that only do one specific task. But we are into having quality tools and equipment so that we can get the job done efficiently and use a minimal amount of time and materials. Think of this chapter as a list of our "Favorite Things" (apologies to Rodgers and Hammerstein—and Oprah) for the kitchen and dining room. You may find that some of our favorites just won't fit your lifestyle or kitchen space, but you'll be able to adapt the concept with a similar tool or maybe no tool at all.

We'll share what we like, why we like it, and how you can get it or something similar, inexpensively. We'll also cover how we buy used appliances without getting burned.

ECONOMIZER TOOLS FOR THE KITCHEN

Annette spends a good deal of time working in the kitchen—but this is not her dream job. She likes to get in, get cooking, and get on to other things in life. To make her cooking time more efficient, she's accumulated some specific tools that help her spend less time cooking and cleaning up. You're not going to find us recommending super-expensive, cutting-edge, chef-quality items. That's just not our style. Several of the items we love can easily be purchased used, and other items are relatively inexpensive. There are a couple that could be costly, but please don't be in a rush to buy something just because we recommend it. Save your money and do your own research and you'll make a decision that you'll be happy with.

Good Pots and Pans

A good set of pots and pans is worth its weight in gold—but needn't cost that much. Our set was a wedding present, and many years later they still function as if they were brand-new. A few years ago, we were told that Farberware products carried a lifetime warranty. One of our pot handles had broken and with a simple phone call to their consumer relations department, we received a replacement handle in the mail the next week! What a deal. We also like the fact that the set we have are *not* nonstick. On the rare occasion when something gets burned onto the bottom of the pot, they clean up good as new with a little soaking and the application of a stainless steel scrubbing pad. A friend of Annette's purchased an expensive set of nonstick pans and needed a whole new set within three years—those surfaces just don't last.

We recently clarified Farberware's warranty policy with their public relations department and discovered that their Aluminum Clad products manufactured before January 1, 1986, only had a five-year warranty, but those products manufactured since then carry a lifetime warranty. Other Farberware products have different warranties. Contact their consumer relations department at 1 (800) 809-7166 for details.

We do have a couple of nonstick pans though. We use a medium-sized nonstick pan to cook over-easy eggs during the week and a large one that we use on Sunday mornings when we cook up a good-sized batch of scrambled eggs for the whole family. We store our nonstick pans carefully, putting a large piece of butcher wrap inside the pan so we can stack other pans in it. And we only use plastic or wooden spatulas or utensils with them to minimize scratching. But even with careful use, we usually replace them every three or four years. You can find them inexpensively at Walmart, Kmart, Target, or Ross.

There has been some concern about dangerous fumes being emitted from non-stick pans. We've researched the information provided from two sources: the Dietary Managers Association (www.DMAonline.org) and the Environmental Working Group (www.EWG.org). Both organizations agree that heating up a nonstick pan to a high temperature can cause it to emit toxic fumes that have been fatal to household birds. The DMA website cautions against heating these pans, without food in them, to temperatures above 600 degrees. Butter or margarine will start to smoke at 350 degrees, and most cooking oils will start to smoke between 400 and 450 degrees, both well below the 600-degree danger temperature. Both of these websites encourage the use of stainless steel or cast-iron pots and pans. Farberware and Revereware are the two most popular brands of pots and pans, and both have products that are stainless steel with either copper or aluminum bottoms to help conduct heat evenly.

We also make use of a cast-iron skillet, usually on our once-a-month cooking day, to brown Italian sausages or ground beef. We also use it for cooking frozen veggies. The cast iron imparts iron into foods, which many experts have concluded to be beneficial to our health. It's also really heavy, so lifting it will increase your arm strength—saving you the cost of a gym membership (wink). Cast iron is easy to care for; we gently wash it to eliminate any food particles, rinse, and then place on the stove on a low heat to completely dry it out. If "unseasoned" cast iron is put away even slightly wet, it will rust. Seasoning cast iron is relatively easy. Put a thin coating of lard or shortening on it, and heat it in the oven at 350 degrees for sixty minutes. Remove the pan and let it cool. Wipe out any excess lard with a paper towel. It will have a shiny appearance, will resist sticking, and won't rust as easily.

Spoonulas

We don't know who invented these rubber spatulas with curved-up edges, but they are wonderful tools. They're great for getting the last little bits of food out of most containers—yogurt containers, peanut butter jars, spaghetti-sauce pots, and the list goes on. Spoonulas can actually stretch the yield of a recipe. We can usually scrape enough batter to make an extra cupcake or muffin. The only downside is that our kids won't share our fond memories of cleaning out the pudding pot after mom cooked up a delicious batch of chocolate pudding. We have purchased our best quality spoonulas from a restaurant supply store. The ones sold in grocery stores tend to be either too flimsy or too stiff with weak handles. We have a whole array of spoonulas, ranging in size from small to large and even have one made of silicone rubber that is designed for high heat applications.

KitchenAid Mixer

We considered this a luxury item when we purchased it with wedding money in 1982. The rest of the money was saved for a down payment on our first house. But Annette has never regretted this investment. Not only can it mix up terrific butter cookie dough—a holiday favorite—but when we have a large crowd for Thanksgiving and need a huge batch of mashed potatoes, this mixer does a fabulous job. This mixer is so powerful that it can even knead bread dough, although Annette prefers to do this by hand.

Over time we've purchased a couple of add-ons for the mixer, including a clear "splatter shield"—it clips to the rim of the stainless steel mixing bowl and keeps ingredients from splashing out onto us or the counter. It really keeps the mess down. The second attachment was our meat grinder. It cost less than $40 and saves us hundreds of dollars each year on ground beef purchases.

A quality mixer can be an expensive investment, but the time you'll save and the years of use you'll get out of it will really produce some great dividends for you—not to mention some delicious food. If you don't have the money saved, it's always a great item to put on your Christmas wish list. But if you keep your eyes peeled, you're likely to find it on sale throughout the year.

Mixing Savings

In December 2003 I was shopping at my favorite department store and walked by the KitchenAid mixers. I just loved looking at them and thinking, "Some day!" It was about that time that I noticed that they went on sale for as low as $159. I was determined to have enough money saved by the end of 2004 so I could purchase one. The mixer normally retails for $249, but as much as I wanted one, I could never pay that price.

In March, I was cleaning out some magazines and found a picture of the mixer. I cut it out and taped it on a large brown envelope. My husband and I try to stick to our household cash budget of $300 each week. So, I decided that any leftover money that I had at the end of the week would go toward my mixer fund. I usually only had $3 or $4 to add to the envelope each week. I also added any extra money such as birthday money or rebate money to the fund. By November, I had $140 in cash to apply toward my mixer.

After Thanksgiving I started watching for sales. About the middle of December I saw the mixer on sale for $189. But during early bird hours one weekend this store offered an additional 15 percent off all purchases. That brought the price down to $161. I also had been saving an MVP coupon for 15 percent off any purchase—just for such an occasion. That saved me another $28. So, in the end, I was able to purchase the mixer for $133! I had saved $116 off retail. I was thrilled.

I used my store credit card so I could keep my MVP status (notification of special sales and more discount coupons), but immediately walked over to customer service and paid off the balance with the cash I'd saved. There was no way I was going to give back any of my savings by carrying a balance. Now, I make sure to use that mixer to bake up yummy recipes at least once each week!

JENNIFER—NORFOLK, VA

Food Processor

If you are cooking meals from scratch every day, you'll find a food processor to be a real pain to use. It simply takes too much time to clean on a daily basis. But if you have a large quantity of something to cut up, or do once-a-month cooking as Annette does, this small appliance is a must. Our food processor is an old one that we found at a garage sale, to replace a similar one that we already had. The cool thing is that all of the blades from our old one fit on the "new" one. On cooking day Annette will cut through eight onions and twelve carrots in no time at all. It's also handy when she is making her annual batch of Spanakopita—Greek cheese triangles—for New Year's Eve. She uses the processor to crumble about five pounds of Feta cheese nice and fine in just a few minutes.

Joe's Favorite Kitchen Gadget

Since they were about four or five years old, our kids have helped on our once-a-month cooking day. They start out with simple tasks like mixing ground beef or cutting celery, and as they grow, the jobs become more complex.

In October 2004, we had a camera crew from *Budget Living Magazine* in our house to chronicle our lifestyle. We were demonstrating different aspects of cooking day, and Joe was tasked with peeling several onions before they were to be chopped in the food processor.

We've tried every trick in the book to keep onions from making our eyes tear. We've lit candles (marginally successful), covered the cut onions with a wet dish towel (sort of worked), put the cut onions in a bowl of water (better), but Joe didn't think any of those things helped. So he went to his bedroom and came out with a vintage military gas mask that Steve's dad had given the kids several years earlier. Joe donned the mask and proceeded to peel the onions without tears. The photographer snapped a photo. Months later Joe and his favorite kitchen tool were reproduced in living color for all the world to see! (We have a photo on our website—search for *Budget Living Magazine*.)

Wooden Cutting Board with a Gravy Moat

This is a real mess saver in the kitchen. We've heard all the stories about the dangers of bacteria and wood cutting boards, but we've never encountered that problem in over twenty-five years. Whenever we cut raw meat on a cutting board, the board is immediately washed with hot soapy water with a little bleach in it. The best part of a wood cutting board is the gravy moat. When cutting up a roast or steak, it provides a place to hold the juices that run off. It's also useful when chopping veggies if you want to put the discarded tops and other trimmings off to the side. These end up in our compost bucket and later in the garden. The downside of wooden cutting boards is that they can be heavy, hard to clean, can harbor bacteria, and can crack or split when they have been left in water too long. They do require a periodic coating with mineral oil to protect the wood from absorbing too much moisture.

Plastic Cutting Mats

We read about these in *Consumer Reports* magazine and thought they looked intriguing. When we finally bought them on sale at Walgreens and started using them, we became impressed with how versatile they were. It's so easy to go from cutting to pouring whatever you've cut up into a pot or into a plastic storage bag. You simply bend the cutting mat into a conical shape and pour the contents. Nothing spills off the sides—it's just great. Plus they're easier to sanitize than wooden cutting boards. We wash them in soapy dishwater with bleach in it and have never had a problem. They aren't good for cutting any items that are juicy, like certain meats or some fruits. They are usually sold in sets of three and are relatively inexpensive.

Good Knives

We aren't knife aficionados, but years ago, Steve was building a website for a client named Cliff, who owned a knife shop in Phoenix and definitely was an expert. He gave Steve a thirty-minute lecture that traced the history of knife making and the various kinds of metal currently used in knife blades. Basically Steve came away with the understanding that there are cheap knives (made of stainless steel), modestly priced knives (made of high-carbon stainless steel), and expensive knives (made of carbon steel). Cliff also described knives made of ceramic and titanium, but those just weren't even a consideration for us. Cliff said that the more carbon that was used in making the steel, the easier the knife would be to sharpen and the better it would hold a good cutting edge. We have two brands of knives that we really like, neither of them are expensive: Chicago Cutlery (which was rated a best buy by *Consumer Reports*) and Old Homestead Cutlery. Both are high-carbon stainless steel and are easy to sharpen and use. We use a handheld sharpening steel to sharpen our knives, and you can really tell the difference when sharpening a "good" knife versus an inexpensive stainless steel one. The better knives feel a little gritty and a little soft when we're sharpening them, and the less expensive ones feel hard and don't seem to be affected by the sharpening steel. We've got several sizes of our good knives, from small paring knives to large slicing knives.

One other knife style that we love are those with serrated blades. We have a cheap "Ginsu"-styled knife that is great for slicing tomatoes without squishing them, and bagels too. The downside of serrated blades is that they have a tendency to cut at an angle—especially when cutting watermelon.

Glass Cookware

Another thing Annette couldn't live without are her ceramic CorningWare French White and Pyrex glass baking dishes. Glass cookware is extremely versatile; it can go in the microwave, in the oven, or on the stovetop. And it even looks nice on the table as a serving dish. We store most of our once-a-month cooked meals in 13 x 9-inch Pyrex glass baking dishes. We cover them with plastic wrap that sticks nicely to the rim, creating an airtight seal. Glass is safer than other cookware because it transmits no toxic chemicals in the cooking process. The only drawback is its breakability—especially if you have kids helping you in the kitchen.

We've picked up glass cookware at thrift stores and garage sales.

Plastic Storage Containers

Having an ample supply of plastic storage containers is a must. When we were first married, Tupperware was the rage and you couldn't go two months without being invited to a Tupperware party. In the last few years, we've switched to Rubbermaid storage containers. They are easier to find in stores and less expensive than Tupperware. We use them to store things in the freezer and refrigerator, they stack nicely, and because they are clear, we can easily see their contents. The only problems we've had are that they are brittle when frozen and will crack if you drop them.

Hand Mixer

When you have a simple job like beating pancake batter in a large bowl, whipping cream from scratch, or beating egg whites, this little machine is a must-have. Over the course of our marriage we've only had two; the first one was a wedding shower gift and the second was an upgrade for us. These are inexpensive and great if you do a lot of cooking from scratch.

Manual Can Opener

We have a simple handheld can opener with a rubber handle that we store in a utility drawer near the pantry. It's simple to use, works great every time, and because it doesn't require electricity, we could even open cans during a power outage . . . that is, if we could see to do it. Our friend Lyn who helps in our office bought a handheld smooth-edge can opener that cuts the can with a horizontal blade below the can lid. There are two nice things about this can opener: (1) the lid doesn't fall into the can, (2) and it doesn't create a dangerously sharp edge—great if you have kids helping you in the kitchen. These smooth-edge can openers are a bit more expensive than the traditional ones, but as more companies are selling them, the price will likely drop.

Blender

We have an old but faithful Hamilton Beach blender. We love making smoothies with fruit that is past its prime, by adding some ice, fruit juice, and a little ice cream or yogurt. We also use it for mixing up non-instant powdered milk (added to whole milk to "stretch" it) and to puree whole tomatoes for homemade spaghetti sauce. If you cook from scratch, you'll eventually find ways to use a blender.

Stainless Steel Cookie Sheets

For years we had some cheap steel cookie sheets that had some sort of coating on them. Eventually the coating wore off and every time we washed the cookie sheets, they rusted. Ugh! A couple of times we left some pizza dough on the old cookie sheets only to find that they had started to rust and transferred the flavor to the dough. So a few years ago we started looking for stainless steel cookie sheets. This may sound really strange, but Annette put them on her Christmas wish list. We now have a full complement of large, non-rusting cookie sheets and never worry about rust anymore.

Cooling Racks

We use our cooling racks all the time—especially on cooking day. They speed up the cooling process for 13 x 9-inch glass baking dishes full of hot meals—allowing us to get meals into the freezer faster and protect our counters too. We especially love it when daughter Becky uses them . . . because it usually means lots of fresh, homemade delicious chocolate chip cookies. Then around Christmas each year, they get another workout when Annette bakes dozens of loaves of pumpkin bread to be given to teachers, neighbors, family, and even the garbageman and mailman. Now that's "cool"!

Bread Pans

We have a bunch of large and medium metal bread pans and a few glass ones too. We've collected these over the years from thrift stores and garage sales.

Step Stool

If you're taller than 5 feet 7 inches you can skip this handy tool. But Annette is height challenged (she's 5 feet 2 inches) and has a tough time reaching things on our seldom-accessed top cabinets and pantry shelves. We have a couple of step stools near the kitchen for her to use. It keeps her safe and makes getting to those things a lot easier than having to climb up on the counters if the guys in the house aren't around.

Air Popper

These handy gadgets are relatively inexpensive brand-new and also can be found at most thrift stores. If you love popcorn, but hate to heat up oil and cook it in a pot, because of health or cleanup reasons, try an air popper. We've had one for years and it works great. This is a great alternative to expensive microwave popcorn.

Slow Cooker—It's Not a Crock!

We saved one of Annette's favorite time- and money-saving tools in the kitchen for last. No, this one isn't flashy either, but if you're a busy family or single parent, this is a must-have appliance. The slow cooker or Crock-Pot is a great tool for making dinnertime easy—all year round. In the winter it fills the house with its wonderful aroma and in the summer it fills the whole outdoors as we let it slow cook on the patio—this keeps the house cooler.

Singles can load up a smaller slow cooker with a batch of meat and when it's done, freeze it in single-serving containers for future meals. For example, cook up four to six pork chops in a yummy barbecue sauce. The first night you eat one chop. The remaining chops are put on the menu once a week for the following month. For a complete meal you can combine the meat with a variety of side dishes. As we write this, a steamy baked potato (microwaved) and some frozen or fresh green beans (steamed) sound particularly appealing. This same plan on a larger scale works for our family too. So don't be shy about giving your slow cooker a try.

Some people are hesitant to leave a slow cooker unattended. We suggest testing it a couple of times while you are home. Since they are lower-wattage devices, using between 70 and 300 watts, the fire danger is quite remote. Once you're sure your cooker works okay, place it on a heatproof surface, plug it in, head out, and let your meal cook.

Here's a list of simple meat and sauce combinations. Remember to stock up on different sauces when they're on sale.

Pork or Chicken

BBQ sauce

Sweet & sour sauce

Orange marmalade

Garlic, onion, salt, and pepper

Beef

Cream of mushroom soup

Onion soup mix with yellow mustard

Red wine and teriyaki sauce

Garlic, onion, salt, and pepper

A Handful of Other Kitchen Tools

We'll wrap up our list of favorite things for the kitchen with a quick list of several other kitchen necessities that need little explanation: wooden spoons, stainless steel cooking spoons (solid and slotted), spatulas (metal and plastic), a set of plastic funnels, measuring spoons, Pyrex (glass) measuring cup, plastic measuring cups, stainless steel teapot, cowbell cheese grater, vegetable peeler, colander, rolling pin, and a pastry mat (although waxed paper can be used just as well).

There you have it, a list of our favorite tools that keep us singing in the kitchen. They get the job done for us year in and year out and haven't required much maintenance beyond a periodic cleaning. Take your time in deciding what tools you need, and shop around and get the best value you can for the least amount of money. Your family may even be surprised when they see your Christmas list this year. These things can really be gifts that keep on giving!

Here are a few tips from visitors to our website:

Handy Veggie Cleaner

I have tried a variety of vegetable brushes for cleaning produce, but never felt like I was getting it cleaned thoroughly or fast enough. So I purchased a pair of nylon exfoliating gloves from the beauty section at a drugstore. I slip the gloves on and wash all the produce by rubbing my hands over it. I wash it in a pan of water or under the faucet. The gloves are very effective, especially for large items like potatoes, celery, and cucumbers. When I'm done, I drape them on my dish rack to dry.

LAYLA—WILMINGTON, DE

Cooking Under Pressure

My grandmother, my mom, my sister, and I are big fans of pressure cookers. We all own more than one. Except for rice, pasta, pastry, and soups, we cook almost everything in a pressure cooker. The cooking time is significantly reduced, thereby cutting your time spent in the kitchen and your energy usage. Most veggie dishes take ten to fifteen minutes; meats take around twenty to forty-five minutes depending on the cut. The initial investment may be a bit expensive, but the cookers last a very long time, so it sure is worth it.

CANAN—ISTANBUL, TURKEY

We haven't used a pressure cooker, but have heard that they are great time savers in the kitchen.

Having great tools is wonderful, but if you can't keep them clean, they simply won't be as effective. We conducted an experiment with dish soap to see which one really helped us clean up the best. But before we give you those results, here are a few other ways to save money as you clean your kitchen.

Recycle Paper Towels

My smart daughter-in-law does something I have now copied. Next to her sink she has a decorative ceramic container that she puts lightly used paper towels in—e.g., those used in zippered bags with veggies and fruit. They are crumpled up and dry quickly. Later, when there is a pot or dish that needs to have grease or sticky residue wiped out, or a mess on the counter, sink, or floor to clean up, these are the paper towels she uses. My husband and I do this now, and I notice that our rolls of paper towels last much longer.

SALLY—BOERNE, TX

Phone Books Clean Up

Instead of throwing out the out-of-date phone books, keep them and tear out several pages at a time. Store them in a big plastic cup under your sink. Use these sheets instead of paper towels when you peel vegetables, etc. You won't buy paper towels nearly as often.

S. C.—Palm Springs, CA

WASHED-UP SAVINGS

Have you ever thought, *Hmm, this name-brand product costs twice as much as the generic; is it twice as good? Oh, it's all just advertising hype, there can't be that big of a difference—I'm going to save the money and buy the generic.* Well, when it came to dish soap, that was our general opinion until recently. We would buy the pricier name-brand products only if there was a sale and we had a good coupon, but we had no idea if we were just buying a name or if we were buying more cleaning power.

Our curiosity finally got the best of us, so we devised a simple test. It's not a controlled test, because no family has a controlled method of leaving oatmeal on their bowls or burned onto the bottom of their pot. No, we figured that the best test would be a family field test. We selected a different dish soap for each of three weeks. We changed no eating habits and no washing habits. Everyone in the family was involved. We put a specifically measured amount of detergent into a generic bottle, used it for a week, and measured how much we had used at the end of the week.

Before we give you the results, we want to describe how we wash dishes. It may not be revolutionary or earth-shattering, but where else have you ever read how a family washes their dishes?

First, we use our dishwasher for washing plates, bowls, glasses, silverware, and smaller miscellaneous plastic storage containers. We run the dishwasher about once a day.

The items that don't go into the dishwasher are stacked in the "staging area"—the counter to the left of our double-bowl sink. We stack our pots, pans, casserole dishes, spatulas, large serving utensils, reusable plastic zippered bags, and other cookware there.

How We Wash Dishes

We fill the left side of the sink with hot water, and add about three squirts of dish soap and one glug of bleach. While the sink is filling up, we load in serving utensils (usually on the left side of the sink), then pots or smaller pans or casserole dishes. The water is still running to fill the sink when we start to wash.

We use a scrubbing sponge (with a scouring pad on it) and apply a small amount of dish soap directly on the sponge. Each item is scrubbed on both sides, dipped back in the water to rinse off the majority of the soap, and then put into the right-hand bowl of the sink for rinsing.

We usually soak an item with burned-on food in water and a little soap prior to washing. We'll scrape it with a metal spatula to remove most of the food waste. We do the same thing with oily or greasy items, wiping them with either newspaper or a paper towel before submerging them in the wash water. Our goal is to keep the wash water as clear as possible to provide us with maximum cleaning power—this also reduces the amount of water we use.

Once the right-hand sink is filled with washed items, we rinse them under a slow-running stream of water. Rinsing one item under the faucet splashes clear water on the items below, providing them with a partial rinse also.

Items are stacked on the dish drainer, and plastic zippered bags are hung on a special dish rack with vertical spines that hold them open and allow them to drip dry faster.

Teamwork Saves Time

Usually one of us washes, another rinses, and two or three others dry and put things away. Working together we can usually tear through a pile of dishes in twenty minutes. Done solo it would take over an hour.

When Steve was a kid, his parents introduced the concept of "Kitchen Duty." Basically each of the four boys was assigned to clean up the kitchen after dinner for one week. While the other members of the family went off to do their activities, finish homework, or relax, one lone person would wrestle through the pile of dishes. We swore that it would not be that way in our home. Washing dishes, like making a bed, is always easier when it is done with someone else. We like the team building and the cross training it provides. Everyone knows how to wash and rinse, and almost everyone knows how to put away all of the dishes. (Okay, Steve sometimes needs some assistance from the kids.)

The Test

Here's what we discovered in our liquid dish soap test:

PRODUCT	AMOUNT USED IN 1 WEEK	RETAIL PRICE	EFFICIENCY	ACTUAL COST PER OZ.
Dawn	100 ml.	38 oz. $3.99 / 10.5¢ per oz.	100%	10.5¢ per oz.
Ajax	175 ml.	34 oz. $2.99 / 8.8¢ per oz.	Used 75% more	15.4¢ per oz.
Generic store brand	262 ml.	25 oz. $1.99 / 8¢ per oz.	Used 162 % more	20.96¢ per oz.

As you can see, even though Dawn costs more initially, because it is more concentrated and contains more grease-cutting ingredients, it cleans more dishes for half the price of the generic store brand.

International Approval

We have some friends who are missionaries in Papua New Guinea. We talked with them recently about this dish soap test. Debbie said, "Whenever someone visits us from the States, we always ask them to bring Dawn with them." We were amazed. She went on to tell us that the dish soap they can buy there is worse quality than the weakest generic stuff. It doesn't clean anything. But because Dawn is so powerful, one bottle lasts a very long time. Consequently someone could bring her four bottles of Dawn, and Debbie would be fully supplied for several months.

One Word of Caution

Another friend saw her naturopathic doctor for some skin tests. The naturopath asked if she was using Dawn detergent. She said that she was. The doctor said that she had some toxins in her body that he had traced to the degreaser used in Dawn. He recommended that she either stop using this product or wear rubber gloves when washing dishes because this ingredient could be toxic to some people.

Washing dishes is a regular part of life. So if we've got to do it, why not use a product that gets the job done and costs less to use? Our test was limited to only three detergents, so if yours wasn't included, conduct your *own* field test. Track your results and let us know what you find. You may spend a little more initially, but when combined with a money-saving coupon and the knowledge that the product will last two and a half times longer than the competition, you can *really* be cleaning up.

Here are a couple of more ways to save money while keeping your kitchen clean:

Diluted Savings

I find that a squirt of full-strength liquid dishwashing detergent is usually too much for my needs. So I fill an old bottle of dish soap halfway with detergent and then the other half with water. Now I have two bottles full of detergent for the price of one (it's even less expensive because I usually use cents-off coupons).

ELAINE—PITTSBURGH, PA

Squeaky Clean

When I was younger, I worked for a deli, where it was extremely important for us to have not only scrupulously clean counters and equipment, but also shiny counters and sinks! We put straight isopropyl (rubbing) alcohol into a spray bottle. Spray it on the counters, plastic surfaces, stainless steel sinks, anything that's glass, including windows and mirrors. It works like a charm, doesn't streak, the excess will evaporate, and you will have surfaces that have been disinfected too! Hospitals have also been using rubbing alcohol to disinfect for years. The only type of surface that you need to be careful with are painted surfaces (always test first!) There are some types of paint that will be lifted by the alcohol. Any time you use it on a new surface, it doesn't hurt to test in an inconspicuous spot first. I never use alcohol on wood surfaces because it could dry it out. (Murphy's oil soap works great on wood!)

DARLENE—NEW ORLEANS, LA

Now that all of your dishes and kitchen utensils are clean, let's head from the kitchen sink to the kitchen table and save some money.

THE ESTATE OF YOUR TABLE LINENS

Years ago we started using cloth napkins on our table. We did it strictly as a money saver, and it is definitely a benefit to the environment. We really didn't like the idea of putting paper napkins on the table for each meal and then tossing them in the trash even if they weren't used. We've found cloth napkins at several garage sales and on closeout tables in household supply stores. We don't wash them after every meal for family members, but if you're a guest at our table, we promise, you'll get a clean one. Washing them costs virtually nothing, as they are included with a load of similarly colored clothes.

A few years ago we received an e-mail that took our understanding of cloth napkins to a new level. In the e-mail, the writer shared her knowledge and experience with cloth napkins and tablecloths. Here are some of her ideas:

⌒‿⌒

Table Linens Save Several Ways

Table linens are one of the cheapest items to find at estate sales when people are cleaning out a lifetime of stuff. I own six damask linen table-cloths, each purchased at estate sales, and each purchased for less than $3.

A little history: Tablecloths were originally made from linen because it is one of the longest lasting, toughest wearing fabrics around. A good quality linen tablecloth should last for thirty to fifty years. It can be bleached and washed in hot water as much as you like. It will not stain or pill the way polyester fabric does. They do need ironing, but I don't mind that.

After hosting a dinner party for sixteen guests, I noticed that cran-berry sauce, wine, gravy, and other items were spilled on my tablecloth. Because it was white—and could be bleached—and because it was 100 percent linen, it went into the washing machine and came out looking new. This is another advantage that linen has over polyester. Polyester fabrics absorb grease stains forever.

I had a few linen napkins—purchased from a lady who had used them for fifty years—that got to the point where I thought they were too thin. I didn't throw them away. They make wonderful window clean-ing rags. Linen, unlike regular cotton, is lint-free and is great for sparkling clean windows.

DEIRDRE—CALIFORNIA

One thing we'd add to Deirdre's great tips is that paper towels, plastic and paper tablecloths and paper napkins eventually end up in landfills. Are you con-vinced that cloth napkins and tablecloths are the way to go? If so, we'll see you at the estate sales!

So your kitchen is organized, cleaned, and you're ready to cook. But what happens when one of your trusty appliances dies? Is it time for a loan and a trip to the local appliance store, or is there a better way to get a replacement appliance? We've got a few tricks to share about buying appliances at huge discounts.

DON'T GET SOAKED BUYING USED APPLIANCES

It's time versus money. New versus used. When it comes to home appliances, you can save a boatload of money if you invest some time in research. Sometimes we have bought new appliances, but we always consider the option of buying used. To ensure we don't get soaked, we use the following strategies.

Know the Value

Check the store ads for retail prices of different sizes and kinds of the appliance you want. Call the stores to see if there are any unadvertised sales or coupons. When we were researching freezers, we found that upright freezers were much more expensive than chest freezers of the same size. The biggest drawback was the amount of floor space the chest freezer used.

Scour the classified ads in your newspaper and online for a few weeks to learn the price range for used appliances. Once you've determined the price range, you can decide whether you want or can afford to purchase new or used.

We've always purchased our used appliances from individuals selling their own items. While there are reputable businesses that sell used equipment, we have heard only negative stories from friends who have gone that route. We want to trust people, but we live in a large city and the chance of being "soaked" or taken advantage of is greater than in a small town. As a result, we've put the following guidelines on our appliance purchasing habits.

Research the Brand Name

We use *Consumer Reports* to research which brands are rated as most reliable. We may not purchase the exact model it rates as best, but if a company has several models in the top ten, we will look for a similar one with fewer "bells and whistles." Next we call a few appliance repair companies and ask which manufacturers they have found to be more reliable and easier to maintain. Armed with this information, we start the hunt.

Find the Original Owner

When we call on an ad, we ask the seller if he or she is the original owner and has the original receipt and instruction manual. We have discovered that most people can't remember exactly when they purchased their appliances. We once bought a gas dryer in a hurry—our old one died and we needed to dry cloth diapers. The owner told us the dryer was eight years old. We later discovered the true age was closer to twenty. Since that time, we have either bought from the original owner with a receipt or confirmed the age in another surefire way.

Get the Serial Number

Another way to determine the age of an appliance is to ask for the serial number and manufacturer's name and either call the manufacturer's toll-free number or visit the Appliance411 website—www.Appliance411.com/service/date-code.php. Either source can tell you the year the appliance was manufactured from the serial number. On one occasion, we discovered the serial number plate to be missing. We passed on that item because of the likelihood of its being stolen. Another time, the seller told us that a refrigerator was nine years old. A call to the manufacturer revealed the age to be twenty-five. When buying a used appliance, we like to buy one that is no more than four or five years old—newer is better.

Haggle and Cash Out

We usually negotiate the price. Knowing, from our research, what the fair market value is gives us leverage. But if the price is fair and the seller resolute, we will purchase at the asking price. Always bring cash for the purchase. With so many bad-check writers, don't expect a stranger to take a chance on you. If you don't want to carry a large sum of cash, get a cashier's check from a nearby bank after you've finalized your negotiating. Write out a receipt with the date, amount paid, serial number, and buyer and seller's names.

Getting It Home

When buying used you usually don't have the option of home delivery. If you don't have a vehicle large enough to carry the appliance home, you'll need to factor in the cost of renting a truck (or baking cookies for a friend who will loan you a truck). You'll also need a cart or an appliance dolly. If these resources are not available to you, you'll have to get creative—call an appliance repair store for a referral or rent a truck by the hour from Home Depot or U-Haul and enlist the help of a strong friend or two.

Some sellers will deliver their appliance for a small fee, but we would never buy the appliance from a person who wanted to deliver it to our house before we actually saw the appliance. You can learn a lot about a person's integrity by visiting his home.

With dangerous assaults being reported for people who buy things off of CraigsList, we always recommend taking someone with you when you visit a potential seller's location, and if a situation doesn't feel right, don't proceed—just go home. Being safe is more important than saving a few bucks.

No matter what kind of appliance you want, use these tips to find the best deal on a new or reliable used item. You may spend a bit more time than the average, credit-card-toting consumer, but as you sail into the sunset with your boatload of savings, you'll know "for sure" that you found the best deal possible.

THE DISHWASHER DEAL

We'd set aside $400 to replace our old dishwasher. Our goal was to get the best quality for the least amount of money—we were looking for a dishwasher that had a stainless steel tub and nylon racks. After consulting *Consumer Reports*, we called several appliance stores in our area looking for a particular brand and model. We discovered that most large distributors in our city have "scratch and dent" and discontinued units, which they sell at discounted prices. So we called a few more stores looking for these deals. We struck "pay dirt" at a Maytag clearance outlet, and walked out of their downtown warehouse with a brand-new, $800 stainless steel dishwasher (in an open box) for $400. We stayed within our budget and ended up getting the quality we wanted for half of the retail price!

Please remember that if you don't have the money saved to buy the items you think you need, be patient. Patience and planning combined with saving and sleuthing produce the best results. Make a list of the tools you want to buy and keep a watchful eye, and you'll see miracles as you wait. Don't believe us? Listen to this story.

About seven years ago our gas dryer started smoking. Some lint had accumulated underneath it and started smoldering. Steve and Roy moved the dryer to the garage, laid it on its back, and cleaned it out. The heat from the "fire" melted one of the rubber rollers that turn the drum. As a result, for the next five years the dryer made a constant thump, thump sound every time the drum turned. We didn't think much of it; the clothes dried and the noise wasn't that bad. Steve checked into getting replacement parts, but discovered that it would be a huge undertaking and the parts cost close to $100. So we let it go.

Two years ago, the dryer started making a screeching sound. Steve checked inside the drum and found that it had been cut in two. Apparently the thump, thump sound also meant that the drum was constantly being scored and scraped by a metal fitting on the wheel. Eventually the fitting cut through the drum—no small task. What did we do? No, we didn't run out and buy a new dryer—we didn't have the money saved for that. We waited and prayed and thought and waited some more. In reality it was about three days. Steve was at a friend's house. Our friend had just torn down his old house and rebuilt a new one. He lived on a huge lot and in the back of his lot he had many things he was getting ready to either throw away or give away. One of the items turned out to be a gas dryer. Johnny, who is in some ways more frugal than us, wouldn't take any money for the dryer; he was glad that he didn't have to run an ad to try to get rid of it. When we took his dryer home, we thought it would just be something to hold us over until we found a newer model. But when we went to the Appliance411 website and punched in the serial and model numbers, we found out that the dryer Johnny had given us had been manufactured in December of 2000. It was only seven years old!

Patience, waiting, and building reciprocal relationships with friends can really help you out in a time of need. If you have a need for a tool, an appliance, or anything in life, write it down . . . wait and watch—amazing things happen when we're patient.

Building an arsenal of the right tools, bought at the right price, can really streamline your food preparation and cleanup. Plus they can really save you money—especially if they can be used for multiple tasks. Be sure to do your research before you buy and please don't go telling your spouse or friends that you need to buy anything in this chapter just because we said so. Take time to really evaluate your need. It is a complete and utter waste of money to buy a tool that is used once and then spends its life on the shelf or in a drawer gathering dust.

If you do find that you have a kitchen gadget that you aren't using, give it away or sell it at a garage sale. Reducing unused things means you have less to store, less to clean, less to move, and less to worry about. Achieving a goal of having the right tools in the right places will take time and mental energy to accomplish. But, rest assured, the effort you put forth to organize the control center (the kitchen) of your home will produce years of benefits.

WHAT CAN YOU DO ABOUT KITCHEN TOOLS AND APPLIANCES NOW?

 Timid Mouse

1. Pull out a piece of paper and write "Kitchen Wish List" on the top of it and post it on your fridge. Whenever you think of something you need, or want, for your kitchen (large or small, inexpensive or costly) write it on the list. If someone asks you for a Christmas list or wants to buy you a birthday present, share one or two items from your wish list with them.

2. If the item is costly or large, research it through *Consumer Reports*, call a repair shop, and talk to friends about what works best for them.

3. Whenever you go out to discount stores, thrift stores, or garage sales, take your list with you. Also check CraigsList.org and FreeCycle.org. Track prices and when you know it's a great deal, buy what you need. Cross off items you've purchased.

 Wise Owl

1. Do you have tools that you seldom or never use? Either move them to less accessible places, sell them, or give them away.

2. Evaluate what you throw in the trash. Can you eliminate some of your paper waste by using cloth napkins, eliminating paper plates, or reusing paper towels? Can you recycle aluminum foil or zippered plastic bags? Create a system for reusing and recycling these disposable items and help your bottom line and the environment.

 Amazing Ant

1. The next time you need to replace an appliance, do some research and consider buying it used or from a scratch and dent store.

2. When one of your kitchen hand tools breaks, pull out the warranty booklet (or check with the company's website) to see if it has a lifetime warranty. If it does, call for a free replacement!

8

Family Dinnertime—Building a Stronger Family at the Table

We've talked about the steps we take in planning, shopping, storing, and cooking great meals. But what is the use of going through all of these steps if no one is ever home to eat what is prepared? Many families are running so fast that they rarely sit down together to eat a meal. We know the struggle, because with five kids, we are constantly being tugged to join the soccer-mom or baseball-dad crowd in the drive-through lane of a fast-food restaurant. Family dinnertime just doesn't get much respect from those who schedule lessons, practices, club meetings, or sporting events. What is a busy family to do? Do we surrender to the culture or can we, dare we, take a stand to defend our family turf? And if we do take a stand, will we miss out on the good things in life?

There are lots of things that we know are good for us. Things like drinking lots of water each day, exercising, eating more veggies and fruits rather than chips and soda, and getting some sunshine on a daily basis. Intellectually, we all know these things. But it's in the daily application, the fleshing it out, where we encounter the biggest struggles and resistance. The same is true with the concept of eating together as a family—no matter what size your family is.

Will eating together save you money? It could, depending on how you are currently "doing dinner." But more important this chapter is about actively building stronger family bonds. Bonds that will ensure healthier relationships and help you weather the storms of life.

Annette grew up in a traditional Italian family, with five kids and a dad who was an engineer. Each day her dad would come home from work at the same time, change out of his work clothes, and wash up before dinner. Mom had the meal ready and they all sat down to dinner at the same time every day. Conversation around the dinner table was often animated and loud as each sibling vied for attention to share something about the day or a funny observation. When Steve first became acquainted with Annette's family at a Thanksgiving dinner in 1980, he was amazed at how boisterous the table conversation became . . . and how much fun it was.

Steve's Greek family consisted of four boys and his parents. His dad owned a photography studio with several employees and often worked late at night in downtown Chicago before tackling the thirty-five-minute commute home. The family often ate dinner without dad. When the boys entered high school, they each got involved with a gymnastics team that practiced after school, usually until 7 p.m. Once again the family was fragmented with the remaining siblings and mom left alone to eat dinner, while dad and the athletic high schoolers came home later to heat up dinner in a microwave.

Knowing the different backgrounds we grew up with, it's no wonder that we had numerous battles over the importance of our family dinnertime. Steve thought that following his dad's pattern of coming home whenever his work was finished was fine, while Annette insisted that we have dinner together as a family every night. It took several years until Steve saw the value of Annette's desire—but he finally did. And the result of her persistence has been a blessing to our family for years. You'll have to keep reading to find out what she did to change Steve's mind.

THE DISAPPEARING DINNER HOUR

Does eating meals together really promote healthy families? We think so, and so do numerous experts who have conducted surveys that investigated this very idea. It seems that most families want to eat dinner together, but many are finding it too challenging to obtain.

Many good activities are stealing precious time from families: work schedules, school activities, sports, church activities, music lessons, computer games, online communities, and TV. A book Annette read several years ago, *Traits of a Healthy Family* by Dolores Curran, really cemented her thinking about the idea of actively protecting our family dinner hour.[4] Ms. Curran surveyed over five hundred working professionals from five institutional areas: education, church, health, family counseling, and volunteer organizations. They each were asked which positive traits they most frequently observed in healthy families. Her book expands on the top fifteen traits the professionals identified. A few of the healthy family traits they identified are these: they communicate and listen; they affirm and support each other; they trust each other; and they respect each other. Included in that list was that a healthy family "fosters family table time and conversation." None of the traits were money or possession related. All of them had to do with spending time together and valuing each other. And family meals provide a perfect vehicle and the time to strengthen our families.

When our kids were younger and Steve was working long hours as an advertising account executive, Annette wanted to come up with ideas to keep the family dinner hour fun and exciting. Since we were homeschooling our kids and were with each other most of the time, our mealtimes weren't used to find out what happened in each other's daily lives. So Annette started reading chapter books to the kids. Many of these have become family favorites that the kids love to read over and over. But we made a family rule that we couldn't read any portion of the book unless everyone was home and at the table—this became a powerful encouragement for Steve to get home for dinner. We also started playing some thinking games at the table, and the kids really enjoyed those (we'll give you a list of resources we've used later in the chapter). Other times, Steve read a Bible passage or a story he discovered in the newspaper or on the Internet and we discussed its relevance to our lives. We work very hard to schedule our activities—kids and adults—to protect our time together at dinner.

So, how can you make mealtime a priority? First make a choice that you're going to look for more ways to help your family sit down together for meals. Read our list of suggestions for things to make family mealtime fun. Then read the fifteen most common excuses that we've heard why some families can't get together for dinner. As you read through these lists, you'll start to get some ideas of what will work best for your family. Maybe it's a family time at breakfast or dinner or maybe it's tea at 10 p.m. (this is what one single mom decided worked best for her and her two teenage daughters). Maybe it will be breakfast three days each week. It really doesn't matter when you sit down together, just that it becomes a priority, everyone shows up, and it's done consistently.

Over the past few years, around the start of the school year, we've heard radio news stories about a survey from the National Center of Addiction and Substance Abuse at Columbia University (CASA) that encourages families to eat meals together. In their fourteenth annual report, CASA shared the results from surveying 1,000 teens between the ages of twelve and seventeen and 452 parents of those teens. They looked at things like dinner and academic performance; the relationship between family dinner and substance abuse; and the effects family dinnertimes play in the development of relationships at home.

The most powerful conclusions we came away with from reading this study are: Children who eat dinner with their families fewer than three times each week are 61 percent more likely to use alcohol, tobacco, or illegal drugs. By contrast, children who eat dinner with their families at least five times each week are 20 percent less likely to drink, smoke, or use illegal drugs. And if that isn't enough encouragement to work at having regular family meals, here are a few more reasons:

Reasons That Eating Together Is Better for Your Family

1. **It's cheaper than eating at a restaurant**. With a moderately priced restaurant meal costing anywhere between $7 and $20 per person, you can easily serve up a great meal for your whole family for the price of one restaurant meal. And with many families eating out two or more times each week, the

savings can really add up. A family of four spending $30 twice each week for dinner out will spend about $3,000 annually.

2. **It promotes better health**. Family meals are usually more nutritious than fast food or restaurants. A survey from the Obesity Prevention Program at the Harvard Medical School revealed that kids who ate dinner at home ate more fruits and vegetables and less soda and fried foods. And eating together also provided more opportunities for parents to discuss the value of good nutrition with their kids.

3. **It's faster to eat at home**. When you factor in drive time, waiting to be seated, waiting to be served, waiting to receive the bill, and driving back home, simple meals at home take less time and provide more time for conversing.

4. **It builds intimacy**. You have more privacy and better family interaction at home. It's difficult to have conversations that are in-depth when you are constantly interrupted by waitresses or people busing the tables. Plus, at least for our family, we tend to feel the need to tone down our laughter when we're out at a restaurant.

5. **It allows you to pass down your family heritage**. Family meals are a great time to prepare some ethnic dishes or meals that have been passed down through your family for generations. We've got to fight the homogeneous nature of our culture and keep special and unique meals and traditions alive. We eat great Italian (Annette's heritage) and Greek (Steve's heritage) meals, and our kids have come to appreciate the different flavors and names of several of the meals. Annette learned to cook many Greek dishes from Steve's mom, and, of course, the Italian meals from her mom and some other relatives. Keeping family traditional meals alive gives you roots and memories.

Our bottom-line encouragement is this: if you make family mealtimes a priority, and you work through the resistance and other obstacles, you will come to enjoy it immensely. Don't give up! Find activities that your family loves and looks forward to. (Even if you are empty nesters, you're still a family.) It takes time and commitment, but with perseverance you can discover that rather than disappearing, your dinner hour becomes a favorite time of the day.

More Dinner Surveys

Here are a few more surveys to give you added encouragement to pursue this ideal: Wylers Bouillon Fast 4-Ward Dinner Data Survey:

- 62 percent of American households with children described their typical dinnertime as hectic.
- 77 percent spend less than half an hour eating dinner.
- 26 percent eat dinner in fifteen minutes or less.
- 19 percent said they very often eat alone.
- 7 percent said that they very often eat standing up in the kitchen.

Kraft Foods and the National Pork Board survey of 1,045 moms:

- Only 39 percent of moms said their families turn off the TV during mealtime and even fewer families—30 percent—refuse to answer the phone.

WestSoy survey of 592 adults:

- Only 10 percent of families eat together four or more times each week.

MAKING DINNER FUN

The ideas we are going to present here are things we've done, but we're sure with your creativity, you'll come up with more and even better ideas.

Have a Question of the Day

If you come up with enough questions, you can put them in a basket and take turns drawing one question out each day.

- What was the most _____ [funny, weird, surprising, sad, boring— choose one] thing that you saw today?

- What was the nicest thing you heard today?
- Tell us a joke that you heard recently. (Joe loves telling jokes, so sometimes we've had to limit him to just one a day—otherwise he'd go on for hours.)
- Read a short news story and then ask, "If you were the president, what would you do about this?"
- If you could take a trip anywhere in the world, where would you want to go, and why?
- If you could have dinner with any person in the world, who would you want to meet and talk to?
- When was the last time you were completely overwhelmed and you saw a miracle happen that turned your whole situation around?
- Try playing "Thorns and Roses." We learned this from our Boy Scout troop. This is a time when each family member tells one good thing and one hard thing about his or her day during dinnertime. You'll hear things you might not otherwise know, and it also helps to cultivate an attitude of gratefulness.

Read a Book Out Loud

Whether you have kids or not, reading aloud is always a good thing. We've read various books including: Little House on the Prairie series by Laura Ingalls Wilder; Little Britches series by Ralph Moody; American Girl books; Christmas in My Heart series by Joe L. Wheeler; Jim Kjelgaard animal stories; *White Fang* and *Call of the Wild* by Jack London; *Where the Red Fern Grows* by Wilson Rawls; and *Riverboat Adventures* by Lois Walfrid Johnson. Another great book with short selections is *The Rest of the Story* by Paul Harvey. If you need more ideas, we have lots of our favorite family books listed on our website, www.AmericasCheapestFamily .com.

Play a Game

We often played a simple little game called Geography from Educational Insights. The cards gave us clues and random facts to help us guess which state the clues were describing. We kept score and learned about U.S. geography. The kids especially love to play it when guests come over for dinner. Now, whenever they talk to Uncle Bill (Annette's older brother), he always teases them, saying, "I want to play Geography!"

We also love playing Mad Libs, a fill-in-the-blank story game. Mad Libs is a way to learn different parts of speech and have fun at the same time. There are various stories based on historical figures or sports or TV shows. Participants are asked to give nouns, verbs, pronouns, adverbs, and other parts of speech to fill in the blanks of a story they haven't heard yet. The results are always hilarious—many times we end up laughing so hard we have tears in our eyes. If we have dinner guests, they are invited to participate—though often they have a harder time with the parts of speech than our kids do.

Read a Letter

We love reading Christmas letters from friends and family. It's a great way to remember them and discuss what they are doing. It also helps our kids to connect more quickly with our extended family when we get together with them. We keep in touch with a number of friends who serve as missionaries in foreign countries. It's fun for all of us to read their letters and learn about the work they do and the uniqueness of the culture where they live.

Make It Different for Holidays

We've tried several different ideas centered around the holidays to make dinner special. At Thanksgiving time, we write on index cards special things we're grateful for about other members of our family. At Advent, we've put a special wreath on the table with candles in it. We light one candle each of the four weeks of Advent. At Easter, we have a special basket of twelve plastic eggs, each with a different Bible verse and symbol that pertains to the Resurrection story. For Christmas dinner, we usually cook a leg of lamb, and for Christmas breakfast, Steve makes super-delicious cheese blintzes. On each family member's birthday, we cook a special meal—a favorite, requested by the birthday person. There are always ways to make dinner special around holidays and special occasions, which will create memories that will last a lifetime.

Let Kids Prepare the Meal

When Abbey was about seven years old, she wanted to cook dinner for all of us. She had a little help from Nana and made a complete meal from recipes in her *Beanie Baby Cookbook*. Becky did the same thing using Civil War era recipes from an Abe Lincoln cookbook she found at a used bookstore. Getting the kids involved in planning and preparation will increase their interest and pride in eating together as a family.

Listen to Something Fun or Educational

We've listened to old-time radio shows, Bill Cosby CDs (we've laughed until we've cried with these), and podcasts that Steve has heard and thinks would be interesting to all of us. One in particular described the life of a South American tribal shaman and how his life and his tribe were changed by an encounter with a missionary family. We've also enjoyed listening to a series called *Adventures in Odyssey* produced by Focus on the Family—these dramatizations are fun to listen to and always have a strong moral and spiritual message.

Tell Family Stories

Giving our kids a sense of their roots is really important. So sometimes we just recount things that happened to our family years ago, like the time we had a flat tire on a dirt road in southern Arizona, thirty miles from the nearest city, and how the jack broke and the spare tire rolled and almost knocked five-year-old Becky over. We were eventually rescued by a rural mailman who said that he never traveled that particular road without three spare tires. Whenever we have Annette's parents over, we inevitably end up sharing stories from Annette's youth, their youth, or their memories of WWII. Our kids love hearing those stories over and over.

THINGS WE DON'T DO AT DINNER

There are a few things that simply are not allowed at our dinner table. You could label us as crazy parents, but we call the following items distractions and things that tend to isolate individuals rather than reinforce relationships.

No TV

It's hard to watch TV and communicate. So we don't do it. Beyond a lack of communication, a lack of nutrition is linked to eating in front of the TV. A survey commissioned by the New York State Department of Health surveyed 1,300 families about their dinnertime habits and found that when families watched TV during dinner they tended to eat fewer fruits or vegetables and have fewer conversations.

No Technology

. . . unless you're going to share a song, a story, or a podcast with the whole family. We know this might be a radical idea, but this means no laptops, iPods, and no texting on cell phones.

No Newspapers or Books

This is just a rule we have. Everyone in our family loves to read, and we each are often in the middle of a couple of books (fiction and nonfiction). We also get the newspaper periodically, and Joe loves to read the sports section, Steve loves the business and news section, Annette loves the ads, Abbey loves to look at the classified ads for pets, and Becky always has her eye out for any horse-related articles or things for sale. But we don't read anything at the dinner table. It's okay to read at breakfast or lunch, but not at dinner—that's the time to talk, laugh, and connect.

Don't Leave the Room

We stay in the same room. We don't just grab a plate of food and go off somewhere else in the house to eat alone.

Don't Answer the Phone

We let the answering machine get it, and screen all calls. We usually don't answer, unless there is some family emergency, or someone calls with whom we've been playing "phone tag" for several days. Most things simply can wait until dinner is over.

These ideas of what we do and don't do at the table have served us well for many years. Interestingly, we often have extra people at our table, friends of our kids, family friends, or relatives, and they really do enjoy the things we do at dinnertime. They feel like they are a part of the family.

In this next section we're going to encourage you to overcome some of the more common obstacles to eating together.

AVOIDING DINNERTIME DISRUPTIONS

Eating together won't just happen—it takes planning and perseverance. You may have to fight like a lioness to preserve it. Trust us, it's worth every ounce of effort you put into it.

Here are fifteen excuses we've heard about the impossibility of insisting on a consistent, daily family meal. If you see yourself in several of these statements, don't despair, but work to conquer them one by one.

1. *"My kids don't like what I cook—they're picky eaters. It's not worth my time and effort to prepare a meal."* It *is* worth the effort to prepare meals and eat as a family. Someone is sure to enjoy what you've cooked, so keep trying a rotation of different meals and eventually everyone will find a favorite. Picky eating should be discouraged as much as possible. We've got to teach our kids to try to enjoy many different foods. It's much better for their health and their future. Experts say that it takes anywhere from ten to fifteen exposures to a new food before it is readily accepted.

   One other interesting tidbit we recently found—breast milk slightly changes flavor depending on what the mother ate four to six hours previously. Breast-fed babies are accustomed to a variety of tastes, whereas formula-fed infants get the same flavor at every feeding. Could an increase in breast-fed babies bring about a reduction in picky eaters?

2. *"We're always at church for various activities and don't have time to eat together in the evenings."* Church-related events (or any other good activities, for

that matter) can unintentionally destroy a family. Many churches today focus on segregating families into various age groups with everyone going in separate directions, rather than offering family-centered activities. You must make choices to keep your family a priority. So, unless you're a clergyman, family mealtime should be a higher priority than church activities.

3. *"My kids' club activities occur in the late afternoon or early evening."* You simply can't allow these activities to disrupt your dinner schedule every night of the week. One of our family rules was that extracurricular activities could be scheduled only one night each week. Additionally, until the age of fifteen, each child could be involved in only one activity besides school. Try contacting the leaders and ask to change meeting times. We've done it and sometimes we prevail. Your other options are to eat an earlier or later dinner or to find a different activity for your kids to be involved in.

4. *"My teens' work schedules conflict with sitting down to dinner."* We've dealt with this issue also. If your teens absolutely have to work a shift that overlaps the dinner hour, talk with your teen and his or her manager about doing it less frequently—perhaps once each week—even in the summer. It might be helpful to find a job where your teen can work afternoon shifts or after an early dinner. We've helped two of our kids negotiate this issue and both times they received the schedules they wanted. One employer actually changed a scheduled shift time permanently. We believe all teens should work, but limiting it to two or three shifts per week during the school year should allow them to earn enough money for their needs.

5. *"My spouse has a very demanding job, works long hours, and can't make it home for dinner very often."* We worked through this issue together and came to a better place for our family. Perhaps you can convince your hardworking spouse to limit late nights to only one or two each week. If he or she absolutely must work later, then consider bringing the work home to do after the kids are in bed. No job is worth the sacrifice of time with your family. Exceptions to this might be a doctor in residency or a CPA during tax season. All exceptions should be for a limited, well-defined time.

6. *"We both work outside the home full-time and are too exhausted to prepare a meal each night. If I buy prepackaged things like taquitos, the kids can fix themselves dinner."* Whoa—this sounds like an abandon-ship mentality, and the family's going down to a watery grave. When both spouses work outside the home, meals need to be planned for and prepared the night or weekend before. Spouses should take turns cooking and coordinating dinner. And the kids should be included in preparing and cleaning up the meal. Families have to work together like championship teams instead of letting meals become a solo exhibition. With a little teamwork, you can pull off a sit-down dinner and get some "me time" too. While prepackaged meals are not our preference, if your budget can afford them, fine—just eat them together as a family.

7. *"It's just too overwhelming to think about shopping each day for a meal, then cooking it, and then cleaning up afterward."* If we had to shop and cook from scratch every day, we'd be overwhelmed too. Many families are finding it beneficial to modify the once-a-month cooking concept we use to prepare about fifteen dinners in one day. Some folks cook once a week, others once every two weeks. No matter how you do it, having meals (main dishes) prepared and sitting in the freezer makes dinner prep much easier. Shopping can easily be done once a week if you take fifteen minutes to plan a menu— even if it's only for dinners. Just remember that learning and perfecting a new skill takes some time, but it will eventually pay off.

8. *"I'm home with toddlers, infants, or preschoolers every day, day in and day out, so even if I wanted to, it seems impossible to pull something together each night."* By the time our fifth child came along, we were using playpens and baby back-packs to help carve out time for dinner preparation. These two tools were lifesavers. We also assigned some of the older kids to play with the younger ones. They'd pull out a special box of toys, reserved for use only before dinner each night. A couple of their favorites were paint-with-water coloring books used inside the house or sidewalk chalk used outside—all of the kids had a great time. Another lifesaver is once-a-month cooking. Remember, the meals don't have to be gourmet quality, just balanced nutritionally. Simply having them prepared in advance will take a lot of the stress out of your day.

9. *"I have absolutely no cooking skills, so preparing a dinner is beyond my ability."* Early on Annette felt this way too, but she resolved to change. And so can you. Start with a simple seven-day menu until you learn to "really cook." Repeat it several times and slowly add new recipes as you build your repertoire of meals. Start off with something as simple as the sample dinner menu below. (There is a different dinner menu in Chapter 2, "The Power of the Plan.")

Sample Dinner Menu

> *Monday:* Macaroni & cheese with pickles
> *Tuesday:* Tacos and rice
> *Wednesday:* Spaghetti & meatballs with salad
> *Thursday:* BBQ chicken in the slow cooker with baked potatoes and frozen green beans
> *Friday:* Soup with muffins
> *Saturday:* Hamburgers, buns, corn, and carrots
> *Sunday:* Chicken and rice with broccoli

10. *"The family I grew up in didn't make dinnertime a priority, so I don't even know what it's supposed to look like!"* Okay, it looks like this: a terrific meal, with everyone taking turns talking (well, we're talking about the ideal; sometimes at our house it gets pretty rowdy and we need a chairman to keep things in order) about what they experienced that day, a little teasing, some bantering, maybe a little arguing, lots of laughing, and sometimes even crying about something sad. Often we include reading short stories, telling stories or jokes, and playing games.

11. *"I don't have a mother, mother-in-law, or anyone else I'm close to who can coach me through learning this cooking thing, so how can I possibly do this?"* There are hundreds of cookbooks in the library that will take you through every step of the way. Don't be afraid of failure; every great cook has a few flops. Annette's mom told her, "If you can read, you can cook."

12. *"Restaurants are on every corner, and besides, we have the extra money, so why not eat there?"* Just because you *can* doesn't mean you *should*. Eating

at restaurants takes a lot of time, provides limited privacy for family conversations, and simply wastes money. If someone in your family learns to cook, the food would be tastier and healthier. We've never had a case of food poisoning in our home in the past twenty-eight years—can that be said for the restaurants in your area? How much more could you put in your retirement plan, college savings plan, or pay on your debts or mortgage if you ate out less often? Try cutting your eating out in half for one month and see how much excess you can generate. If you truly don't need the money you've saved, donate it to a local food bank or other worthy charity.

13. *"Fast food is not nearly as expensive as a sit-down restaurant, so what's wrong with this as an alternative?"* This alternative involves all of the reasons above and will compromise your health too. If you have young kids and feed them a regular diet of fast-food fare, you'll also blow the opportunity to teach them to eat a variety of foods.

14. *"My kitchen is so small, and I have so few cooking implements, I couldn't possibly cook a full meal!"* Size isn't the issue; neither is the number of gadgets you have. Annette hates kitchen gadgets and tries to use as few as possible. If you try once-a-month cooking, you may need to set up a card table or two for extra counter space. It only takes a few basic things to get started cooking: cutting board, dish soap, dish towels, glass baking dishes 13 x 9-inches or 8 x 8-inches, a good set of pots and pans (garage sale fare is okay), ladle, measuring cups, mixing bowls, pot holders, sharp cutting knife, slotted spoon, spatula, sponge, and wooden spoons, etc. Not one of these items is overly expensive, and many can be found at discounters, thrift stores, or garage sales.

15. *"I get absolutely no support or gratefulness from my family, so why should I break my back trying to pull this off day in and day out?"* This is when you have to decide what is really important to *you*. Annette sees family mealtimes as a cornerstone to a healthy family. No one person in a family should be breaking his or her back over anything. Enlist the kids' help and lavish plenty of praise. Minimize your concern for spotlessness—kids will be messy at first. Remember you are training them in teamwork, not merely using them as slave labor. Turn off the TV and the computers if you have to. You can even

go so far as to take away iPods and cell phones until the meal is completely prepared, eaten, and cleaned up. If they complain, you can tell them that Annette said this was how we do it in our house.

Standing Firm for Family

We have some dear friends who run a very demanding family athletic business. They struggle desperately to get family time with their two teens. A while back they were over at our house for dinner and Annette was drawn into a debate between the teens and their parents. The parents wanted Sunday to be their family day—no friends, just their family. Their kids thought they'd be considered absolute freaks by their peers and wanted to be able to see their friends on Sunday. Then the kids made a tactical error. They said, "No one does what you're asking us to do!" Annette smiled and said, "That is exactly what *our* family does every Sunday and for dinner almost every night!" That ended the debate and the teens just sulked away, licking their wounds.

Family mealtimes are important and worth fighting for. We laugh and yell and pray and shout at dinnertime. Sometimes we even jump for . . . well, we jump to avoid the glass of water spilled by some arm-swinging storyteller talking about their day. It's worth every bit of effort put into it, and it's never boring—that's for sure.

Here's a tip from one of our website visitors—with more options for stimulating conversation at the dinner table:

Laughter in the Dining Room

We collect a whole lot of jokes or other funny stories from The *New Yorker* or *Reader's Digest*. We each take turns being the person to read them. They make us laugh and aid digestion and table conversation. It makes dinner a fun family time. A couple of favorite books I draw from are: *Politically Correct Bedtime Stories* and poetry from *Where the Sidewalk Ends*.

ANNE MARIE—HOUSTON, TX

We asked our kids what they liked most about our family mealtimes. Here's what three of them said:

Abbey loves playing Mad Libs—especially when we have friends over. She said, "It's the most _____ game ever!" (Just in case you need some help, an adjec-
_(insert adjective here)
tive describes a noun—words like: *cold, gooey, smelly, awesome, fantastic*)

Becky shared that whenever she had friends over for dinner, they'd say that it was a "real experience." We think that's a good thing—it must have been, because they keep coming back.

Joe said that he loves to tell jokes or stories. Especially jokes or stories that get Mom laughing so hard that she can't breathe!

Making family mealtime a priority will be a constant battle. You can't let your guard down . . . ever. Will your efforts permanently scar your kids or your spouse? Will they miss out on the good things that life has to offer? Our experience is that they may miss out on a few of the fun things, but as you persist, your entire family will discover not something that is good, but something that is better. A strong family bond in the short and long run will be of more value than all of the Little League, soccer, dance, and academic trophies and awards they'll ever earn. And it will be worth more than all of the overtime and bonuses you think you need from working extra hours. When all of the paychecks have been cashed and spent, the certificates have been long filed away, and the trophies have gathered dust, family relationships will still be strong and of greater importance and relevance. Invest in your family mealtime and you'll reap rewards for decades to come.

WHAT YOU CAN DO NOW ABOUT FAMILY MEALTIMES

 Timid Mouse

1. Track your restaurant habit for two weeks and find out how many times you eat out.

2. If you're doing the fast-food restaurant thing, bring it home and eat it together, sitting at the table as a family.

3. If your kids aren't proficient with mealtime manners, such as, using napkins or silverware properly and asking politely for things to be passed to them, start now. Make a game out of it and lavish lots of praise and rewards when they succeed. Good table manners can win a job or even a spouse.

 Wise Owl

1. Track your restaurant habit and set a goal to cut that number in half for one month.

2. Gather some resources to make at-home mealtime more interesting. Select age-appropriate books, games, and stories to share with the family.

3. If your kids are older and dinnertime has too many schedule conflicts, settle on another time during the day when you can connect.

4. Start reading aloud a book or a series of books to your family at dinnertime.

 Amazing Ant

1. Help one or more of your kids to plan and cook a meal to share with the family. Be sure to take pictures and brag about it to all of your relatives.

2. Learn to cook some traditional or ethnic meals from your family's past. Then teach your kids to cook them.

3. Invite a family friend with an interesting life story to come to dinner and share in your family mealtime. (We've invited lots of foreign missionaries to our home—their stories are always encouraging and life changing!)

9

Feeding Your Kids
for Less

T he USDA says that it will cost over $200,000 to raise your child from birth to age seventeen. They base this figure on the "fact" that every child requires so many square feet in your house, a certain amount of cubic feet in a car (on payments of course), a predetermined amount of food (the same for every child, of course—especially Cocoa Krispies), and designer clothes from birth to high school graduation. We aren't going to tackle the designer clothes in this chapter (we already did that in our first book, *America's Cheapest Family Gets You Right on the Money*), but we are going to tackle the expenses related to feeding your kids and how you can save a boodle in this one area.

Most of society looks at children as a liability—they cost you money, and lots of it. We have a different attitude. We view our kids as an asset—kind of like farmers and ranchers did hundreds of years ago. Once our kids start walking, we incorporate them into the everyday workings of our household with age-appropriate chores and activities. Initially the chores and activities take twice as long, but after a while, the kids become proficient at it and some even do a better job than we do. Our goal is not to get free labor from them, but to train them in the skills they'll need to survive and thrive when they have families of their own.

When it comes to feeding our family, we get the kids involved too. No, we don't take them shopping with us very often before they are old enough to really help, but we do involve them in many other aspects of the food cycle in our house. From storing it, to cooking it, to eating it, to cleaning it up—they are involved.

But before we share some of the ways we involve our kids, we want to offer some ideas on dealing with two of the more expensive feeding times in a child's life: the infant stage and the teen years. If you don't have a handle on these expenses you'll be driven to the brink of:

☐ bankruptcy
☐ homicide
☐ the drive-through lane at McDonald's
(Please select only one.)

FEEDING YOUR BABY

If you've got an infant in your home, your menu planning takes on a special twist. The great thing is that you have options. You can go with formula, breast feed, or a combination of both. You can buy prepared baby food, make your own, or do a combination of these also. The U.S. Department of Health Services reports that 68.4 percent of women breast-feed their infants. This number is up over 30 percent from 1990 statistics. The number of moms choosing to nurse their children until six months of age has increased from 18 to 31 percent in the same period. Not only is nursing free (with the exception that mom has to feed herself well to stay healthy), but it is much better for your child than bottle-feeding. We've never regretted going this route. With average annual costs for formula ranging from $1,500 to $2,000, it's really worth considering. Here are more ways to save on feeding your infant.

~~~

Nursing Benefits

If we look at it from a purely financial perspective, it is much cheaper to nurse a baby than not. I was able to nurse our second baby, but not our first. Many people supported my decision to try again and it was a totally different experience—I would encourage every mom to seriously consider it. Take a class, get support from your spouse and friends, and then go for it. Every week you nurse reduces formula costs. Also, spilled breast milk does not stain nearly the way formula can, so you'll save on cleaning costs too. If you can't nurse, you can't, but if you can, wow! What a way to save!

ANN—BRIDGEVILLE, PA

To learn more about breast-feeding, visit LaLecheLeague.org. We differ with their ideas for setting schedules for babies and a few other issues, but their feeding information is right on.

~~~

Formula Savings

To save money on formula, contact the manufacturer and get on their mailing list—they'll usually send you coupons for their products.

SUSAN—WINCHESTER, VA

~~~

DIY Baby Food

Making my own baby food saved a lot of money. I used regular ice cube trays to freeze pureed fruit, veggies, or even casseroles that the rest of the family ate. I stored the food by type in zippered bags and pulled out two or three cubes for each meal. I could use two or three of the same type, or mix different foods together for variety. The book *First Meals* by Annabel Karmel describes the process and has some great ideas for every stage of feeding.

Erin—Phoenix, AZ

We hardly bought any "real" baby food for our kids—maybe a few jars when we had "killer" coupons. They loved puffed rice and wheat cereals, which are inexpensive and virtually melt in kids' mouths. As they grew teeth and showed interest in eating, we mashed some of the food we were serving during our meal and gave them little bits to chew on. We were always careful to introduce only one new food at a time and to watch for any type of adverse reaction. This is also a great way to minimize the picky-eater syndrome we mentioned in Chapter 2.

Feeding your baby doesn't need to be a huge expense or take hours and hours of preparation each week. Hanging out with like-minded parents who can give you even more ideas about feeding your baby is another great way to ensure your savings and sanity.

Don't think you're out of the woods when Junior is able to eat table food though. You'll have a few years when the cost to feed your child is reasonable, but then he'll enter the gulping stage—the teen years. That's the time when you need to have a locked refrigerator where you store food for family meals or it will all mysteriously disappear (just kidding). But don't despair, there is hope; your food budget can survive with a teen in the house.

FEEDING A BOTTOMLESS PIT: SNACKS FOR TEENS

How do you feed a bottomless pit? We're talking about those teens with "hollow legs." Remember when they were babies and we fed them every two hours? Well, the two-hour feedings start all over again in the teen years. You want to provide nutritious snacking food without going broke, but how? By the time your kids reach their teens, if you're like many parents, your brain is just plain tired. You've weathered the trials of toddlerhood; you've seen them grow through three pairs of shoes in a year and wear through even more pairs of jeans. You've spent hours on your knees bathing them; you've powdered, changed, and rocked. They've grown and are able to do more and more on their own—they're almost on autopilot. Then one day they come to you with that crazed look in their eyes and you know that if you don't think up something fast, they're going to eat everything in the house that has a hint of sugar in it. It will be like a swarm of locusts descending on a field of grain—nothing will be left except a couple of rocks. And certainly not a single scoop of ice cream. To ward off a plague of biblical proportions you've got to be well armed. Take a few minutes to memorize this list of snack options . . . okay, don't memorize it, your brain is already overloaded. Just post it on the refrigerator for quick access in moments of panic.

Here's a list of things we do to fend off the "munchies." Remember a little suggestion can go a long way to distracting a hunger-possessed teen.

- **Fruit in season**
  Summer: cherries, melons, peaches, nectarines, plums, and apricots
  Fall: pears and apples (a special treat for apples is to cut them in quarters and sprinkle cinnamon sugar on top or dip in peanut butter)
  Winter: all types of citrus
  Spring: strawberries
  If you have your own trees (apple, peach, pear, and apricot)—take your bumper crop of fruit and dry some to store for snacking throughout the year.

- **Hard-boiled eggs**. We store them in specially marked egg cartons to avoid cracking the wrong ones.
- **Bananas** cut in slices with peanut butter
- **Celery** with peanut butter and raisins (ants on a log)
- **Nuts**. These can be expensive, so stock up when on sale.
- **Homemade trail mix**. Include things like peanuts, almonds, walnuts, raisins, sunflower seeds, edamame (dried soybeans), M&M's, granola, and whatever else they like.
- **Pickles**. We buy spears in gallon jars.

- **Popcorn** from scratch, not microwave. Sometimes we use an air popper—they can usually be found at thrift stores or garage sales. Margarine and salt make it great; add a little sugar or honey and you've got kettle corn. We also pop it with hot oil in a large sauce pot, but for the sake of safety, encourage kids to use an air popper.
- **Pretzels**. Some of the warehouse clubs sell huge bags.
- **Yogurt** with fruit mixed in.
- **Pumpkin seeds** roasted from free pumpkins collected at Halloween time.
- **Quick breads and muffins**. We bake banana, pumpkin, zucchini, and other quick breads. We make muffins three dozen at a time, half to freeze and half to eat this week. Tip: Remember if you've got bananas that are turning brown and mushy, put them in a zippered bag and store them in the freezer. You can use them for banana bread or for smoothies. (See some of these recipes in the Bonus Material at the end of the book.)
- **Smoothies** are a great way to use up aging fruit. We mix together crushed ice, fresh fruit, milk, and a little jelly. Protein powder can be added for extra nutrition. Other "mix-ins" include pineapple juice (from canned pineapple), older bananas, oranges, peaches, and yogurt. We avoid pears and apples; they tend to make the smoothie grainy.
- **String cheese**. We stock up when it is on sale. Because it is vacuum-sealed and processed, it stores well for months.
- **Sunflower seeds**. Buy or grow your own.
- **Tortilla chips and salsa**. Purchase 5-pound bags at warehouse clubs and use coupons for the salsa.

As you can see, snacks don't have to come prepackaged and be potato chips or Cheetos, no matter what the kids say. Look for items that can be purchased in bulk or made in bulk and easily stored. Involve your teens in assembling a list for your refrigerator. And if you include them in preparing some of the nutritious snack foods they eat, they'll also be learning to cook and plan ahead. You can help them grow up healthy and fill their hollow limbs without it costing you an arm and a leg.

INVOLVE YOUR KIDS IN THE FOOD CYCLE

Steve was listening to a radio broadcast many years ago when a child psychologist said something that stuck with both of us ever since. The psychologist mentioned that many parents he worked with felt guilty for asking their kids to do chores. He said, "The greatest form of play for a child is working with his parents." Hmmmm, so it doesn't hurt our kids to teach them to work? We won't scar them for life if we give them chores to do? . . . Hmmmm, it's actually like playing to them, when they work side by side with their parents? Well, we wouldn't say that they equate working with us as playing, but we have noticed as we've worked with our kids in the kitchen and around the house, that they have developed a quiet confidence, a self-reliance, and a sense of accomplishment. They know that they can do just about anything they set their minds to and also many things they didn't want to set their minds to. Some of the tasks our kids help us with in the kitchen are:

Dishwasher jobs. On a weekly cycle our kids rotate between emptying the top rack of the dishwasher, silverware, and bottom rack. We start them putting away nonbreakable items as young as four or five years old. For safety, we wash all sharp knives by hand. This not only protects the kids, but also the wooden handles of the knives. We keep track of who does which jobs each week on a kitchen calendar.

Cereal boxes. When we stock up on cereal, we always label the top of the box with the month and year it was purchased. It's an easy job for a child with good handwriting. Once labeled, the boxes are stored in the pantry room.

School lunch. To save money, your kids can help prepare their own lunches. Avoid using prepared, prepackaged lunch meals—they're really expensive. Younger kids can prepackage snack foods in zippered bags; older kids can make sandwiches or scoop yogurt into smaller containers. With your kids' help you can create a rotating lunch menu and post it on the refrigerator.

Whenever we plan a day trip or long outing, we almost always pack a lunch. Our kids all know how to pitch in and get the job done quickly.

Coupon preparation. Kindergarten-aged kids love to use scissors—especially on their hair. Giving them a productive and positive task like clipping coupons not only makes them feel grown-up, but also helps develop fine motor skills.

As they get older they can help sort coupons and weed out expired ones too.

Abbey is our fifth child. She learned by watching her older siblings and imitating them. We asked her what she remembers about learning to clip coupons. She said, "Mom used to cut a little slit where I was supposed to clip, and I would just cut around the coupon. I felt bigger because I was helping. Of course, I also thought that since I was "legally" allowed to use scissors on coupons, that I could also use them on other things too . . . like my hair and my doll's clothes. I got in trouble for that, but not for clipping coupons!"

Cooking meals. In the cooking chapter we briefly mentioned how we involved our kids in the kitchen. Cooking is an important life skill that we want to pass on to our kids, so we start them young. When Steve made humongous batches of pancakes, the kids helped get out the ingredients and every kid (especially the little ones) wanted a turn using the hand mixer. Of course, you may need to guide little hands to keep from having batter all over the kitchen. And on cooking day everyone pitches in (once they're old enough) with age-appropriate tasks. Our kids help wash veggies, grind beef, dice turkey, cube beef, cut up green peppers, slice celery, peel onions, mix meat loaf, roll meatballs, make dough for shepherd's pie, label meals, wash dishes, and lots of other things. You should see their faces when we serve a meal they've helped prepare! It's a priceless thing.

Even when a dinner is pulled out of the freezer, there are usually veggies or a salad and another side dish to prepare. Young kids can tear up lettuce or wash carrots or potatoes. Older ones can cut the veggies and even cook them. Now our kids (and a somewhat kitchen-challenged husband) can prepare the entire meal if Mom isn't home to get it going.

As they've gotten older, each of our kids has learned to cook, if not an entire meal at least several components. Both Abbey and Becky have prepared entire themed meals for our family. And John made some special cherry turnovers on an outdoor fire one Thanksgiving—it was a recipe he had learned on a Boy Scout outing. Joe has developed his own specialty—making French fries—mmmm, they're as good as the ones from McDonald's!

Involving our kids in meal preparation has provided great opportunities to discuss good nutrition, teach planning and cooking skills, and minimize their dislike of many foods.

Table setting. Just like dishwasher jobs, we've divided setting the table into two categories: plates and silverware; and cups and napkins. When it's time for dinner, each child knows his duty for the week and does it almost flawlessly.

Kitchen cleanup. We all help wash dishes. It's amazing how quickly a huge mountain of pots and pans, used on once-a-month cooking day, can be reduced to nothing when we all work together. Younger kids can easily dry and help put things away. Older ones can wash and rinse.

Your kids are one of your greatest assets. If you take the time to involve them in the food cycle at your house, you'll not only lighten your load, but you'll also be preparing them for a life of healthy independence (and good eating habits!). Expect much from your kids and you won't be disappointed.

WHAT YOU CAN DO NOW ABOUT INVOLVING YOUR KIDS IN THE FOOD CYCLE

 Timid Mouse

1. If you have an infant, research making your own baby food.
2. If you have several kids, assign them age-appropriate tasks for helping with the dishwasher and setting the table.
3. Let your kids help you clip and sort coupons.

 Wise Owl

1. Make a list of available snack foods and post it on your refrigerator for a quick reference for your kids.
2. Have your kids help you prepackage snack foods and items for school lunches.
3. Involve your kids in meal preparation and cleanup.

 Amazing Ant

1. With your kids, plan a five-day rotation of lunches that they can help pack.
2. Work with your older kids so they can cook an entire meal for the family.

10

Where and How to
Eat Out for Less

Weare realists. We know that even the best-laid plans, menus, dinners in the freezer, and family dinner hours can fall victim to the unexpected. Whether it's exhaustion from a grinding schedule of errands and kids' activities, or unexpected emergencies, or it's 5 p.m. and you haven't even thought about dinner yet, there are still ways to feed your family without spending a fortune.

It shouldn't happen often, but when your dinner plans go up in flames, you need to have some resources in your back pocket so you don't end up blowing your budget. We'll share some of our resources and those of some of our frugal friends. And we'll offer some ideas to get the best deals at sit-down restaurants too!

Just because this chapter is included in this book doesn't mean that we're encouraging you to go out to a restaurant every night. So please don't post a blog or Tweet and say that America's Cheapest Family told you to stop cooking at home. We simply want to arm you with enough information so that you can make wise choices when life throws your dinner plans a curveball.

TEN WAYS TO "DO DINNER"

Feeding your family can be accomplished in myriad ways ranging from ridiculously expensive to really cheap. But expensive isn't always better, cheap isn't always bad, and eating out isn't always faster than eating in!

We think nothing beats a home-cooked meal or just eating at home (that is, unless someone else does the cleanup). But if you're having a rough day and cooking from scratch is out of the question, we've got a few other options for you. In reality, there are a few times each month when either our schedule is so hectic or we're so tuckered out that we choose other options rather than cooking from scratch. Because we usually have prepared meals in the freezer (thanks to once-a-month cooking), the other options are seldom exercised. Here is our Top Ten list from most expensive to most economical ways to calm your growling tummy.

1. **Sit-down restaurants**. Call for a reservation and pay full price plus tip.
2. **Sit-down restaurants with a two-for-one coupon**. Cuts the price a bit, but still includes a tip. We use the Entertainment Book, Restaurants.com, or a coupon from a mailer. (Or find a place where kids eat free with an adult-purchased meal.)
3. **Carryout from a restaurant**. Chinese is our favorite, but we've heard that there are other options (we can't imagine what they would be, though).
4. **Carryout fast food—pick it up and bring it home**. For us, this includes pizza (special deal or with a coupon) and fried or rotisserie chicken from a grocery store deli counter.
5. **Fast food.** McDonald's, Taco Bell, Wendy's, Burger King, Chick-fil-A, Subway, etc. If we go to a fast-food restaurant, we usually order from the dollar menu (if they have one) and skip the drinks and fries, or we use a discount coupon,
6. **Frozen-food section/prepared meals**. This is the largest and fastest growing section in the grocery store. They do the cooking; you just reheat. We think it sounds a lot like leftovers—but most people won't believe us. These

include TV dinners, frozen pizza, stuffed pockets, sandwiches, and the list goes on forever.

7. **Easy-to-cook prepared meals**. These meals, from your grocer's meat or frozen-food section, require a little more work but are basically prepared for you, including stir-fry in a bag, chicken kiev, chicken cordon bleu, stuffed pork chops, etc.

8. **Canned meals: SpaghettiOs, canned beef stew, soups, or chili**. These aren't our first choice (because of their high sodium and preservative content), but stock a few cans in your pantry for those crazy days to avoid the drive-through.

9. **Easy throw-together meals**. Now you're cooking, but this is easy stuff. We're talking about roasted chicken breasts, a bag of frozen corn, and a bag of green salad—voilà—an instantly delicious meal. Or how about grilled steak or chops, baked potatoes, and a bag of frozen green beans? Easy enough, scrumptious, and cost effective.

10. **Send out an SOS**. If your mom lives nearby and you have a good relationship with her, ask if she can bring over a pot of chicken soup or bowl of pasta. In Italian families this is not an imposition, there's always extra food.

We eat out at restaurants on our date nights and a few times each year when we have a family vacation, a weekend alone, or on Annette's birthday. To be honest, the food is okay, service ranges from laughable to fair, but nothing compares to the comforts of home and Annette's good cooking.

We've purposely kept this section short and sweet. We just want to give you food for thought. People often overspend because they're too stressed to think of other options. So make your own list of options, post it on your refrigerator, and next time you don't feel like cooking, take a minute and read down your list. You might just find a less expensive option that tastes great and is easier on your wallet.

If you keep your eyes open, there are always ways to get discounts on eating out, as this website visitor discovered:

Dinner Out for Less

I had two thousand frequent flyer miles on United Airlines that I had forgotten about. I was able to redeem them for $100 in credit at Restaurant.com.

Find out more at www.United.com and search for Restaurant.com dining certificates.

With Restaurant.com you purchase gift certificates for a discounted price and then when you go out, you only spend about $10 for $25 worth of food. Also, they have a "diners club." For $10 per month you get a $25 coupon and an additional gift certificate each month. Memberships are three, six, or twelve months in length. Also, CouponMom.com regularly sends out "discount" codes for Restaurant.com. I've received codes for as much as 80 percent off, and the gift certificates from Restaurant.com are good for a full year. Last Christmas that's what everyone got and it only cost me something like $8 for the whole family. This is the ONLY way we go out!

Jeannie—USA

EXPENSIVE ISN'T ALWAYS BEST

Since we started writing books and being interviewed on national TV shows, we've experienced a different way of living. No, we haven't changed what we buy or where we live, but we have traveled to New York and L.A. several times to appear on TV shows. We are usually given a food allowance per person each day. We normally buy some snack and breakfast foods to eat in the hotel room and end up going out to a restaurant for two meals each day.

One late night after five long hours of taping for an ABC *20/20* news special, we wandered the streets of New York looking for a restaurant near our hotel. In this part of Manhattan, not much was open and we didn't have anyone to direct us to a good restaurant. We were really hungry and we picked a nearby Portuguese / Spanish restaurant that was listed in our hotel's in-room guide. It looked popular, as there were a bunch of people at the bar watching soccer on TV and several people in the dining area of the small, white tableclothed restaurant.

We were hankering for a good steak-and-potatoes type of dinner. Six of us were eating that night (including two ravenous teenaged boys), so we ordered a plate of appetizers, main dishes, and soft drinks (it was a special occasion—normally we just drink water). Time passes slowly when you are hungry, and this night it was interminably slow. After about forty-five minutes the food finally arrived, and what met our eyes was not at all what we envisioned. The chicken was rubbery and swimming in a tomato and water sauce, the steaks looked like they had been boiled, and overall the food was just plain awful.

Our international dining experience is limited, consisting mainly of Chinese, Mexican, and lots of homemade Italian and Greek foods. We didn't know if what we were experiencing was authentic Portuguese or Spanish food, so we choked it down and waited for the bill. We ended up spending $168 for a subpar meal (an astronomical amount in our minds—but probably cheap by New York standards).

On our next trip to New York, we found a diner on a back street in the theater district and it has become one of our absolute favorites. It's nothing fancy, vinyl booths, simple lighting, no tablecloths, paper napkins, and a huge menu. But the service, the food, and the prices are absolutely fantastic. We can completely gorge ourselves with main dishes and dessert, have food left over, and not spend over $100 for six of us. The owner is Greek, our favorite waiter is Italian, and the food is delicious (that's a combination that you just can't beat!). If you're ever in New York, you've just got to try the Cosmic Diner—888 Eighth Ave. (Fifty-Second and Eighth). You'll love it too! (www.CosmicDinerNYC.com).

The point of this story is that price is not always an indicator of quality, and sometimes the best dining deals are in the least likely places.

We are not your average family. We enjoy nice things, but we don't have to eat at the fanciest restaurants or spend a lot of money to be happy. Are you average?

According to the Bureau of Labor Statistics, the average family has 2.5 people in it, with 1.3 wage earners, and spends $6,133 on food. Of that total, $2,668 is spent on food eaten away from home—restaurants. That's over $200 each month! And if you're a couple with no kids at home or if you're single, you're likely to spend even more than that. Based on these figures we're definitely not average, nor do we want to be. We eat out occasionally, but we don't do it like most "normal" people.

EATING "OUT" FOR LESS THAN $18

"Eighteen dollars or less for a family of six to eat out? You've got to be kidding." Nope, that's our threshold for "eating out." Look, just because fast food is "fast" doesn't mean it's cheap. We've stood in line at some of these restaurants and have regularly seen a family of three or four drop $50 or more for burgers, fries, and drinks. Fast food is no bargain at $12 to $15 a person. And after hearing about our New York dining experience, you might think we've changed our ways and are eating at more expensive restaurants now. Nope—nothing could be further from the truth.

About two times each month, when Annette is tired of cooking or after our once-a-month cooking day, we utilize one of several fast and easy dinner options to feed our family. But we don't go out to eat; we buy dinner and bring it home.

Here's our list of fast-food resources:

Option 1: Fried chicken. A nearby grocery chain, Albertson's, has absolutely the best deal in our area—and the chicken tastes pretty good too! The regular price is $4.99 for eight pieces of chicken. It goes on sale for $3.99 at least once each quarter and many times around holidays. We supplement with a loaf of French bread for 99 cents and either a bagged salad or coleslaw from the deli. Total price, $10 to $12 dollars. If you want a healthier option, many store delis are now selling roasted chickens (either whole or pieces) for about the same price as fried chicken.

Option 2: Arby's. In the mail, we regularly receive coupon ads touting their specials. The best deal we've found is the "Five for $5" deals. The downside is you have to buy the roast beef sandwiches in quantities of five, so we usually buy ten and sometimes will have one left over for the next day's lunch. Add a bag of tater tots and either bagged salad or unsweetened applesauce and you've got a quick, easy, and inexpensive dinner for about $14.

Option 3: McDonald's or Burger King. No Happy Meals here. We only buy the 99 cent or $1 specials. Add some home-cooked tater tots or baked potatoes and pickles or fresh fruit and you've got dinner for $13. When the kids were younger, Steve came up with a cute idea for a special fast-food night out—we'd take the kids to the "King and Queen." It sounded really exciting for the kids and it was an economical, fun time for us too. We took them to Burger King for dinner and bought items off the dollar menu, then for dessert we went to a nearby Dairy Queen and bought inexpensive ice cream treats.

Option 4: Pizza. There are always pizza chains running discount deals. We go with whoever has the best special sale. Most of the time it's Little Caesars' large, one-topping pizza for $5 each, other times it's Domino's three medium pizzas for $5.55 each. We can feed our family with three medium one-topping pizzas—of course, the ravenous teenage boys get a couple of extra pieces. To complete the meal, we add bagged salad, applesauce, or dill pickles—$17.

Option 5: Chinese buffet carryout. When the kids were smaller, we used to go to a nearby Chinese buffet and order three dinners to-go in those large square Styrofoam containers, for a total of between $12 and $16. Each one weighed about five pounds and three of them easily fed the entire family. Now, with price increases and three teenagers, we usually need to purchase four meals, but this is still an affordable option especially if you can pick up the meal early and get the lunch price. We don't put any rice in the containers—it takes up too much space—and we'd rather fill the containers with tastier Chinese favorites. It's easy to cook up a pot of rice or pull some out of the refrigerator and reheat it. Total cost $16 to $20.

Another option for those days when the cooking blues hit was sent in by some dear frugal friends of ours:

~~~

Fast Food for Fatigued Families

With three kids and homeschooling, my life has been busy. I generally cook from scratch, but some days I'm just too tired. So as not to buy fast food or the like, I have resorted to buying some ready-made foods on sale to keep on hand. Items such as frozen pizza, canned tamales mixed with canned chili, macaroni and cheese, or other canned soup make an easy meal. This saves money and the kids think it is a treat.

CHRISSY—PHOENIX, AZ

Just be sure you conquer the picky-eater syndrome. If you have, you'll be able to pick one dining option and your whole family will be on board to enjoy it!

So there you have it—the next time your dinner plans take a dive, don't picture a sit-down restaurant as your first option; think of "eating out" at home as a family. And if you follow our advice, dining out will be less of an emergency and you'll be able to walk away with dinner in the bag, money in your pocket, and a smile on your face.

We realize that fast food doesn't appeal to everyone. And there are times when you'll want to go to a nice sit-down restaurant for a special occasion. Even then you don't need to spend a fortune. Here's what we do when we go out for dinner.

DINING OUT FOR LESS MONEY AND MORE ENJOYMENT

It used to be a monthly date night—especially when the kids were younger and Steve was working out of the house for long hours. It was a great time for quiet conversation, some planning and dreaming—without any interruptions. Now that we both work out of the house, spend just about every day together, and are able to have some longer conversations without being asked twenty questions by inquisitive toddlers, we don't feel a need to go out as often. But when we do, you know we're not going to pay retail. Here are the things we do as a matter of course to minimize our dining-out expenses.

Use a Coupon

There are always coupons in the mail, newspaper, on Restaurant.com, and in the Entertainment Book. Using a two-for-one coupon doesn't mean your entire bill is half price—it just means that you get a second entrée for free. If your coupon says one menu item is free, be careful to clarify with your server or you could be paying full price for your entrées and getting your drink for free. Remember, you're still going to have to pay for tip, tax, and any extras you order. But it is a good way to cut $10 to $20 off your bill. Be sure to tip your server generously on the total bill before the discount.

When using a two-for-one coupon issued by someone other than the restaurant, we usually call in advance and ask if they are still honoring these specific coupons. There have been a couple of times when, due to a management change, specific coupons were no longer being accepted. In those cases, we changed our dining plans.

We keep our clipped restaurant coupons in an orange file folder next to our Entertainment Book. It makes finding discount dinner options much faster and easier.

Keep the Drinks Simple

Alcohol puts us both to sleep, and too much caffeine (from sodas, teas, or coffee) can keep us awake all night. So we tend to avoid both when we go out. Our drink of preference is water with a slice of lemon.

When we were celebrating our twenty-first anniversary in Cancún, we ordered dinner at a nice restaurant and asked for water (*agua*) with lemon. We were surprised when the waiter brought back glasses with a slice of lime perched on the rim of the glass. We learned that in this particular Spanish dialect, the word for lime is *limón* (lee MON). If we truly wanted lemon in our water we should have asked for *lima*.

No matter how you say it, in most restaurants water is free, unless you want the bottled type, and they usually don't charge for lemons either.

Watch for Up-Selling

Be on your guard when your server asks if you'd like something additional with your meal (cheese, avocado, etc.). Sometimes they are trying to up-sell, and you'll be charged an additional amount for their suggestion. We always ask, "How much does that cost?"

Find Early-Bird Specials

Many restaurants encourage dining off-peak hours by offering special discounts for early diners. One fancy hotel restaurant we ate at offered a discounted early-bird dinner along with a free dessert bar. We used a two-for-one coupon, enjoyed a fantastic dinner seated by a window that overlooked the golf course, and watched a beautiful sunset as we dined. Around our home early-bird discounts mean ordering between 5 p.m. and 6 p.m. Check with your local restaurants and see what they offer.

Split a Plate

Some restaurants are known for serving large portions. If that's the case, order one meal and an extra plate. There may be an additional fee for the plate.

Go Out for Dessert

One restaurant near our house serves a super-rich, super-chocolaty, delicious dessert—they call it mud pie. The slice is huge and so is the calorie count. Splitting a piece of mud pie saves more than just money and still tastes delicious.

If money is tight, but you still want to go out, make it a special occasion and do dessert. It's less expensive than a full meal, and still affords you a nice atmosphere and time to unwind. We try to avoid going during peak dining hours when tables are scarce.

Take Savings in the Bag

Many restaurants serve so much food that we can't or shouldn't eat it all. In those cases, we always ask for a doggy bag and take the delicious leftovers home. Think about it . . . a two-for-one meal that provides not only dinner, but lunch the following day . . . that's four for one!

Double-check the Check

Mistakes are common in restaurants. We always review the bill and make sure that we were charged correctly. But this is a two-way street; if we are undercharged, we always bring it to the server's attention.

OUR FIRST SPECIAL DINNER

Back in 1982 when Steve was still earning about $7 per hour as a graphic design paste-up artist, we planned a special dinner with some friends. It was going to be expensive—we calculated the cost to be around $30 per couple (about 4 percent of our monthly take-home pay)! We planned to go to Benihana's—a Japanese steak house where you sit in a group of eight or ten people around a teppanyaki table—a special grill where the chef prepares the meal in front of your group. We'd heard that these chefs perform daring deeds with their knives and put on quite a show.

It took us three months to save enough money to go on this extravagant date, but the fun we had, laughing and sharing the memory with our friends, still brings a smile to our faces to this day.

Don't just go out for dinner. Save for and anticipate a special experience that will create great memories for years to come.

We thought we had covered all of the options on where to eat inexpensively until we read these great tips:

Great Food Operations

Here's a great way to get a tasty meal for just a few bucks. Try out your local hospital cafeteria. Here is what I've had. For breakfast: Two eggs, toast, hash browns, and bacon for $2.50. Lunch is almost a better deal, hamburger, fries, and a 20-oz. drink for $2.50. Dinner prices range any-where from $4 to $6—the prime rib was delicious. They even give a 10 percent senior discount. We've heard the same thing from friends who have done this in other parts of the country while traveling in their RVs.

SYLVESTER—SCOTTSDALE, AZ

Dinner for Lunch?

When we get a craving for Chinese take-out food, we plan it for a day I can pick it up while already out on errands. I go during the restaurant's lunch hours. It costs about two-thirds the price of a dinner meal, and the lunch specials usually include extras such as soup or egg rolls that the dinner meal does not.

ANN—BRIDGEVILLE, PA

Speak Up for Cash

I like to pay with cash instead of using other methods. However, there have been several times when I've run into difficulties at a store or restaurant when paying the cashier. After I've handed them a $20 bill, they'll forget what I've given them and start making change for a ten! They swear that I only gave them a ten! This is really frustrating. Since it's my word against theirs, the business always seemed to win. So, I came up with an alternative strategy when paying.

Now when I pay the bill with a twenty, I say out loud, "And here Sir (or Ma'am) is my $20 bill that I'm paying with." I say this loud enough for my wife and usually several others to hear. No more mishaps and everyone stays honest. In all fairness, there are many "quick change" artists who do pay with a ten and insist that it was a twenty, so I can understand the retailers' caution.

Curtis—Spokane, WA

Here are some more tips for saving money when you are eating "on the road."

Take One for the Road

Years ago when we were just starting on our frugal trek, we discovered many ways that we were wasting money. One of them was soft drinks. When we'd go out for a weekend drive and get thirsty, we stopped at a fast-food place to get a soft drink. On a daily basis, it didn't seem like a lot of money, but on a monthly basis, it really started to add up. We decided to start taking our favorite drinks with us. A little planning in advance can really save dollars.

Mike—South Holland, IL

~

Food for the Long Haul

When we take car trips, rather than pay for expensive fast foods, we pack up a small cooler with healthy lunch favorites and snacks—fruit, vegetables, cheese, and drinks. Besides easing the stress on the pocketbook, we feel good about what we are putting in our bodies too!

KIM—KINGWOOD, TX

~

Very Smart Vacation Victuals

Limit eating out to one or two meals a day by staying in a hotel that offers a decent continental breakfast: cereal & milk, fruit, muffins, pastries, coffee & juice. Don't be afraid to ask for a detailed menu, hours it is served (e.g., 7 a.m. to 9 a.m.), and if it is replenished. Alternatively, stay in a place that has a kitchenette so you can cook some easy meals: cereal, toast and eggs, chicken Caesar salad, or a taco bar. Pack good snacks to nibble when you are out sightseeing, i.e., trail mix, jerky, nuts, dry cereal, canned fruit cups, or fresh fruit from a local market. Lastly, pack a water bottle like a Platypus or Camelback. Without the pouch, the bottles easily tuck into a smaller space; the water is a little warmer but still wet.

ALANA—REDMOND, WA

EATING ON VACATIONS

Just because you're traveling doesn't mean you have to eat out at a restaurant for every meal. Vacation dining can be really expensive for several reasons: you don't know the area or the restaurants; you have no cooking tools in your room; and you want some time off from meal preparations.

Here are four things we do to save when we travel.

1. **Coupons**. We order an Entertainment Book for the city we are traveling to. Usually Entertainment Books are half price in the summer, so the cost is minimal. As a result of the book, we have an idea of restaurants in the area with discount coupons to boot.

2. **Cook in**. If we're going to spend several days there, sometimes we buy a slow cooker. Most thrift stores have several. We did this on an extended vacation to Washington, D.C. The slow cooker was only $5 and it allowed us to prepare several lunch or dinner meals in our hotel room. When we headed home, we gave the slow cooker to a sweet young lady who worked at the front desk.

3. **"Free" breakfast**. If you stay at a hotel that offers a continental breakfast, for larger families this can save $30 or more per day.

4. **Eat out less**. We try to only eat out one meal each day. If your hotel room has a refrigerator, buy sandwich fixings and pack your lunch, then go to a restaurant for a nice sit-down dinner. Or bring in a meal to your hotel room and put your feet up after a long day of sightseeing.

You can see that with a little planning (yup, there's that word again) you can definitely get more food for your dining dollar. We know that most of you won't want to unreservedly adopt our dining philosophy (and we don't expect you to), but at the very least, consider changing the way you view restaurant food. Make it an occasion instead of a habit. Annette is such a great cook, and all of us know how to help with food preparation and cleanup, so we simply don't eat out that often. The infrequency of our dining out saves lots of money, hours of time, and helps make the times we do go to a restaurant much more memorable.

WHAT YOU CAN DO NOW ABOUT EATING OUT FOR LESS

 Timid Mouse

1. Make a list of your dinner options and post it on the refrigerator.
2. If your dinner plans go up in smoke, consult your list and try something healthier than going out for fast food.
3. Collect a bunch of restaurant discount coupons and put them in a file folder so that you can find them quicker and easier.

 Wise Owl

1. Try one of our $18-or-less dining-at-home options on a hectic night.
2. Save sit-down restaurant dining for a special occasion.
3. Research restaurants that have early-bird specials.
4. Use a two-for-one coupon or discounted gift certificate from Restaurants.com for dinner.
5. Think of doggy bags as a way of getting another meal out of your dining experience.

 Amazing Ant

1. Create a memory. Save for and plan a special dinner with friends at an expensive restaurant.
2. Plan your vacation dining by getting an Entertainment Book and planning to eat out only one meal per day.

11

Gardening—Grow It Yourself and Be Healthy

ccording to the National Gardening Association (www.Garden.org) in 2009 almost one-third of all American households were growing a garden, reflecting a 20 percent increase over previous years. And a good portion of those home gardeners were digging in the dirt for the first time ever. Many reasons are given for planting a garden: saving money, growing more nutritious food, recreation, exercise, or socialization. Regardless of the reasons, more and more gardens are growing and more and more families are finding it beneficial to their health and lifestyle.

This chapter isn't designed to be an exhaustive resource for gardening. We want to provide you with just a taste of how inspiring, rewarding, and totally awesome this hobby can be! While we're talking about exhaustive material, please understand that starting a garden *can* be an exhausting process. It's a good thing to do, but it does take quite a bit of elbow grease and physical labor to get started. The reason we're mentioning this is not to scare you away from it, but to help you put it into perspective. If you're new to many of the planning, shopping, and cooking tips we've shared, then you may want to hold off on starting a garden. You're going to see your savings increase as you perfect the skills we've discussed in the previous chapters. Reducing your grocery bill by gardening will take some time—not just the time for the seeds to germinate, the seedling to mature, and the fruit to ripen, but time to learn how much to plant, how to make it produce well, when to harvest, and how to store what you harvest. Gardening to reduce your grocery costs is one of the more advanced strategies and requires a large time commitment. But that said, if you really want to give gardening a try as a hobby, go for it.

If you live in a smaller home, a town house, a condo, or an apartment, don't just dismiss this chapter thinking that you don't have space. There are lots of different ways to garden, and we'll touch on many of those options. Whether you have a large property or not, you can receive some benefit from growing your own food—so let's get growing!

DOES YOUR GARDEN GROW—AND HOW!

Most economizing people we know have a garden. They garden to produce not only food and flowers, but a healthier lifestyle and a better understanding of nature and life.

If you haven't yet discovered the thrill of sinking your hands into a plot of soft, rich loam or picking homegrown veggies or flowers, we want to encourage you to give it a go. If you're an avid gardener, we hope you'll pick up some tips or be inspired to share some of your own.

As kids, we both experienced gardening in climates with cold winters and a growing season that sped from late April through early September. Moving to Arizona was like moving to a different planet as far as gardening was concerned. We can garden year-round, but we had to learn which plants will produce during each season. Once we overcame the different seasonal schedule, we discovered that many of the same basic gardening principles apply.

We've learned that three basic elements can make or break our garden: soil, exposure, and timing.

The Dirt on Dirt

Our dirt in Arizona is basically clay. It can be hard as a rock—after all, didn't many Southwestern Native Americans make bricks out of it to build their hogans and adobe huts? The soil here definitely needs improving.

Over the years, we've gathered gobs of information on composting. Our first attempts were rather feeble—we dug a shallow hole in the corner of our garden and threw stuff into it. We've now graduated to a three-bin system. One bin holds fresh material, one contains material that is "cooking" (or decaying) and one has compost to be used. Our bins are separated by cement blocks and lie a good distance from the house and the garden beds. To generate enough heat within the compost piles, they need to be at least 3 feet tall by 3 feet wide and deep. Heat and moisture help the bacteria break down the waste on the piles, so in Arizona, because we have so little rain, we actually have to water our compost piles.

Our compost is made up of leaves, grass, pine needles, and nonfatty food waste. Even though our family is large, the food waste accounts for no more than 10 percent of our total compost mixture. We even solicit yard waste from our neighbor Rob—he's glad to contribute. In a small way, we are reducing the volume in our landfills.

Many people have the misconception that compost stinks. When it's "cooking," we cover any freshly added material with older material already on the pile. It doesn't smell, but it does attract insects. If the compost is too dry, ants will make it their home. When the compost is fully broken down, it looks and smells like dirt. The magic of it is the nutrients it contains. Compost adds organic matter to the soil and keeps it from becoming compacted. Imagine soil so soft that you can just reach in your hand and pull out a sweet potato. That's the kind of soil we now have. Your county extension service should have specific information about composting and gardening in your area.

Here are a few more ideas for inexpensive ways to amend your soil.

No-Turn Compost

You can make your own compost without turning the pile. Collect garden debris and leaves in the fall and moisten the pile. The pile can be huge, as it will settle over the winter and lose up to two-thirds of its size. In the spring, rake the pile into a heap and then plant directly into it. You may need to place the plants or seeds into small pockets of the garden dirt.

K. C.—Seattle, WA

~~~

Grounds for Frugality

I thought of you guys when I found out about this program. I've tried it and it's great! Nationwide, the folks at Starbucks are glad to give their used coffee grounds away. I call ahead—about four hours—and when I arrive they usually have a huge trash bag full of Espresso grounds ready for me. I take the grounds and work them into our vegetable beds, and around our roses and citrus trees—the worms love them too! For more details visit www.Starbucks.com and search for "grounds for your garden."

<div align="right">Susy—Scottsdale, AZ</div>

~~~

I Shred to Mulch

I always mulch around my garden plants to reduce the need for weeding. Unfortunately, I don't have a ready source of free mulch, such as grass clippings. But I do shred my receipts and bank statements. My Dad gave me the idea to use the shredded paper! Now I shred everything that comes in the mail that's on regular plain paper as well as all financial paperwork. I'm delighted to recycle right into my own garden. Also, if you put newspaper down before you mulch, you'll not have to mulch as often.

AnnMarie—Oshkosh, WI

No Indecent Exposure

No, we're not talking about skimpy clothing, but about locating a plant in the right type of light and temperature to allow it to thrive. In our climate with mild winters and sizzling summers, we do things a little differently. Our main garden beds are located on the east side of our house, protected from the blazing afternoon sun—the hottest time of the day. We have other beds in front of our house where we put plants that thrive in direct sun and tolerate high heat. Our atrium, in the middle of our house, receives reflected, indirect light. It has taken years to find plants that will flourish there. We finally settled on a giant philodendron, foxtail ferns, and sword ferns.

Other considerations are proximity to the house, frost, heat retention, proper drainage, and having a long enough hose to reach the plants.

If you're a beginner and want instant success, plant zucchini. Just beware: although it's easy and fast to grow, you'll need to collect numerous recipes to use up what you produce. Beyond zucchini, identifying heat-loving plants and cool-weather crops is just as important as differentiating tall plants from shorter ones and trailing or vining plants from bushy ones. We usually make a diagram of our garden areas and sketch out approximate locations for what we intend to plant. We place taller plants toward the rear of beds against walls and in the center of round beds. Frost-sensitive plants go by the fence, and the frost-hearty out on the edge of the garden area.

Tomatoes and eggplants take a long time to grow, favor warm weather, and need to be either started indoors or grown from plants purchased at the nursery. Tomatoes send their roots deep, and are great for breaking up harder soil. Squashes, melons, cucumbers, and green beans like warmer weather. These vining plants are great producers all summer long.

Root veggies, such as beets, carrots, and radishes, don't do well in our high summer heat. So we grow them in the spring and fall. Lettuce and spinach don't tolerate the heat either—they tend to "bolt" (go to seed) when the temperature rises. You've got to know your climate. Visit your library for books that deal with gardening in your specific climate zone. Once you learn what will flourish in your area, grow lots of it and enjoy.

Our kids love spinach salad throughout the spring months. They've also come to love a Greek cucumber salad called Tzatziki (zod zeek'). Annette makes this recipe throughout the summer when our cucumber production is at its zenith.

For a couple of years, we grew sweet potatoes in our front beds. The vines made a beautiful ground cover. One year we harvested over fifty pounds from just a few sprouting sweet potatoes.

Cool-Weather Crops

These plants take a bit longer to grow, but the results can be rewarding. These include Brussels sprouts (we were amazed at how they grow), broccoli, cauliflower, and collard greens. Although carrots are relatively inexpensive, we still grow them because we have been given free seeds and we use the greens for feeding our box turtles.

Conserving Water

Being smart about water usage will save you time and money. In some parts of our property we have installed an automated watering system (mostly for our fruit trees and shrubs) with a timer and drip emitters that put water only where we want it to go. It's a good way to conserve water unless the system springs a leak—which happens a couple of times each year. These systems are costly and require constant monitoring and maintenance, but they also help water a large number of plants consistently and accurately.

If you're just starting out, use a hose, a watering pitcher, or a manual drip system. Flood irrigation works for long rows of plants or areas where you have many plants grouped close together. We also place large pots or planters with easy-to-grow plants like mint or aloe vera under our hose reels so that when we are done watering and water drips out of the hose, it does more than just get absorbed into the ground.

Save Your Back

Our main garden beds are 12 feet long and 4 feet wide. The narrow width allows access from both sides without stepping on the soil and compacting it. In retrospect, we should have made them a bit narrower. We built the borders of the garden beds out of 4-by-6 landscape timbers that a neighbor was throwing away. If you have back problems, consider building small, raised beds that can be cultivated and harvested from the sides. Or, try gardening in pots and containers. Container gardening also works well for smaller families or those with limited space.

We were visiting a friend's home a few months ago, and she was just bursting with pride as she showed us her garden—the first she'd ever grown. She's in her sixties and had decided to use a system called Earth Boxes (EarthBox.com or at your local gardening store). You can purchase the entire package for about $60. It comes with a large plastic container on wheels, potting soil, and a watering system built in. She had fabulous success growing tomatoes and green peppers. It was perfect for her, as she could move the plants on her patio to get the perfect amount of sun. The Earth Box concept is easy on her back because of the height of the boxes, and with the use of special covers for the soil, there are virtually no weeds. These are an excellent choice for apartment or town house families who want to garden, but don't have a lot of space.

Indoor Gardening

For those of you who live in smaller spaces, you can grow plants and veggies indoors either using Earth Boxes or containers from simple Styrofoam cups to flowerpots. Depending on the location of the plants in your house, you may need to supplement sunlight with indoor grow lights. Don't spend a lot of money on these; simple compact fluorescent lights (CFLs) will work fine.

When gardening indoors, you may need to help pollinate some plants because you won't have the benefit of insects doing it for you. Most gardening books will tell you how to do it.

Our son Roy worked at a gardening supply store for a few years and brought home all kinds of flowering bulbs and other plants. We've created a one-shelf garden in front of a window to our atrium. Plants flourish there, and it adds a lot of color to our house.

Community Gardens

Many cities have dedicated areas for residents to garden—usually for a small fee. Near the community college where our kids have attended, there is a large community garden. When we visited Washington, D.C., we parked our car behind the Smithsonian's National Air and Space Museum; there was a small community garden there too. The biggest advantage to this type of gardening is the camaraderie that forms as you work side by side with green thumbs from all walks of life. Many of these gardeners grow so much food that they donate their excess to food banks.

Companion Planting

When we started our home garden, we emulated the mass production farms with long rows of one type of plant. After years of reading and learning, we stumbled upon the concept of companion planting—mixing flowers and herbs with vegetables. The purpose is not merely to add color and variety to your garden area, but properly selected flowers and herbs attract beneficial insects that will increase pollination and reduce plant-devouring pests. Our top five flowers are bachelor's buttons, alyssum, nasturtiums, zinnias, and hollyhocks—the last attracts butterflies. The herbs we plant are borage, dill, anise, chives, oregano, and basil.

The only drawback we've had is cross-pollination. This occurs when pollen-gathering insects go from one plant to another and mix the pollen. We've ended up with cucumbers that are shaped like eggplant (they taste like cucumbers, they're just rounder), and lemons that have orange skins (they still taste like lemons—but can be easily confused with oranges until you take a bite!). So be aware that if you plant a lot of different veggies in the same area, you may end up with some unique items.

Laughter in the Garden

We've had some humorous experiences in the garden. When John, our oldest, was about four years old, he wandered into the garden and plucked up a handful of seedlings. He marched into the kitchen with his fist extended, and proudly proclaimed, "I was picking posies for the girls!" We didn't harvest much that year. Another time we espied our 80-pound German shepherd jumping the 3-foot fence we had erected to keep her out of the garden. She emerged, proud as a peacock, with a small orange pumpkin in her mouth. But her all-time favorites were zucchinis—she ate them like popsicles.

Kids in the Garden

When our kids were younger, Annette would give them a 1-foot square of the garden and allow them to plant flowers. They loved watching them grow. Later, we put in a couple more plots and the kids got to grow things they wanted. Nothing inspires children more than working with their parents and seeing things they planted grow. We still laugh about Joe's "monkey face" green pepper, and Roy's jumbo cauliflower plant.

Then there are the wonderful "mistakes." One year we discovered a vine growing next to an old pine tree stump. We watched and watered, wondering what it was. As it grew, we discovered that it was a watermelon vine. The seed had been "planted" by Becky as she rinsed out our kitchen compost bucket. She would bang it against the stump, as she rinsed it out, to dislodge the last little seeds from the bucket. Those watermelons were crisp, red, and delicious.

A couple of our favorite books on gardening are: *Square Foot Gardening* by Mel Bartholomew and *How to Grow World Record Tomatoes* by Charles Wilbur. Mel gives you simple ideas for starting an easy to grow and easy to maintain garden. Charles presents his experience in growing huge tomatoes. His tips can be used to grow any garden bigger and better.

The Bumper Crop

One of the liabilities of gardening is that some years you have an abundance of a particular crop. What do you do with the excess? We've done several things. While we aren't expert canners, one year we had a huge crop of Armenian cucumbers (they handle our summer heat better than other varieties), and Annette researched making pickles—she canned dozens of jars of bread and butter pickles. They were delicious. Another time we had huge quantities of zucchini growing. We made zucchini muffins, bread, fried zucchini, and even put it in salads. Still we had more growing. Annette called a friend, and Sue told her about a recipe for zucchini relish. Once again Annette canned dozens of jars of relish. We enjoyed it for a couple of years.

Canning is a fantastic way to extend the use of your fresh produce. You can also freeze it—which is what we do with cooked pumpkin after Halloween. It is saved for use in our annual pumpkin bread baking day just before Christmas.

And the last thing you can do is share your excess with others. Consider food banks and friends at work, clubs, and church. Most people are grateful for homegrown produce—that is, of course, unless *they also* had a bumper crop of zucchini—if that's the case, just laugh and work together to find someone else you can donate your excess to.

Gardening is a terrific way to reconnect with nature. Children can learn about science and develop patience as they watch and wait for their seeds to become something delicious or beautiful. The National Gardening Association estimates that for every dollar you spend in seeds, you can anticipate harvesting between $8 and $25 in food value. Although we've never determined the monetary value of our harvest, we know that we are eating healthier, fresher, and tastier food. Plus the exercise and the time in the sun and fresh air add to our overall mental and physical health. So how does our garden grow? With silver bells and cockle shells and *lots of elbow grease and sweat.*

Just because gardening is a lot of work, doesn't mean that you have to spend a lot of money too. Keep reading.

CONTROLLING START-UP COSTS

If you're thinking about starting a garden for the first time, go slowly and do your research. It's very easy to be sold lots of things you simply don't need or won't use. As you become more experienced with gardening in your geographic area and with your property, you'll discover what works and what doesn't. We've had our share of flops that were somewhat costly—like the avocado tree that we moved a couple of times (which later died), the banana tree that didn't make it in our atrium, the hybrid blueberry bushes that croaked, and the fig tree that we planted in the wrong place. Just because a nursery or home improvement store sells a particular type of tree or plant doesn't mean it will do well in your area. And finding the right location on your property is crucial.

Enthusiasm about gardening is a good thing, but spending loads of money isn't. Here are some great ways to save on your start-up costs.

Growing Guidelines

I saw that you suggested starting a garden as a means to save money on vegetables. Yes, it sure can be, but like anything else, expenses can expand to the size of your pocketbook. I'm an avid seed-starter myself and here are a few ideas for saving money in the garden:

1. **Advice**. Good advice on gardening is free from your county extension agent or the local library.

2. **Finding seeds**. Watch for community seed and plant exchanges and get there early for the best selection. Seed packets are the least expensive at discount stores, dollar stores, and home improvement centers for between 10 cents and $1 per packet. Catalogs have a better selection, but a packet is usually at least $2 (a steal compared to the cost of plants). Find a friend to split a packet of seeds and share in the shipping charges. I love poring over seed catalogs, comparing prices, and dreaming of a beautiful garden— it's free to look and a great way to spend a snowy January evening. This is such an enjoyable activity that we charge seed purchases to our entertainment budget and not our gardening budget.

3. **Sowing seeds**. Some flower and vegetable seeds can be sown directly into a garden after the danger of frost has passed (zinnias, sunflowers, marigolds, cosmos, green beans, squash, and basil). Others should be put into a starting soil mix to grow better. Garden soil is usually too dense and contains pathogens. Purchase a $2 box of 3- or 5-ounce cups and a $3.50 bag of seed starting mix. With some seeds from your local discount store you can start a garden for less than $10.

4. **Soil preparation is a must**. Start your own compost pile. I've been caught "trash picking" bags of leaves and grass clippings from my neighbors' curbsides to feed our compost. Vegetable peels also make a good addition.

5. **Use drip irrigation**. Water is expensive—use it wisely.

CINDY—ASHBURN, VA

Cindy is right: if you're new to gardening, you can go broke buying all of the "must have" tools and plants. We recently talked to a single dad who wanted to start a garden and spent well over $100 getting started with topsoil, plants, and fertilizer. Start small, and see if you really like tending a garden, then build on your successes.

We mentioned the book *Square Foot Gardening* earlier; it's great for beginner gardeners (and experienced ones too), and if you want some instant free information you can visit Mel Bartholomew's website SquareFootGardening.com where he's got lots of great info and even some instructional videos.

Does growing your own food need to be limited to a garden area "out back" of your home? That's what we used to think, but recently we've discovered the concept of edible landscaping—no, we aren't talking about eating the bark off your trees— keep reading.

IS YOUR LANDSCAPE EDIBLE?

Producing enough food for your family to actually live off of may seem like a far-fetched concept, rooted in the past when most people lived on farms. The growing interest in healthier food options coupled with falling wages and higher unemployment may have created the perfect incentive for growing more food yourself. Add to that tainted-spinach scares and recalled foods, including pretzels, potato chips, pecans, and cream of mushroom soup—you might want to stop eating altogether (for up-to-date information on U.S. food and drug recalls visit www.fda.gov/Safety/Recalls/default.htm). But there is a way you can start producing more of your food and the answer is right in your own backyard (maybe even your front and side yards too).

If you own or rent a house, you already have some type of landscaping. Instead of spending time and water maintaining a typical inedible landscape, you could decorate your property with delicious, healthy food with minimal effort. You can adorn areas as small as an apartment patio with beautiful, eye-pleasing, and scrumptious vegetation. And the satisfaction of walking into your yard and picking fresh fruit off a tree, bush, or vine can't be beat.

Here are a few things to consider.

Research

Visit a local nursery where knowledgeable gardeners can assist you with the selection and placement of plants suitable for your climate. Or go to your local library and check out books specific to your area. Also look for books by Rosalind Creasy, the author of *Edible Landscaping*, and many other gardening books.

Knowing what easily grows in your area will keep you from wasting money on plants that simply won't produce for you. We've learned to ask the experts, do the research first, and add only a couple of new things each year, allowing us time to learn how to grow them properly.

A few years ago we met Greg Peterson. He lives on a small lot in central Phoenix. But he has transformed his residential property into what he calls The Urban Farm. We've learned much from Greg about planting fruit trees, composting, and getting lots of food production out of a little space. He has a very informative website called www.yourguidetogreen.com/TheUrbanFarm/—it's full of great articles and videos. If you search, you'll easily find other gardening enthusiasts in your area who are brimming with great information for you to use.

Yard Space

Obviously those with more property have more options for what to plant. Our three-quarters of an acre accommodates numerous trees and berry bushes. Over the years we have diversified from just citrus trees to include strawberries, grapes, blackberries, peach, plum, Asian pear, fig, almond, pomegranate, and apple trees. We love the fact that various types of fruit ripen at different times. As a result, we have some sort of fresh fruit virtually all year long. If your space is limited, consider purchasing dwarf varieties of trees. These trees won't grow as large and don't produce as much fruit as full-sized versions. But they're great for patio homes and container gardening (in some cases). Because of their smaller size, they allow you more variety in less space. A smaller space may seem limiting, but with a little creativity, you'll always find a great solution.

Time Factor

Not every kind of tree or plant requires as much attention as a home garden does. There are several edibles that can be planted once and return each year as annuals, such as, asparagus (this takes a few years to start producing), rhubarb, arti-chokes, bush plums, and berry plants. Several herbs are also relatively easy to grow: thyme, rosemary, mint, chives, anise, tarragon, dill, and parsley.

Most of our trees require less than one hour per year for pruning and fertilizing (adding compost and other organic supplements). If you don't have an automated irrigation system or live in an area with sufficient rainfall, watering will add consid-erable time to your maintenance, but once established, most trees will do well with once-a-week deep watering. If you have young children at home and both parents are working, committing to a large-scale organic landscape may have to be put off for a few years. Including your kids in the maintenance of your fruit-bearing plants is a great family activity, but if you're already tapped out for time, wait a few years—there are many seasons in our lives, and organic gardening can wait until the kids are a little older.

Regional Plant Selection

In Arizona, grapevines, pomegranate, fig, citrus, pecan, and almond trees all require very little fuss, as our climate is perfect for growing them. In colder regions, stone-fruit trees, which need more chill hours to produce good fruit, do well. Consider, among others, peach, cherry, plum, apricot, nectarine, and apple trees.

Over the years, horticulturists have created hybridized versions of most fruit-bearing plants, allowing them to be grown in "foreign" climates. We recently harvested several pounds of apples from our three-year-old Anna apple trees—apples in Arizona—who would have believed it! There are even some container-sized citrus trees well suited for you orange and lemon lovers in the northern climes. Science is amazing!

Bonus . . . Energy Savings

Besides providing yummy-tasting fruit, strategically planting fruit and nut trees around your house can also keep your home cooler during the summer months. Unfortunately, most fruit trees don't do much for winter windbreaks, but a few evergreen trees will do the trick and provide plenty of compost material with cast-off needles and berries.

Learning what types of plants are suited for your area and nurturing them is a rewarding project. Remember that most young trees and fruit-bearing plants take a few years to reach their bearing potential, so you need some patience. But the prospect of attractive trees and ground cover full of fresh, organic, healthy, wonderfully juicy fruit is enough motivation to keep us going. Let us know what you've planted and grown successfully!

Edible Landscape Resources

W. Atlee Burpee & Co.
300 Park Ave., Warminster, PA 18974
1-800-333-5808
www.Burpee.com

Gurney's Seed & Nursery Co.
P.O. Box 4178, Greendale, IN 47025
(513) 354-1492
www.Gurneys.com

Henry Field's Seed & Nursery Co.
P.O. Box 397, Aurora, IN 47001-0397
(513) 354-1495
www.HenryFields.com

Johnny's Selected Seeds
955 Benton Ave., Winslow, ME 04901
(207) 861-3900
www.JohnnySeeds.com

Plants of the Southwest
3095 Agua Fria St., Santa Fe, NM 87507
1-800-788-7333
www.PlantsOfTheSouthwest.com

Visitors to our website provide a never-ending stream of ideas—here are some great ones to use in your garden.

———

Reseed and Save Money

Beth (my wife) and I saved money in planting flowers. While neighbors were visiting the garden centers to buy 4- to 8-inch-high perennials, we just replanted what we grew from our seeds. Of course we had to start about three weeks before our neighbors were planting their new plants. However, the gardens around our house looked every bit as nice.

At first it was our own science experiment. We bought three packets of flower seeds. Used plant-starter trays were available at the local garden center. All we had to do was add dirt, water, and create a warm enough environment for the seeds to germinate. Our sun-drenched, closed-in back porch served well as a warm room. For about three or four evenings we used a little space heater overnight to keep the room at about 85 degrees. The seeds grew. It was exciting seeing three hundred small plants growing from just $2.25 worth of seeds. When the plants were about 3 to 4 inches tall we planted them in two beds in our backyard. While freezing was possible, sheet plastic worked well to protect the plants. When our neighbor was planting her store-purchased plants, we transplanted again, all around the yard. We had so many plants that we gave some to neighbors and friends. We had blue flowers along the west side of the house, yellow flowers in one hot bed, purple flowers in another hot bed, and blue and red flowers in pots on our porch. Then in fall, we harvested seeds and did it again the next year. This is our third year of doing this. We enjoy beautifying our yard while we save in the process. Annual savings about $75.

CURTIS—SPOKANE, WA

The next two tips are great to use at the end of the gardening season.

~~~

Shake, Jiggle, and Plant

At garden time I always let the last of my spinach and lettuce go to seed. I also give the dead plants a good shake before the snow falls. In the spring, I have volunteer plants coming up even before the garden is tilled. Then I transplant the spinach and leave the lettuce and parsley in their beds to mature. I've heard that some people even do this with potatoes and carrots.

PATTI—NEWPORT, WA

~~~

Green Tomato Pie

Last night we had our first freeze. That means it's time for one of my produce favorites. Green tomatoes! I use them like apples to make green tomato pie or green tomato crisp. Just follow your favorite apple pie/crisp recipe, adding 1 teaspoon baking soda to the spices that you put on the apples before baking. If you didn't know it was tomatoes rather than apples, you would never guess!

AMY—LINCOLN, NE

No matter where you live or how many people are in your household, you can receive incredible health benefits from growing and eating what you've grown in your garden. Sure it takes time, planning, effort, and a little money, but the benefits far outweigh the costs. Start small and get educated and soon you'll be teaching others what you know. We can dig it—can you?

WHAT CAN YOU DO ABOUT GARDENING NOW?

 Timid Mouse

1. Check out books from the library and contact your county extension service to learn about gardening in your area.
2. If there is a community garden near your home, visit and learn from the people who are growing things there.

 Wise Owl

1. Get a couple of small pots and start growing some herbs or veggies.
2. Evaluate what you'll need to create a compost pile and start recycling your kitchen and yard waste.
3. Design and install a small raised garden bed and start planting.

 Amazing Ant

1. Research and plant a couple of fruit or nut trees this year. Use your compost to amend the soil and watch those trees grow!
2. Walk your property and determine areas that are suitable for growing fruits or veggies. Design the new areas to be landscaped with edible plants.

12

Bag Up the Savings

Some people turn to the last chapter of a novel to find out how the story ends—they simply can't stand the idea of having to read through all of the chapters before they know how the hero or heroine fares. If you're one of those people, we'll tell you how the story ends—only remember this isn't fiction—this is real life, and the only hero or heroine in this story is you. And how the story ends depends on you and the choices you make.

We have no idea what's going on in your life right now. You may be experiencing total chaos or intense physical or emotional pain—there is hope. Some of you may be facing life as a single parent with no idea of how you're going to survive financially—there is hope. You may be recently widowed and wondering how you're going to get through tomorrow—there is hope. You may be wondering how you're going to dig out from under a huge mountain of debt—there is hope for you too. We know there is hope because we've experienced hopeless feelings, feelings of being overwhelmed (more often than you'll ever know), and feelings of inadequacy, and we've made it through and our story has taken us to a better place. Sure there have been some tears, and yes, there have been periods of uncertainty, but over time, the laughter, joy, and sense of fulfillment have far outweighed the feelings of frustration and sadness. We have hope that you will experience the same joy that we have and that as you write the story of your life, you'll end up in the same good place that we have.

Theodore Roosevelt said many profound things, but this one quote has stuck with us for years:

> It is not the critic who counts, not the man who points out how the strong man stumbled or where the doer of deeds could have done them better. The credit belongs to the man [or woman] who is actually in the arena, whose face is marred with dust and sweat and blood . . . and who, . . . if he fails, at least fails while daring greatly, so that his place shall never be with those cold and timid souls who know neither victory nor defeat.

The key to surviving the tough times and getting to the better times is being persistent. If you've ever been involved in sports, you know that the players who win are those who stay in the game. They stay in regardless of how hard, overwhelming, or difficult it is. They stay in even if it looks like they'll lose. Someone said that the one difference between a winner and a loser is that the winner gets up one more time than the loser.

You've got to persist and keep on persisting. It takes time to develop new habits. Remember that each changed habit moves you closer and closer to the success that you desire. So hang in there. Focus on one thing at a time and become proficient at it. Then move on to the next. Step-by-step, you'll become an expert—and no one will be able to stop you.

If you follow any or all of our advice, you'll feel an incredible sense of accomplishment. You'll know how to plan, not just your shopping trip or a weekly menu, but you'll know how to plan other events and activities in your life. You see, the skills and habits you're learning and perfecting in the grocery arena can be used just about anywhere—at work, in a club, at church, and at home.

But if your success is going to be long lasting, you'll need to have a way to lock in your savings, and that's what this chapter is all about.

LOCK IN THE WIN

Our son Joe loves to play baseball. Some seasons his team has played great and won the championship, and others, well, let's just say that their record was nothing to brag about. The winning seasons were punctuated by many games when his team was able to get more hits, score more runs, and lock in the lead, more often than their opponents.

Winning takes not just one thing, but a combination of lots of little things: it takes hits, smart base running, skillful coaching, precise pitching, good defense, and finally scoring runs. If Joe's team gets hits and gets players on base, but those players never score a run, all of their efforts won't earn a win. To win, they can't strand players on base. They have to cross the plate; they have to score!

Winning at the game of cutting your grocery bill in half has some similarities to baseball—you can plan a menu, clip coupons, shop carefully, cook at home, and have dinner together but still not cross home plate—if you don't have a way to capture your savings.

If all of the money you save is frittered away and you have no lasting memory of where it has gone, how have you won?

Now, we don't want to freak anybody out. But we want to, very briefly, share with you the one financial tool that we've used for over twenty-five years that has allowed us to capture and use just about every penny we've saved. This isn't some grand financial planning software or program, and you don't need to be a math wizard or a CPA to use it. And like everything else we've shared in this book, it may be tough at first, yet will get easier to use as you become more disciplined.

What we're talking about is utilizing some sort of budgeting system. This is how we know, without a doubt, that we've only spent $350 on groceries each and every month for years and years. When a writer from *People* magazine interviewed us, she wanted us to prove what we were saying about our grocery expenses. So we pulled out our budget notebook and showed her our record of grocery expenses. She could easily see that each and every two weeks we deposited (on paper) $175 into our grocery budget account. And she could also see that each and every month we spent $350 or less on groceries. There was absolutely no question.

But more important, and what most people don't understand, is that because we have this kind of control over our finances, we can lock in the savings. Because we control our grocery expenses and all of our other expenses in much the same way, we know when we have extra money each month. And when we have extra money, we choose to use it to reach the goals we value most.

In the past we used the excess in our household budget to accelerate the payments on our first house—it only took nine years to pay off. We've also used the extra money to pay cash for our cars, take great vacations, put our kids through college, remodel our kitchen—and a lot more.

If you're new to budgeting, read our first book, *America's Cheapest Family Gets You Right on the Money*. Hundreds of people have blogged or written us saying that the explanation of how we set up our budgeting system is the easiest to understand and implement that they've ever read.

Simply stated, our budgeting is similar to a cash envelope system but maintained on paper (we keep very little cash in the house). Every paycheck, we deposit a predetermined amount of money into several budget categories ranging from mortgage to food and from clothes to pets. Because we save in advance of all of our anticipated expenses, we simply consult our budget categories to see how much money we have saved for a particular purchase. Our bottom line is this: if the money isn't there, we either don't buy or we look for other options. We choose to exercise creativity rather than credit. All of the benefits of how this system has protected, provided, and helped us lock in the win would fill an entire book.

We maintain our budget on paper, but if you're more computer oriented you could try Mvelopes.com. Their system works similarly to our budgeting system—we've written a more detailed review and have a link to them on AmericasCheapestFamily.com.

Remember your goal is to get the money you've worked so hard to save at the grocery store across home plate. You can lock in the win and earn the family savings championship!

Be Patient and Grow Strong

We've talked about a lot of different new habits for you to implement. Change is never easy—but positive changes are always good. A wise man said, "At the time, discipline isn't much fun. It always feels like it's going against the grain. Later, of course, it pays off handsomely" (*The Message* by Eugene Peterson).

Learning new habits takes time, so we're begging you to be patient with yourself. Sure you're going to have to struggle to overcome old habits and fight to resist tempting marketing ploys. You're sure to get frustrated when you forget to buy something on your list. We struggle against these things too. But as you persist, you *will* make progress. Weeds are incredibly easy to grow—and so are bad habits. They can sprout up without even trying. Oak trees take a lot longer and require more nurturing and care to bring them to maturity. Your new skills are like an oak tree—nurture them, feed them, and they'll provide shade for many years to come.

Remember, we've been doing this for a long time. Many of the steps we've outlined fit into our lifestyle like a pair of comfortable old slippers—we hardly notice we're wearing them. Stick with your plan and your new habits will become second nature—and it will be good—very good!

Be Excellent

Annette started our marriage without any domestic skills, but she did have one driving, motivating attitude that carried her through those first years very well. She took her job seriously and wanted to be excellent at it. She read books (and still does—we have over three thousand in our house), she talked to other women who were excellent in what they did, and she pondered problems and came up with solutions.

It's hard to be excellent at anything the first time you do it. Have you ever watched a young child brush his teeth for the first time? *Some* of the toothpaste actually gets in his mouth! It's a funny picture to imagine—toothpaste on the cheeks, hair, and clothes. But given a few years of practicing several times each day and soon that same child will be carrying on full conversations, walking around, maybe even texting while brushing his teeth. Over time your new skills will become so ingrained into your life that you'll forget that they were ever difficult.

Any action that you repeat regularly can be refined and perfected. Creating a shopping list and menu, taking inventory of your pantry, going to the store, or cooking up several meals in one day—all of these repetitive tasks will become faster, easier, and more streamlined as you work. And as you become excellent at these tasks, people will notice and you'll move from being the student to being the instructor—helping others learn what you've learned. So, work to be excellent in all that you do.

Be Generous

As you grow in your skills, you'll discover that you have an abundance of food in your house. You might not believe it is possible, but trust us, it will happen. We've taken our excess food and used it to help others. Having an extra person at our table for dinner is a regular occurrence. Years ago when we ran a financial coaching ministry at our church, we'd regularly send single moms home from our house with bags of groceries pulled from our pantry shelves. Did we miss the extra food? No. Did it cost us something? Sure it did, but we still never exceeded our budget. If you do once-a-month cooking, you can easily pull a meal out of the freezer for a sick friend or someone experiencing a time of pain or grief.

Take the excess you have and bless someone else. Maybe it will be a food bank, a church pantry, your grown kids, or a family who is struggling with unemployment—anything you do to help others will eventually come back and bless you.

Focus on What Really Matters—Faith and Family

We've shown you how we find bargains and save all kinds of money. We've told you how we work efficiently and save all kinds of time. But in the end there really is more to life for us. All through this book, we've talked about striking a balance between activities that help you save money and spending time with significant people in your life. Having loads of money in the bank, but no loving relationships, unfortunately has become the sad fate of many wealthy people. Please don't let this become true of you.

Years ago, before we were married, we both experienced a time in our lives when faith in God became a foundational part of our lives. We could tell you lots of awesome stories of times we've seen God provide for our needs, but those will have to wait for another time and another book. Through this change, we've learned that all of the savings we can amass in the bank and all of the possessions we can cram into our house are *nothing* compared to our relationship with God, the one who loves us more than anyone else. Knowing we are completely loved in spite of our weaknesses helps us keep money, possessions, and people in a healthy perspective.

We're in the stands, cheering for you as you run the bases in your game of life. Keep your eyes on what really matters, and run so you can score and lock in the win! Just be sure you're playing the right game—don't substitute what really matters for what merely seems important today.

We'll see you in the checkout lane.

P.S. We love hearing success stories from people who have read our books, so send us a message through AmericasCheapestFamily.com or send a letter to America's Cheapest Family, PO Box 12603, Scottsdale, AZ 85267, so we can celebrate with you.

More Ways Singles and Empty Nesters Can Save a Boodle

Many singles and retirees simply don't want to fuss with preparing their own meals. We hear this reasoning all of the time, "It's just no fun to cook for one!" Or they'll say, "It's too much work to cook a full meal just for the two of us." We totally understand those feelings. We know that your life as a single or empty nester is different from those with larger families. But being different isn't bad, and it definitely doesn't mean you don't have options. You do have choices, probably more than people with large families. Everything we've written in this book can be modified to fit your lifestyle. It may take some time or thought to adapt it to your routine, but with time you'll be amazed at what you can do. You can plan your meals, shop smarter, shop less often, cook in bulk and freeze your meals, and make your dinner hour fun by including others. And yes, you can save money and still enjoy delicious meals. But like anything else, it will take some effort. Hopefully this short bonus section will spark your imagination and motivate you to find specific ways that you can cut your grocery bill.

We'll divide this section into three areas: cooking quicker, storing smarter, and sharing savings.

COOKING QUICKER

Finding ways to minimize your food preparation time will go a long way to helping you want to eat at home. Once-a-month cooking or once-a-week cooking can successfully be modified for your lifestyle. Having whole meals or partially prepared meals already in the freezer is a great way to make your eating time delicious and nutritious.

Using a microwave oven to reheat previously cooked meals (from the freezer) is one of the quickest ways to make sure you're eating a balanced diet. Frozen veggies can easily be cooked in a microwave also.

A slow cooker is an invaluable tool for working moms or families on the go, and you can use it to your advantage too. Putting dinner in the slow cooker in the morning and knowing that there's a hot meal waiting at home for you will minimize your urge to go out to eat.

One-pot meals like stew or soup are not difficult to make and are easy to clean up.

If you're trying to break the restaurant habit and aren't yet ready to cook from scratch, go to the grocery store and pick up some partially prepared meat from the butcher. Many regularly stock things like stuffed pork chops, shish kebab, and other mouthwatering meal starters. Just pop them in the oven or on the grill and you'll be eating soon afterward. Or pick up frozen prepared main dishes like teriyaki chicken, oriental stir-fry, chicken cordon bleu, or hamburgers. The variety is great and you'll be able to control your portion sizes and your costs too.

———

Cookin' to the Fourth Power

I live by myself and almost always cook four servings for my main dishes—including proteins and vegetables. I eat one serving and immediately put the other three servings in individual-sized serving containers and put them in the freezer. If I cook twice a week, I almost always have healthy, economical frozen dinners on hand for the times when I don't have the time or energy to cook. It's "once-a-month cooking'" on a smaller scale and requires much less freezer space too.

SUE—PHOENIX, AZ

STORING SMARTER

One of the biggest problems for singles and empty nesters is getting a great deal on produce, meat, or other perishable items only to have them go bad before they can be consumed. Here are several ways to keep your great deals from going bad.

Lunch meat. Repackage larger quantities of lunch meat into smaller portions that you can consume in one week. Then store in smaller zippered plastic bags and freeze. Once you defrost a small quantity, insert a paper towel into the bag to absorb moisture and keep your lunch meat fresher.

Fruits and veggies. You want to make sure you eat lots of healthy fruits and veggies. But because fresh veggies don't store for a long time, keep lots of frozen veggies in the freezer. Tests have proven that flash-frozen veggies keep almost as much nutritional value as fresh.

If you decide to make a salad with lots of different ingredients, but can't eat it all at one sitting, store it so that it will last:

- Don't put salad dressing on the entire batch. Salad dressing causes the salad to deteriorate faster.
- Keep things like tomatoes and cucumbers separate from the lettuce until you are ready to eat.
- Store the lettuce in a sealed bag or plastic container with a paper towel to absorb moisture.

Storage containers. Because you'll be storing or freezing food cooked or bought in bulk, you'll want to invest in good, easy to use, stackable storage containers that can be readily labeled. Labeling your containers is critical to being able to use up what you have. It's no fun rummaging though piles of unmarked containers or zippered bags searching for a frozen meal, only to find that you froze it a year ago and it tastes totally freezer burned.

Don't Cry over Sour Milk

Do you buy milk in gallon or half-gallon containers only to have it go sour in your refrigerator? As our kids have grown and left home, our consumption of milk has slowed greatly. We went through a few months when our gallons of milk were constantly going sour because we didn't consume it fast enough. We needed to make a change because we were wasting money. We still buy gallons of milk because they are usually less expensive than half gallons or quarts. But once we get home, we pour the milk from the gallon container into half-gallon containers (leaving a little room at the top for expansion) and then put the smaller containers in the freezer.

If a half gallon is too much for you to use before spoilage occurs, try using quart containers.

Freeze Your Rice

Cook up a large batch of rice and freeze it in individual-serving-sized containers. Thaw in the microwave with your favorite main dish.

Single Chef Prefers Jars

As a single person, I've found it difficult to cook healthy meals and not have disagreeable leftovers or rotting veggies in the fridge. I tried all the plastic thing-a-ma-jigs, free or otherwise, but they have always failed me.

Then I began freezing things in canning jars. It's a fantastic way to store food in single servings. I experimented and found I could freeze many things I never would have considered. I freeze soups, which I cook up sixteen quarts at a time (and never have to buy canned soup), sauces made from garden produce, cooked meat in its juice, peanut butter (purchased by the gallon), and leftover cooked veggies thrown in a jar for some future stew. I have very little waste now and eat much better and healthier. In all these years I've had only one jar break—I cooked a jar of soup in the microwave, then added cold water to it. Stupid, I know. I reuse the lids over and over. Because I'm freezing the contents, I don't have to worry about an air-tight seal.

I've found canning jars at garage sales and thrift store for pennies, and I use them for more than food storage—to carry drinks in my car:

water, coffee, iced tea. They always wash up fine, and I store them in my out-of-commission dishwasher. I prefer the wide-mouthed jars because they make cleanup easier, but regular ones work just as well.

PATTI—NEWPORT, WA

~

Vacuum Sealer

I used to have a large family, but now it's just me. I've had to work to change my mind-set from cooking huge portions to cooking for one. One of the best tools I have in the kitchen is my vacuum sealer. I can take advantage of family-sized discounted meats and then freeze them in individual serving sizes. Sometimes I still cook large portions and then divide them up into single servings and store them in the freezer.

CAROL—PHOENIX, AZ

If you need more information on storing food, review Chapter 6, "Stocking Up and Organizing," and learn which foods freeze well and which ones don't.

SHARING SAVINGS

Everyone knows that you always accomplish more, easier, when you work with someone else. The same rule applies when it comes to shopping and cooking.

Sharing Bulk Buys

Buy bulk fruit and veggies, and family-sized meat packages to split with a friend so you can take advantage of discount prices.

Social Saving

You also can join or create your own food co-op. Working with like-minded friends is great and the savings can be significant.

~~~

Share the Love . . . and the Food!

Though I'm single, I have roommates, as well as friends that stop by frequently. I like to feed them—and that hospitality is returned to me in loads of different ways. There's an obvious spiritual connection here, but it's also practical. We all know the frequent complaint about single life of, "If I'm just cooking for only myself, I don't want to take the time to make anything too involved." I say, make more than you need and then feed your friends. The love and goodwill that is fostered is worth way more than the cost of the food involved! There's a huge economy here!

THEO—CHICAGO, IL

Dining Out

If you decide to go out for dinner, use these money-saving tips with someone:

- Use the entertainment coupon book or Restaurants.com discount coupons with a friend or two.
- Go early and take advantage of an early-bird discount.
- Split an entrée with a friend or divide it in half and take it home for another meal.
- For drinks, order water with lemon.
- Many senior centers have discounted lunches or dinners. You can eat inexpensively and build some long-lasting relationships.
- See our tips in Chapter 10, where we discuss eating out for less.

Getting Discounts

Senior Discounts. Many grocery chains offer discounts on all grocery items to seniors (the age ranges from over 59 to over 65) who shop on a particular day. In our area it's Fry's (Kroger) one Wednesday each month. Take a friend and you'll get through the store faster as you help each other. Other areas have more frequent days or other limits. Do your research and find out when the discount applies to you. Here are a few we've found:

Arby's. 10 percent discount ages 55+ at participating locations.

Burger King. 10 percent discount ages 60+ at participating locations.

Chili's. 10 percent discount ages 55+ at participating locations.

Hardee's. 33-cent drinks for ages 65+.

IHOP. 10 percent off for ages 55+ at participating locations.

Kmart. Gold K up to 20 percent discount on prescription medication. Ages 50+.

Kroger. 10 percent off total order—one day each month. Check your location. Ages 60+.

Long John Silver's. Discount for ages 55+ at participating locations.

McDonald's. Discounted senior coffee and soft drinks.

Mrs. Fields Cookies. 10 percent discount. Ages 60+.

Rite Aid. Discounts from 10 to 20 percent.

Shoney's. 10 percent discount ages 60+ every day.

Taco Bell. Free drinks for seniors at participating locations.

TCBY. 10 percent discount ages 55+ at participating locations.

Wendy's. 10 percent discount ages 55+ at participating locations.

Ask for AARP or AAA discounts if you are a member of those organizations.

Your greatest challenge as a single or empty-nest couple is going to be minimizing your restaurant expenses. It's so easy to decide to go out for a meal rather than cook. But if you prevail in this area by planning, cooking in advance, storing better, and cooking with others, you'll find that you have fewer health issues and lots of excess money to reach other goals. Sure you can still go out for a nice meal once in a while, but with all the success you'll experience eating at home, you may only want to do it for truly special occasions.

Recipes

There is something magical about having family favorite meals—the ones that you, your spouse, or your kids get excited about every time you serve them. This chapter is a small collection of some of the 100+ recipes that Annette has learned and our family has grown to love over the years. This sampling of recipes should just be a starting point to help you discover meals that will become favorites for your family.

Here's a list of what we've included in this Bonus section.

Chicken / Turkey Recipes
- Jane's Nacho Chicken / Turkey
- Dottie's Chicken Cashew
- Sesame Chicken

Beef Recipes
- Tagliarini
- Beef Brisket with Mustard and Onion
- Annette's Ground Beef Hash

Pork / Ham Recipes
- Aunt Harriet's Pork Chops and Rice

- Cheese Sausage Spinach Pie
- Split Pea Soup

Meatless Recipes
- Eggplant Parmesan
- Kathy's French Onion Soup
- Veggie Soup

Quick Breads
- Steve's Killer Pancakes
- Cheese Muffins
- Banana Bread
- Jennifer's Chocolate Chip Zucchini Bread

CHICKEN / TURKEY RECIPES

Because we stock up on inexpensive turkeys around Thanksgiving time, we often substitute turkey for chicken in these recipes. Using either type of meat in these recipes will turn out fine.

Jane's Nacho Chicken / Turkey

This is one of the recipes that Annette picked up from a friend during a group recipe swap the first year we were married. After twenty-eight years, it's still a favorite.

Ingredients

    2 ½ to 3 pounds cooked chicken or turkey, diced or cubed

    2 (10-ounce) cans cream of mushroom soup

    1 cup chicken broth

    1 (4-ounce) can green chilies, mild to hot, you choose

    1 (10- to 16-ounce) bag tortilla chips, broken up

    1 to 2 pounds shredded Monterey Jack or cheddar cheese

    salsa

Directions

Preheat the oven to 350º. Fill a 13 x 9-inch glass baking dish ¾ full with the chicken. Mix in the cream of mushroom soup, chicken broth, and green chilies. Layer the tortilla chips on top of the mixture, then cover with the shredded cheese. Bake for 30 to 45 minutes, until the cheese is melted and starting to brown. Mmmmm delicious! Have a bowl of salsa available for those who want to spoon some on top. Serves 8 to 10 people.

Dottie's Chicken Cashew Recipe

Ingredients

    2 tablespoons butter or margarine

    2 to 3 cups diced celery, including leaves

    1 large onion, chopped

    3 cups cubed chicken or turkey, cooked or uncooked

    1 or 2 (10-ounce) cans cream of mushroom soup (use 2 cans for a creamier sauce)

    1 to 2 tablespoons soy sauce, to taste

1 cup chicken broth

¼ teaspoon black pepper

2 cups Rice cooked (Brown or White)

Cashews and crispy Chinese noodles to sprinkle on top

Optional: 1 (8-ounce) can sliced water chestnuts, drained

Directions

Melt the butter in an 8-quart pot. Add the celery and onion and cook until tender. Add the chicken or turkey, cream of mushroom soup, soy sauce, chicken broth, and pepper, and water chestnuts if desired. Bring to a boil. Turn down the heat and simmer on low for 20 minutes. Serve over cooked rice with Chinese noodles sprinkled on top for a delicious meal. Serves 6 to 8.

Sesame Chicken

This recipe always gets rave reviews from family and friends—hardly ever any leftovers.

Ingredients

juice from 6 lemons

¼ cup teriyaki or soy sauce

½ cup chopped green onions

3 cloves garlic, chopped

¼ cup peanut butter

15 ginger crystals or 1 tablespoon ginger powder

1 tablespoon to ¼ cup honey, depending on taste

All-purpose flour or cornstarch for thickening

2 to 3 cups diced cooked chicken or turkey

½ to ¾ cup sesame seeds, toasted

Directions

In a 10-inch skillet heat the lemon juice and teriyaki or soy sauce with the onions and garlic until tender, about 10 minutes. Add the peanut butter, ginger, and honey, and bring to a boil. Thicken with flour or cornstarch and pour over the cooked chicken. Sprinkle with toasted sesame seeds. Serves 6 to 8.

BEEF RECIPES

Tagliarini

This is another family favorite. Annette prepares everything but the noodles and cheese on once-a-month cooking day, then freezes the meal. When she wants to cook it, she defrosts it, heats it up, and adds the noodles and cheese as indicated below in the directions.

Ingredients

    1 to 2 pounds ground beef

    1 green bell pepper, diced

    1 medium to large onion, diced

    4 cloves garlic, chopped, or 1 heaping teaspoon garlic powder

    2 teaspoons salt

    2 teaspoons chili powder, or more depending on your taste

    2 tablespoons honey

    1 (28-ounce) can diced tomatoes

    2 cups water

    ½ pound dry noodles (we like twirls)

    2 cups shredded cheese, cheddar or a combination of other cheeses your
       family likes

Directions

Preheat the oven to 350°. In a 10-inch skillet mix the ground beef with the diced bell pepper, onion, and garlic and steam to cook. Drain off fat and scoop the meat mixture into a 13 x 9-inch (or larger) baking pan. Stir in the salt, chili powder, and honey. Add the tomatoes and water. Bake in 350° oven for 30 to 45 minutes. When the liquid is boiling, stir in the noodles and top with the cheese. Cook 30 minutes longer. It is delicious! Serves 6 to 8.

Beef Brisket with Mustard and Onion

The name of this recipe is accurately descriptive, but it does not do justice to how delicious it is. We serve it over noodles or with baked potatoes. Plus this is a slow-cooker meal that can be started in the morning and waiting for you when you get home from errands or work.

Ingredients

1 (4 to 6-pound) brisket
yellow mustard
1 (1.25-ounce) package dried onion soup mix
1 to 2 cups beef broth
1 tablespoon granulated lecithin
cornstarch

Directions

In a slow cooker place the brisket fat side up. Cover with mustard (about ¼-inch thick coating) and sprinkle the onion soup onto the mustard. Cook on low, starting first thing in the morning to serve that night.

When it is cooked, scoop off the mustard and onion soup mix "goop" and put in a small saucepan to make the gravy. Peel or scrape off and discard the fat layer. Slice the meat into ¼-inch slices. To make the gravy, pour liquid from the slow cooker into the saucepan containing the mustard and onion soup "goop." Add the beef broth. Blend well and add the lecithin to break up any remaining fat in the juices. Thicken with cornstarch. Serves 6 to 8.

Annette's Ground Beef Hash

This is an easy one-dish meal that satisfies our family every time.

Ingredients

1 pound ground beef

1 (1-pound) chub breakfast sausage

4 carrots, sliced

1 large onion, diced

4 potatoes, cubed

2 (10-ounce) cans cream of mushroom soup

1 teaspoon garlic powder or 4 cloves garlic, chopped

salt and pepper to taste

Directions

Preheat the oven to 350°. Brown the ground beef and sausage. Let cool. In a 15 x 11-inch baking pan combine the meat mixture with the carrots, onion, potatoes, cream of mushroom soup, garlic powder, and salt and pepper to taste. Cover with foil. Cook for 1 hour. This recipe is very flexible and vegetables can be increased or decreased as desired. It has a family rating of 9 on a 10-point scale and there are rarely any leftovers. Serves 6 to 8.

PORK / HAM RECIPES

Aunt Harriet's Pork Chops and Rice

Pork tends to go on sale regularly in our area with sale prices around 99 cents per pound. We thought you'd enjoy a tasty recipe for pork chops and rice.

Ingredients

  1 (10-ounce) can cream of mushroom soup

  1 (10-ounce) can cream of chicken soup

  1 (1.25-ounce) package dried onion soup mix

  1 (10-ounce) can of water

  ¾ cup wild rice

  ¾ cup white rice (You can substitute brown rice, but it must be soaked in
      water for a couple of hours—this softens the rice so it cooks faster.)

  6 pork chops

  applesauce to serve alongside

Directions

Preheat the oven to 350º. In a 15 x 11-inch baking pan mix the cream of mushroom, cream of chicken, and dried onion soup with the water and wild rice. Lay the pork chops on top of the rice and cover with foil. Bake for 1 ½ hours.

Serve with applesauce. The best part of the meal, according to Steve, is the crispy rice that sticks to the sides of the baking pan. This meal is an Economides family favorite. Serves 6.

Cheese Sausage Spinach Pie

This is super-delicious dinner. Annette discovered this recipe as a result of a "bad ad day" back in 1982 when not much was on sale—except Italian sausage.

Ingredients

1 pound sweet Italian sausage, chopped, or sliced links

5 eggs, optional: 1 additional egg for brushing on top crust

2 (10-ounce) packages frozen chopped spinach, thawed and well drained

1 (16-ounce) package shredded Mozzarella cheese (pronounced "moot-za-rrrrrel"—roll your r's)

⅔ cup ricotta cheese ("rrrri-gotah"—put your fingers together on your thumb, hold at eye level, and shake back and forth—for some reason this improves the flavor of the cheese)

½ teaspoon salt

⅛ teaspoon black pepper

⅛ teaspoon garlic powder

pastry for 2-crust 9-inch pie

1 tablespoon water

Directions

Preheat the oven to 375°. Cook the sausage and drain on paper towels. In a large bowl combine the sausage, eggs, spinach, Mozzarella, ricotta, salt, pepper, and garlic powder. Prepare 2 piecrusts. Line a 9-inch pie pan with a crust and fill with the prepared sausage mixture. Cover with the remaining crust and cut 1/2-inch slits in the top. Brush with water or an additional beaten egg. Bake for 90 minutes. Let stand 10 minutes. Serve and enjoy. Serves 8.

Split Pea Soup

Winter is a great time for hot soup. Soup is inexpensive to make and very filling. Even in Arizona's mild winter, we have soup once each week.

Ingredients

8-quart pot filled ⅔ full of chicken broth or water with 8 bouillon cubes

1 large ham bone (saved in the freezer from when we cook a shank ham)

3 cups split peas

4 carrots, sliced

4 stalks celery, sliced

2 onions, diced

2 cups diced cooked ham

½ teaspoon allspice

½ teaspoon peppercorns

3 bay leaves

salt and pepper to taste

Directions

In the 8-quart pot ¾ filled with broth, place the ham bone, split peas, carrots, celery, onions, and diced ham. Bring to a boil. Reduce the heat and simmer for at least 2 hours.

In a cheesecloth "ball" or tea ball, place the allspice, peppercorns, bay leaves, and salt and pepper. (If using cheesecloth, tie with string to form a ball.) Add the spice ball to the soup after it has simmered for at least 2 hours and continue simmering for 1 hour more. Remove the bone and dice any meat still clinging to it. Add the diced meat to the soup. Serve with muffins, biscuits, or cornbread for a delicious meal. Serves 10 to 12.

MEATLESS RECIPES

Eggplant Parmesan

Our whole family loves this recipe—it's delish!

Ingredients

1 to 3 cups peanut oil, other oils can be substituted, but peanut oil handles
    high heat better and may lower cholesterol

1 to 2 eggs, mixed with a little water

1 (16-ounce) container Italian seasoned bread crumbs

2 to 3 eggplants

2 to 6 cups spaghetti sauce

1 pound shredded Mozzarella cheese

½ cup Parmesan cheese

Directions

Pour ½ inch of peanut oil in a 10-inch skillet and heat on low.

Beat the egg in a medium bowl and add 1 tablespoon of water.

Pour the bread crumbs onto a plate.

Cut the eggplant into ½-inch slices and poke several times with a fork on each
side to help absorb the egg and bread crumbs.

Dip each eggplant slice in egg bowl and coat both sides. Then move eggplant
slices to the dish with bread crumbs and flip slices to cover both sides.

Place breaded eggplant slices on another plate until you have enough to fill the
skillet. Turn heat on the skillet to medium and place eggplants into the skillet. Fry
until golden brown and a fork easily goes through the slice.

Preheat the oven to 350º. While the eggplant is frying, prepare two to three 13
x 9-inch baking dishes by coating the bottoms with spaghetti sauce.

Lay the cooked eggplant slices in the prepared baking dish and add a blop of
spaghetti sauce to the top of each slice. Lightly cover the eggplant with the shredded
Mozzarella cheese and sprinkle with the Parmesan cheese.

Bake uncovered for 45 minutes or until the cheese is browned. Makes two to
three 13 x 9-inch baking pans. Serves 6 to 8.

Kathy's French Onion Soup

This is a great recipe to prepare in a slow cooker. It will warm up a cold winter night.

Ingredients

6 to 8 onions, sliced into rings

½ gallon water with 8 beef bouillon cubes, or use beef stock

1 tablespoon Worcestershire sauce

1 teaspoon ground black pepper

8 to 10 slices of bread

8 to 10 slices Swiss cheese

Directions

In a slow cooker or an 8-quart saucepan add the onions, water with bouillon, Worcestershire sauce, and pepper. Cook on low all day. Ladle into ceramic bowls or very large ceramic tea mugs. Place the bowls on a cookie sheet for ease in getting them in and out of the oven. Top each bowl with a piece of bread and a slice of Swiss cheese. Slide the cookie sheet with bowls into the oven. Set oven to broil and cook until the cheese starts to turn golden brown. Serve with baked potatoes for a more substantial meal. Serves 8 to 10.

Veggie Soup

Soup recipes are very forgiving. If you don't measure the ingredients exactly right it will still turn out fine. Also, leftover veggies are a fine addition to the recipe and taste great. When we make soup, we make a huge pot, eat some, and freeze the rest.

This recipe will feed your family for pennies. If you are single, make a large pot and then freeze it in smaller containers. Annette always serves a quick bread with this meal and our house rule is that when your bowl is half-empty, then you can have your bread.

Ingredients

6 quarts chicken broth, Annette uses broth from boiling a turkey carcass. She
   refrigerates it overnight and removes the fat.

2 cups sliced carrots, sliced in rounds

2 cups chopped celery

4 cloves garlic or 2 teaspoons garlic powder

1 large onion, diced

1 to 2 cups miscellaneous leftover veggies from the refrigerator—broccoli,
   cauliflower, green beans, corn, and peas all work great

salt and pepper to taste

Directions

Start with an 8-quart stock or sauce pot. Add all ingredients and bring to a boil. Reduce heat and simmer for 2 hours

Serves 10 to 12.

Options:
- Add 2 cups of cooked, diced chicken.
- Add brown rice into the simmering soup mixture at least 2 hours before serving (don't use white rice since it will turn to mush).
- Add 1 to 2 cups of beans (be sure to soak in water for 2 hours, dump the water and rinse, then repeat the process a second time to reduce the gassiness of your beans and ease digestion) into simmering soup mixture at least 2 hours before serving.
- Add 1 to 2 cups of noodles to simmering soup ½ hour before serving.

QUICK BREADS

Steve's Killer Pancakes

This is our all-time favorite scratch pancake recipe.

We always make a huge batch, eat some that morning, and freeze the rest. We stack the leftovers in 4 stacks, 5 pancakes high in a 1-gallon zippered bag, and pop them in the freezer. They pull apart easily and can be reheated in the microwave or toaster oven.

Ingredients

- 5 ¼ cups flour (mix 3 cups all-purpose flour with 2 ¼ cups whole wheat flour)
- 8 tablespoons brown sugar
- 8 teaspoons double-acting baking powder
- 1 tablespoon salt
- 4 eggs
- 5 ⅓ cups milk (or substitute fruit juice for some of the milk to add sweetness and flavor)
- ¼ cup salad oil
- 1 tablespoon vanilla extract
- 1 tablespoon almond extract

Directions

In a large bowl mix the flour, brown sugar, baking powder, and salt. In a small bowl whip the eggs until fluffy to help offset the density of the whole wheat flour. Add the milk, oil, vanilla, and almond extracts. Then add the liquid mixture to the dry mixture and beat until "lumpless." Cook on a griddle until golden brown. Makes about 48 pancakes.

Options:
- Mix in 1 can of cherry pie filling or 2 overripe bananas—reduce liquid content slightly.
- Drop 5 chocolate chips onto each pancake—slightly cover chips with batter to avoid a messy griddle.

Cheese Muffins

These muffins are light and fluffy and are extra delicious when you eat them still warm out of the oven. Never worry about having leftovers of these wonderful muffins.

Ingredients

¾ cup whole wheat flour

1 cup all-purpose flour

½ teaspoon salt

1 tablespoon baking powder

¾ cup grated cheddar cheese

2 eggs

¼ cup oil

1 cup milk

¼ cup honey

Parmesan cheese to sprinkle on top

Preheat the oven to 400°. Grease 12 muffin cups. Don't use paper liners for this recipe. Stir together the whole wheat and all-purpose flour, salt, baking powder, and cheddar cheese in a large bowl. In a separate bowl combine the eggs, oil, milk, and honey. Stir together the liquid and dry ingredients. The mixture will be lumpy, but that's okay. Fill the prepared muffin cups ¾ full. Sprinkle the Parmesan cheese on top. Bake 20 minutes or until golden brown. Recipe can easily be doubled or tripled for large families or to store in the freezer—package carefully, so they don't get crushed. Makes 12 muffins.

Banana Bread

This recipe is a great way to use overripe bananas. We store the bananas in a zippered plastic bag in the freezer until we have enough to make several loaves.

Ingredients

    4 eggs
    ¾ to 1 cup vegetable oil
    2 cups sugar
    3 cups mashed ripe bananas (about 6 or 7)
    3 ½ cups all-purpose flour (or 2 ½ cups all-purpose and 1 cup whole wheat)
    2 teaspoons baking soda
    1 teaspoon salt
    ½ teaspoon baking powder
    ½ to ⅔ cup water
    1 cup chopped nuts (we like walnuts, but you can use your favorite)
    1 cup mini chocolate chips

Directions

Preheat the oven to 350°. Grease bottom of two 9 x 5 x 3-inch loaf pans or 24 muffin cups.

Mix the eggs, oil, and sugar together. Add the bananas. Add the flour, baking soda, salt, baking powder, and water. Mix and blend until smooth. Finally, add the nuts and chocolate chips, but don't beat too much after adding them.

Pour the mixture into the prepared loaf pans or muffin cups.

Bake the loaves for 1 hour and 15 minutes or the muffins for 20 to 30 minutes. Insert a toothpick into the center. The banana bread is done if toothpick comes out clean. Cool muffins for 10 minutes and loaves for 45 minutes and then remove from the pan/muffin cups.

Makes 2 loaves or 24 muffins.

Jennifer's Chocolate Chip Zucchini Bread

If you're going to plant a garden and grow zucchini, you'll need a great recipe to use up the bumper crop that you'll inevitably have. This is a delicious recipe.

Ingredients

2 eggs

2 cups sugar

1 cup oil

½ cup sour cream or plain yogurt

1 teaspoon vanilla extract

1 teaspoon cinnamon

1 teaspoon baking powder

1 teaspoon baking soda

2 cups shredded zucchini

3 cups all-purpose flour (or 2 cups all-purpose and 1 cup whole wheat)

⅓ to ⅔ cup water

1 cup mini chocolate chips (don't mix too long or chips will get crushed)

Directions

Preheat the oven to 350°. Mix the eggs, sugar, oil, sour cream or yogurt, vanilla, cinnamon, baking powder, baking soda, zucchini, flour, water, and chocolate chips (in that order). Pour into two greased 9 x 5 x 3-inch loaf pans or three 8-cup muffin tins. Bake approximately 45 minutes for the bread and 25 minutes for the muffins. Poke a toothpick into the bread to check if it is fully cooked. It's done when the toothpick comes out clean. Makes two 9 x 5 x 3-inch loaves or 24 muffins.

The meals listed in this chapter are easy to create and are just the start for you to develop your own list of family favorites. Invest some time at your public library checking out their cookbooks and talk with your friends. Picking up a few new recipes each year will soon add up to an amazing repertoire. You don't have to do it all at once, but one meal at a time, you can do it!

Notes

1. From KeepKidsHealthy.com—A pediatrician's guide to your children's health and safety. Vincent Iannelli, M.D., F.A.A.P., President, Keep Kids Healthy, LLC. Dr. Iannelli is the author of several books and hosts the About.com Guide to Pediatrics—www.Pediatrics.About.com.
2. "Where the Rubber Meets the Road: A Model of In-Store Consumer Decision Making," produced by J. Jeffrey Inman—University of Wisconsin-Madison and Russell S. Winer—University of California–Berkeley.
3. Charles K. Brown, VP Marketing, NCH Marketing Services, Inc. Deerfield, Illinois, a Valassis company.
4. Dolores Curran, *Traits of a Healthy Family* (HarperSanFrancisco, 1984).

About the Authors

Steve and Annette Economides were married in 1982. Steve worked as a graphic designer for $6.50 per hour, while Annette stayed home to stretch pennies until they begged for mercy. In just nine years, on an average income of just $35,000, they paid off their first home. They have also paid cash for cars, taken debt-free vacations, spent $350 per month to feed their family of seven, and put their kids through college without school loans.

They are *New York Times* Best Selling authors and are recognized internationally as family finance experts. They have appeared on many national TV shows including: *Good Morning America*, the *Today Show*, ABC's *20/20*, Fox's *Your World with Neil Cavuto*, and *Dr. Phil*. They are regularly quoted on radio and in newspapers and have been featured in magazines such as *Good Housekeeping*, *People*, and *Real Simple*, as well as profiled on Yahoo.com and MSNBC.com.

AMERICA'S CHEAPEST FAMILY GETS YOU RIGHT ON THE MONEY

A NEW YORK TIMES BESTSELLER

Do you have too much month at the end of your money?
Is your credit card screaming for relief?
Are you tired of robbing Peter to pay Paul … whoever they are?

America's Cheapest Family
Gets You Right on the Money,
*Your Guide to Living Better,
Spending Less, and Cashing
in on Your Dreams*
$12.95 paperback
($16.00 Canada)
978-0-307-33945-4

Meet Steve and Annette Economides. They've been called cheapskates, thriftaholics, and tightwads, but in these tough economic times, Steve and Annette have managed to feed their family of seven on just $350 per month, pay off their first house in nine years and purchase a second, larger home, buy cars with cash, take wonderful vacations, and put money in savings. Without degrees in finance or six-figure salaries, Steve and Annette have created a comfortable, debt-free life for themselves and their children. In *America's Cheapest Family Gets You Right on the Money,* they show you how they did it—and how you can do it too.

Steve and Annette share many down-to-earth principles and the simple spending plan that they have used since 1982. They have taught this economizing lifestyle to thousands of people worldwide through seminars and their newsletter, and they include lots of real-life stories to make you feel as if you're having your own private coaching session. Not only will you find solutions to your financial dilemmas, you'll also discover a whole new way of life.

You don't need to be a CPA or a math wizard to learn their revolutionary system, which will teach you:

* *hundreds of ways to save money on everyday household expenses, including groceries, clothing, and health care*

* *how to save in advance for major purchases such as homes, cars, and vacations*

* *how to stop living paycheck to paycheck*

* *how to eliminate debt . . . forever!*

America's Cheapest Family Gets You Right on the Money puts meeting your financial goals—and living well at the same time—in reach for every family.

Available from Three Rivers Press wherever books are sold